## LEICESTER
# TIGERS

# Official Yearbook 2005-06

**Editorial**
Sam Rossiter-Stead, Howard Kahn, Marc Fiszman

**Design**
Teb Scott, Rob Cubbon

**Statistics**
Stuart Farmer Media Services, OPTA

**SIDAN**PRESS
sidanpress.com

# Club Directory

**Welford Road Stadium**
**Aylestone Road**
**Leicester LE2 7TR**

Phone 08701 28 34 30
Fax 0116 2854 766
Email tigers@tigers.co.uk

Chairman Peter Tom

Chief Executive Peter Wheeler

Managing Director David Clayton

Company Secretary Mary Ford

Directors
David Abell, Garry Adey,
John Allen, Bob Beason,
Roy Jackson, David Jones,
David Matthews

President Roy Jackson

Head Coach Pat Howard

Life Members
John Allen, Jerry Day,
David Matthews

Press & PR
Sam Rossiter-Stead
Phone 0116 2171 284
Fax 0116 2171 291
Email srs@tigers.co.uk

Charity Requests
Email charity@tigers.co.uk

Corporate Sales
Phone 0116 2171 287
Fax 0116 2171 292
Email sales@tigers.co.uk

Ticket Office
Andrea Allen
Phone 08701 28 34 30
Fax 0116 2171 263
Email tickets@tigers.co.uk

Conference and Banqueting
Phone 0116 2171 281
Email cab@tigers.co.uk

Community
Phone 0116 2171 221
Email community@tigers.co.uk

Merchandise
Sara Watson
Phone 0116 2171 267
Email shop@tigers.co.uk

Supporter Services
Paul Hayes
Phone 0116 2171 226
Email paul.hayes@tigers.co.uk

Stadium Management
Jack Russell
Phone 0116 2171 255
Email jack.russell@tigers.co.uk

# Contents

## CORPORATE PARTNERS

**BRADSTONE**
OFFICIAL**MAIN**SPONSOR

### STAND SPONSORS

Alliance Leicester

NEXT

### SHIRT SPONSOR

**AGGREGATE**
INDUSTRIES

### TECHNOLOGY PARTNER

hp invent

### ASSOCIATE SHIRT SPONSORS

FLO GAS
people with energy

**BARDON**
CONTRACTING

### OFFICIAL VEHICLE SUPPLIER

 **VAUXHALL**

### PLAYER OF THE MONTH SPONSOR

Lumbers

### KIT SPONSOR

*Cotton*
**TRADERS**

### TIGER CUP SPONSORS

Prima Solutions

### TOURNAMENT SPONSOR

**GUINNESS**
PREMIERSHIP

### OFFICIAL SPORTS DRINK SUPPLIER

Lucozade SPORT

### OFFICIAL ALE SUPPLIER

**EVERARDS**
ESTABLISHED 1849

### RISK MANAGEMENT PARTNERS

OVAL

### LEGAL PARTNER

Harvey Ingram LLP
solicitors

### OFFICIAL SPORTS SUPPLEMENTS SUPPLIER

**EAS**
active lifestyle nutrition

### ASSOCIATE SPONSORS

ORCHARD

Reflex Design
Signs and Graphics

**BAXI**

STARLIGHT AVIATION

The *Nautilus* Health & Fitness Group

MILLINGTON TRAVEL

---

# corporate partners 2005-06

## BOX HOLDERS

| | |
|---|---|
| Aggregate Industries | Harvey Ingram LLP |
| Alliance & Leicester | HSBC Holdings |
| Artisan Press Ltd | KCT Holdings |
| Barclays Bank | Lafarge Aggregates |
| Bostik Findley UK | Masterplug UK |
| Browne Jacobson | Mondiboard Ltd |
| CJC Development | Nexpress Group |
| Cunnington Clarke | Orange |
| David Abell | PKF |
| David Wilson Homes Ltd | PriceWaterhouseCoopers |
| Defensor Fire Detection | Royal Bank of Scotland |
| Eric Wood | Sowden Group |
| FreethCartwright | Spearing Waite |
| Galliford Plc | The Danwood Group |
| Gateley Wareing | Tony Green Associates |
| George Wimpey East Midlands | Vantis Numerica |
| Haas Automation | W R Refrigeration |

## EXECUTIVE CLUB MEMBERS

| | |
|---|---|
| A&P Maintenance | Goy Harris Cartwright & Co |
| AMG | Guinness |
| AON Ltd | Hewlett Packard |
| Flogas | Lucozade Sport |
| Focus Four Ltd | Manor House Securities Ltd |
| Garden Centres of Excellence | Town & Country |
| Forest Gate Corby | Vauxhall Motors Ltd |

## PREMIER CLUB MEMBERS

| | |
|---|---|
| DHL Freight & Contract Logistics (UK) Ltd | Scott Wilson Kirkpatrick & Co Ltd |
| Linde Material Handling UK | VU Ltd |
| Persimmon Homes | Widdowson Group |
| Pick Everard | |

TO DISCUSS PARTNERSHIP AND SPONSORSHIP OPPORTUNITIES AT LEICESTER TIGERS, PLEASE CA OUR SALES TEAM ON **0116 2171 287**

# Honours & Records

## Honours

| European Champions | English Champions | English Cup Winners | Championship Winners |
|---|---|---|---|
| 2001-2002 | 2001-2002 | 1996-1997 | 2000-2001 |
| 2000-2001 | 2000-2001 | 1992-1993 | |
| | 1999-2000 | 1980-1981 | |
| | 1998-1999 | 1979-1980 | |
| | 1994-1995 | 1978-1979 | |
| | 1987-1988 | | |

## Most Points

| Name | Career | Games | T | C | PG | DG | GM | Pts |
|---|---|---|---|---|---|---|---|---|
| Dusty Hare | 1976-1989 | 393+1 | 87 | 779 | 820 | 47 | – | 4,507 |
| John Liley | 1988-1997 | 226+4 | 74 | 417 | 449 | 2 | – | 2,518 |
| Tim Stimpson | 1998-2003 | 141+10 | 29 | 223 | 372 | 2 | – | 1,713 |
| Lez Harris | 1984-1996 | 213+12 | 23 | 165 | 178 | 70 | – | 1,171 |
| Harold Day | 1919-1929 | 212 | 108 | 281 | 81 | 4 | 2 | 1,151 |
| Bob Barker | 1968-1979 | 318+2 | 158 | 92 | 107 | 2 | – | 1,117 |

## Most Appearances

| Name | Career | Games |
|---|---|---|
| David Matthews | 1955-1974 | 502 |
| Sid Penny | 1896-1910 | 491 |
| John Allen | 1961-1975 | 457 |
| Doug Norman | 1920-1933 | 453 |
| Paul Dodge | 1975-1993 | 434+3 |
| Dusty Hare | 1976-1989 | 393+1 |
| Pedlar Wood | 1906-1922 | 388 |
| Barry Adey | 1967-1981 | 381 |
| John Wells | 1982-1997 | 360+7 |
| Steve Kenney | 1975-1990 | 361+4 |
| Les Cusworth | 1978-1990 | 365 |
| George Ward | 1910-1926 | 361 |
| Jacky Braithwaite | 1895-1906 | 359 |
| Billy Foreman | 1893-1906 | 358 |
| Bob Rowell | 1962-1978 | 355 |
| Graham Rowntree | 1990-Present | 324+31 |

## Most Tries

| Name | Career | Games | Tries |
|---|---|---|---|
| Percy Lawrie | 1907-1924 | 318 | 206 |
| Barry Evans | 1981-1995 | 273 | 170 |
| John Duggan | 1970-1980 | 302 | 158 |
| Bob Barker | 1968-1979 | 320 | 158 |
| Harry Wilkinson | 1895-1905 | 233 | 153 |
| Teddy Haselmere | 1918-1923 | 180 | 136 |
| Rory Underwood | 1983-1997 | 236 | 134 |
| David Matthews | 1955-1974 | 502 | 119 |
| Neil Back | 1990-2005 | 311 | 118 |
| Ralph Buckingham | 1924-1935 | 325 | 117 |
| Harold Day | 1919-1929 | 212 | 108 |
| Dean Richards | 1982-1997 | 314 | 105 |
| Pedlar Wood | 1906-1922 | 388 | 102 |

Be a part of it

# Stadium Bar Guide

## Bars & Restaurants

1  Barbarians Lounge
2  Tiger Bar
3  European Suite
4  Leicestershire Room
5  Captain's Bar
6  Droglites
7  Dusty's Bar
8  Underwood Suite
9  Lions Bar
10 Members Bar
11 ABC Bar
12 Crumbie Lounge

⬛ Public

⬛ Corporate

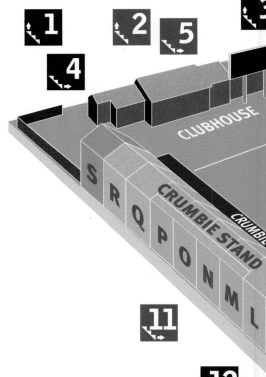

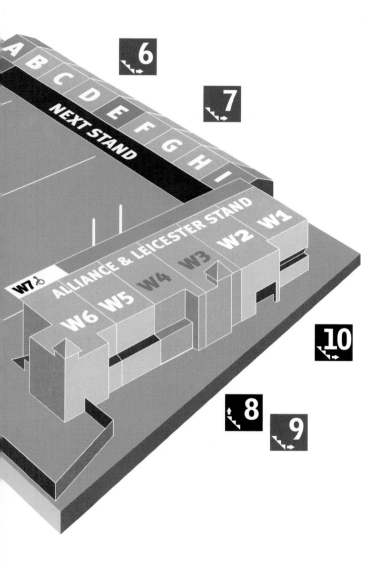

# Local and Area Maps

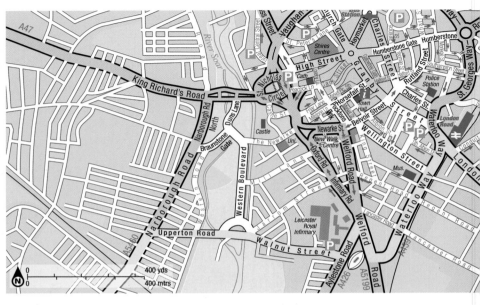

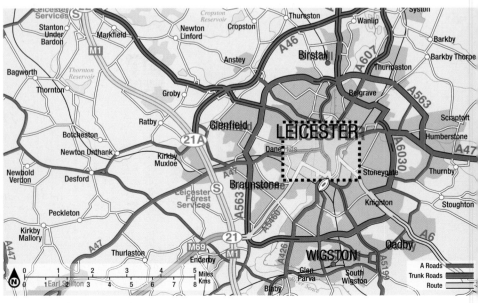

ance & Leicester
LEICESTER FOOTBALL CLUB
Alliance & L
ance & Leicester
Stand
GUINNESS
LAND ROVER
BRADSTONE

# Community

The award-winning community department at Leicester Tigers h. had another excellent year. Building on its strong foundations, we ha delivered more coaching sessions and visits than ever before. T continued growth and expansion of all our existing programmes has be complimented by some exciting new initiatives that have allowed Tige to reach out further into the region and touch more and more supporte and players. The different programmes run target a wide range of grou from school children and primary, secondary and special school university students, rugby clubs, Tigers supporters and communi groups. The community department aims to increase participation rugby, raise awareness of the club and ultimately generate revenue.

### Alliance & Leicester Tag Rugby Programme

The continuation of this nationally-recognised coaching programr has given us an excellent opportunity to forge even closer links with t Leicestershire and Rutland primary schools. Since its inception in Mar 2000, Tigers TAG coaches have coached and introduced TAG rugby over 28,000 10 and 11 year old boys and girls, and enthused parents a teachers alike with this exciting introduction to the game.

As part of the programme each school receives a teacher traini seminar and three coaching sessions which prepare participants for regional festival. The teacher training seminar aims to educate teache on the rules of TAG rugby and therefore allow the continuation of TA rugby after the Tigers coaches have left. This was deemed an importa part of the programme after research showed that less than 10% primary schools in the counties of Leicestershire and Rutland active participated in rugby. The winners of the regional finals are invited Welford Road to play in the district final in front of a crowd of 17,0( Tigers supporters. At the end of each year the final winners are invit back to Welford Road for a grand final to decide that year's champior A unique experience for all concerned!

### Tigers Learning Centre

The Tigers Learning Centre, a Playing for Success study suppc centre, has had another very successful year, having opened its doors the Leicester Primary and Secondary Schools in January 2003. T centre aims to provide out of hours learning and extra curricul. support for disaffected, under achieving pupils from Leicester's inn city schools. Although one of the smallest PfS centres in the count TLC contains 10 flat screen computers, an interactive whiteboard, t printers and table top activity space and accommodates 15 childr

from four primary and secondary schools per term. Each group of 15 participate in a 10-week programme which is broken down into ten, two hour weekly sessions. The education programme focuses upon literacy, numeracy and ICT skills using a rugby theme. Activities include writing their own rugby poems, creating spreadsheets and graphs using Excel, designing their own rugby kit using Paint and creating Powerpoint presentations. The programme also includes a session of TAG rugby in the local park delivered by a community coach.

The 10-week programme culminates with a graduation ceremony held at Welford Road that celebrates the hard work and achievement of all the children with family, friends and teachers. A first team player presents certificates and prizes and stays behind after the ceremony to sign autographs and pose for photos. After the programme each child is given their own free ticket for a Tigers home match where they are looked after by TLC staff and enjoy a lap of honour in front of the home crowd.

So far over 300 children have made it through the programme and received their hard earned certificate at the graduation ceremony. Education in a different environment has opened opportunities for many children and the excitement of being at Welford Road will continue to enhance the chances of our local Leicester youngsters.

### Tigers Leadership Programme

The Leadership Programme visited 24 schools with excellent feedback last season. The scheme targets children who might have behavioural problems and are struggling at school due to various reasons.

The six-week course has been designed to improve children's interpersonal and leadership skills and raise self-esteem. The programme uses TAG rugby to build the confidence of the children involved so that they can coach their peers using a number of simple techniques including 'Demonstrating a skill', 'Giving Instruction' and 'Self Analysis'. In the final session of their six-week programme each child will deliver a three minute coaching session using these techniques. The aim is to ensure that each child not only has fun but also discovers and develops new skills that can be used in future life as well as understanding the strength of good team work and how to help others achieve success. The programme also involves a pre-coaching group discussion, pre-activity questionnaire, feedback from children, parents and teachers, an achievement assembly with a Leicester Tigers player to present certificates and a free ticket watch a Tigers home match and take part in a parade in front of the home crowd.

### Tigers Rugby Courses

Our ever-expanding Tigers Rugby Courses have delivered 18 weeks coaching all over the region during the 2004/2005 season coaching over 1200 children. This year we will be continuing that expansion and have

already planned 22 courses to include a two-week stay at our EPDC Norfolk, Swaffham RFC.

The week-long full contact rugby courses give players aged 8-16 years the chance to experience top-quality Tigers rugby coaching in professional environment. Children receive a rugby ball, t-shirt, poster and photograph along with Tigers memorabilia.

Players are put through their paces and can expect to play up to five hours of rugby each day. Tiger's coaches look to develop individual skills and techniques including: defence, attack, ball retention, ball handling agility, unit skills and conditioned games along with nutrition advice and video analysis work. During the week the children will be put through the 8 Star Award Scheme as a measure of their abilities in line with Tiger Academy expectations. At the end of the week there is an award ceremony where the 8 Star Award certificates are presented.

The courses run throughout the summer and also during the Easter and half term holidays. To find out more about any of the Tigers rugby courses call 0116 2171 221 or email community@tigers.co.uk or look at the Tigers website community pages for a full list of venues and dates

### Matchday Coaching Clinics

Tigers coaching clinics are held on match day mornings and they provide a unique experience for players and coaches, giving an inside look at the life and training habits of a professional player at our brand new purpose-built training ground, Oval Park.

Groups and teams meet early at the training facility to enjoy a one and half hour coaching session from the Tigers coaches and community team. Attending adults and coaches are given written instruction on the sessions planned and treated to a classroom discussion with the senior coach afterwards to assist in their education. Meanwhile the players themselves get to meet one of the Tigers First Team squad in a 15 minute question and answer session before a tour of our million pound training complex where the professionals work throughout the week.

At 12.30pm everyone then makes their way down to Welford Road watch the first XV put all that hard work into practice. Places for the clinics are limited and if last year is anything to go by will be in high demand. If anyone wants to find out more or book a group on the clinic please call 0116 2171 221 or email community@tigers.co.uk

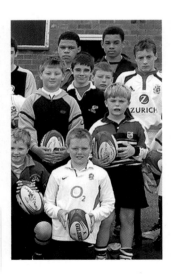

# Members Club

Be part of our success and join the Leicester Tigers members club which offers you exclusive discounts and benefits throughout the year. Tigers membership is ideal for supporters who are unable to commit to a season ticket but want to stay in touch with the club and receive discounts on match tickets.

Without the support of our members we would not enjoy the same level of success and we would not be able to realise the unique ambitions and challenges we have set ourselves.

As an official Leicester Tigers member you will receive:

- £1 off home match tickets
- Free quarterly newsletter
- Priority booking for home cup games
- Priority application for England home internationals
- Exclusive members-only events
- Exclusive members discount in the club shop on match days
- Free tickets for development games played at Welford Road
- Invitation to monthly members' evenings with guest speakers
- Invitation to members' Player of the Season awards
- Discount on function room hire at Welford Road
- Discount on Christmas party bookings at Welford Road
- Exclusive members card

Membership is based on an annual subscription and costs £25 per year for adults. Membership costs £15 a year for full-time students aged 14+. To join, contact Paul Hayes now on 0116 2171 226 or email paul.hayes@tigers.co.uk

# EVERARDS MEMBERS EVENINGS

## August 17th 2005
**Season Preview** with Pat Howard and Richard Cockerill

## September 21st 2005
**Welcome Back the Lions** with Martin Corry,
Graham Rowntree and Lewis Moody

## October 12th 2005
**Meet the New Irish Trio** with Shane
Jennings, Leo Cullen and Ian Humphreys

## November 15th 2005
**Why the Whistle Went** with leading
international referee Tony Spreadbury and Neil Back

## January 25th 2006
**Six Nations Preview** with Ben Kay and
Geordan Murphy

## February 22nd 2006
**Question of Sport 2:
England v Rest of the World**
with Austin Healey, Leon Lloyd, Scott Bemand,
Daryl Gibson, Darren Morris and Dan Montagu

## March 22nd 2006
**Brothers in Arms** with Ollie Smith and Sam Vesty

## April 5th 2006
**Members Player of the Season Awards**

All events are for members only and include a hot fork buffet meal. To
book your place contact Paul Hayes on 0116 2171 226 or email
paul.hayes@tigers.co.uk

N.B. We will try to keep to the above programme of events, but players &
dates may occasionally be changed due to fixtures and training
schedules.

LEICESTER
TIGERS

EVERARDS

## EVERARDS MEMBERS EVENINGS
— SUPPORT YOUR LOCAL —

# Junior Tiger Club

The Junior Tiger Club is a supporters club especially for Tigers fans up to the age of 14 years old. Our club president is Tigers star Harry Ellis. We have loads of fun on match days and get to meet Tigers players when they come to visit us in our clubhouse.

As a Junior Tiger Club member you get:

- The chance to be matchday mascot
- Free Junior Tiger Club gift
- Exclusive membership card
- Entry to the Junior Tiger clubhouse with computers and games
- £1 off all home matches (when booked in advance)
- Free face painting at home games
- Exclusive members events
- The chance to interview a player
- Free quarterly newsletter
- Pre-match parade at the first home game of the season with Welford and JT
- Junior Tiger Club pages in the matchday programme with birthday wishes
- Birthday card

### Be Matchday Mascot

As a member of the Junior Tiger Club you get the chance to be the match day mascot and lead out the Tigers team at Welford Road. Not only that, you will be given your own kit including shirt, shorts and socks to run out onto the pitch. This once in a lifetime chance is available exclusively to our members, who are picked at random or are one of the lucky winners of one of our competitions.

### Clubhouse

As a Junior Tiger Club member you gain entry to our special clubhouse before every home match. Pop in and meet your friends while you enjoy free food, drinks, fun and games. We even have special visitors from the first team squad who meet us at every home game.

### Free Face Painting

Get your face painted for free in the clubhouse on match days.

### Birthdays

To celebrate your birthday we will send you a special card and give you a birthday mention on our pages in the match day programme.

As a member of the Junior Tiger Club you can hold your birthday party at Welford Road with Welford and JT. Enjoy a great day with your mates as you play games and enjoy the food fun. We will even give you a goody bag to take home with you jam-packed with Tigers goodies. To enquire about our birthday parties please contact us on 0116 2171 313.

### Join Us

Joining the best junior supporters' club in the country costs just £15 for the year, so join now by calling Paul Hayes on 0116 2171 226 or email paul.hayes@tigers.co.uk

# JUNIOR tiger Club

## Application Form

**If you don't want to cut up your programme then simply photocopy this form.**

Name......................................................................
Address...................................................................
..............................................................................
..............................................................................
......................................... Postcode ........................
Email .................................... Tel no ..........................
D.O.B........................................................................
School.......................................................................

Were you a member last season? **YES     NO**

Name of parent/guardian.............................................
Signature ..................................................................
Favourite player 1 .....................................................
Favourite player 2 .....................................................
Junior Tiger Club membership costs just £15 per child
for 12 months. Maximum age 15
Parent/guardian's method of payment

I enclose a **CHEQUE        POSTAL ORDER**
*Please make cheques payable to Leicester Football Club Plc

for the sum of £................................................................

**MASTER CARD      VISA      DELTA      SWITCH**

your parent's/guardian's credit/debit card no.

..............................................................................

Valid from ............................. Expiry date ........................

Issue no. (switch) ................................ NB. Please do not send cash

**PLEASE SEND YOUR COMPLETED APPLICATION FORM
TOGETHER WITH YOUR REMITTANCE TO:**
Junior Tiger Club • Leicester Tigers • Aylestone Road
• Leicester, LE2 7TR • Tel: 08701 28 34 30 • Fax: 0116 2171 263
• www.leicestertigers.com

**OFFICE USE ONLY**

MEMBERSHIP NO...........................................................................

DATE PROCESSED .......................................... SEASON.................................................

## Membership Includes:

- ■ The chance to be a mascot at Welford Road – how good is that? You'll walk out with the team in front of the whole crowd and be given a FREE team kit to keep

- ■ £1 off all Guinness Premiership and Heineken Cup pool home games only, when booked in advance. (Under 14's must be accompanied by an adult)

- ■ A special gift for joining

- ■ Your own unique membership card

- ■ A birthday card each year – signed by all the players

- ■ Have fun in the JTC Clubhouse on matchdays with computer games and FREE soft drink and snack (open on first team matchdays only)

- ■ An invite to the Junior Tiger Club Christmas Party

- ■ Four newsletters a year with stories, competitions and much more...

## PLUS

- ■ Discounts in the club shop (available on selected items only)

# Conference & Banqueting

Open seven days a week, Welford Road is a unique venue for business or pleasure, retaining the nostalgia and heritage of a world famous rugby club within modern facilities and luxurious surroundings.

Since opening as a conference and banqueting venue in 1998, Welford Road has fast established itself as one of the premier conference venues in the East Midlands.

Located in the heart of England, the stadium is easily accessible from the motorway network and Nottingham East Midlands Airport and is within walking distance of Leicester Mainline Railway Station.

As a training venue, our Alliance & Leicester Stand offers a unique facility, which can accommodate up to 150 delegates in our main conference room with up to 15 breakout rooms. There is also on-site secure car parking with closed circuit TV.

Tigers' standard conference packages suit the needs of many customers, but our conference and banqueting staff are always happy to tailor any package to suit individual requirements.

And Welford Road isn't just open for business. If you are looking for somewhere to hold a birthday or family party, host a special event, or just want a room to have a disco and let your hair down, there is a function room that will suit your needs. A variety of menus ranging from a finger buffet to a full sit-down dinner means that there is a price range to suit all pockets.

Whatever extras you require for your function, our conference and banqueting team are happy to work with you to arrange additions such as musical entertainment, bar extensions, floral or balloon arrangements for the tables, themed evenings and personalised table plan and menus.

We also cater for wedding receptions, Christmas parties and private functions, as well as offering a room-only rate.

Please contact the conference and banqueting team on 0116 2171 281 for more details.

# Hospitality

### Join the Rush to be a Tigers VIP

If you want to make your day at Welford Road that extra special or surprise a friend or relative, then why not treat them to a VIP match day hospitality package at one of our home matches during the 2005/2006 season.

More and more people are treating their friends and loved ones to an unforgettable day of entertainment that allows them to get up close and personal with some of the Leicester Tigers' stars.

The Tigers experience is meticulously planned with reserved car parking allowing you to arrive in style. Whatever the reason for your day with us, all our guests agree that the three-hour complimentary bar is a great way to prepare for the day ahead. A superb four-course lunch is served fresh from the kitchen by our dedicated catering staff allowing you time to browse the complimentary match day programme and enjoy your personalised gift.

A visit from members of our first team squad is the highlight of the day for many of our guests, young and old. Our Tigers players take part in Q&A sessions and take the time to chat with our guests, sharing a drink and signing autographs. This also provides some great help with forecasting the score for our match day competitions, with great prizes on offer for the lucky winners.

### VIP MATCHDAY HOSPITALITY PACKAGE

This package is for two or more persons.

- Complimentary pre-match bar
- Joined by players for questions/answers
- Four-course pre-match meal with wine
- Souvenir programme for each guest
- Reserved grandstand seating
- Post-match afternoon tea
- Commemorative gift for each guest
- Competitions and prizes
- Reserved car parking

To make sure you don't miss out on celebrating in style during the 2005/2006 season please contact our sales team on 0116 2171 287.

# Milestones

**1880**

**Aug 3** – Leicester Football Club formed in a meeting at the George Hotel in Leicester from an amalgamation of three clubs: Leicester Societies AFC, Leicester Amateur FC and Leicester Alert.

**Oct 23** – First match against Moseley, played at the Belgrave Cricket and Cycle Ground ends in a nil-all draw. Original club colours were black and Leicester were known as "The Death or Glory Boys".

**Jan 8** – First game at Victoria Park, new home venue.

**1882**

**Oct 7** – Return to the Belgrave Cricket and Cycle Ground for one season only.

**1885**

**Feb 21** – The earliest reference to the now famous Tiger nickname appears in the Leicester Daily Post stating "the Tiger stripes were keeping well together."

**1888**

**Sep 29** – Club move back to the Belgrave Cricket & Cycle Ground from Victoria Park.

**1889**

**Apr 4** – Leicester reach their first ever final, but lose to Coventry 0-8 at Rugby in the Midland Counties Cup.

**1891**

Leicester wear their famous scarlet, green and white colours for the first time although in a vertical stripe formation.

**1892**

**Sep 16** – The current home ground Welford Road opens with a game against the Leicestershire Rugby Union, won 17-0.

**1895**

**Sep 25** – Club switch to scarlet, green and white hoops for the first time.

**1898**

**Apr 6** – The Tigers win their first ever trophy by beating Moseley 5-3 in the final of the Midland Counties Cup at Coventry. They go on to win this competition for the next seven seasons until retiring "to give other teams a chance".

**1902**

**Feb 8** – Welford Road's first international match sees England beat Ireland 6-3.

**1903**

Jack Miles becomes the club's first international player

**1909**

**Sep 4** – New Clubhouse opened for game vs Stratford-upon-Avon

containing for the first time dressing rooms at the ground

**29 Dec** – First fixture against the Barbarians ends in a 9-all draw.

**1912**

**Mar 9** – Harry Lawrie becomes the first Tiger to be sent off in a game at Harlequins by referee HA Taylor

**1918**

**Dec 26** – New Members' Stand officially opened for the first Tigers game in 3 1/2 years for the game against the 4th Leicestershire Regiment. On the same day Percy Lawrie with his 154th try overtakes Harry Wilkinson as the club's leading try scorer, he eventually finishes with a still unsurpassed 206 tries.

**1920**

**Oct 2** – New stand (later named the Crumbie Stand) opened by President of the Rugby Union, Ernest Prescott.

**1922**

**Dec 30** – Alastair Smallwood sets a club record by scoring seven tries in the same game in the 36-0 hammering of Manchester at Welford Road.

**1923**

**Feb 10** – England beat Ireland 23-5 at Welford Road in the last England home international played away from Twickenham until 1992.

## 1926

Sep 4 – The Leicester forwards first regularly wear letters as a means of identification against Bath at Welford Road.

## 1927

Mar 26 – Harold Day becomes the first Tiger to score 1,000 career points at home to Old Merchant Tailors.

## 1928

Mar 13 – Tom Crumbie, Hon Sec from 1895 dies in office.

## 1930

Nov 29 – The first BBC radio broadcast of a Tigers game sees Leicester beat Waterloo 21-5 at Welford Road.

## 1931

Sep 5 – Against Bath at Welford Road marks the first occasion that an entire Leicester team is lettered.

## 1946

Dec 14 – Leicester's first replacement is Haydn Thomas who takes over from JCK Campbell at Blackheath when the former is late in arriving.

## 1951

Feb 3 – First TV appearance against London Scottish on the Richmond Athletic Ground, won 14-0.

## 1956

Nov 18 – Tigers first game on a

Sunday sees them lose to Old Belvedere in Dublin 3-23.

## 1959

Oct 22 – Clocks unveiled on stands as a tribute to the late Eric Thorneloe who was Honorary Secretary between 1928-57.

## 1960

Feb 13 – Tigers' first game under lights was at Newport, which they lost 9-19.

## 1963

Dec 14 – David Matthews misses the visit of Blackheath to Welford Road and thus breaks his run of 109 successive first team appearances stretching back to January 1961.

## 1964

Oct 8 – Floodlights first used at Welford Road for a game against a Midlands XV, won 31-8.

## 1971

Nov 21 – Leicester's first 'modern' cup tie sees them lose 3-10 to Nottingham at Beeston on a Sunday in the first round of the RFU Knockout Cup.

## 1973

Apr 21 – David Matthews breaks Sid Penny's club appearance record with his 492nd First XV game at Broughton Park. He goes onto to make 502 appearances.

## 1977

Sep 6 – New scoreboard unveiled.

## 1978

Apr 15 – The club reach their first Twickenham final but are beaten 3-6 by Gloucester.

Dec 27 – Clubhouse extension opened.

## 1979

Apr 21 – Leicester win the John Player Cup for the first time, beating Moseley 15-12 in the final at Twickenham.

## 1980

Apr 19 – Dusty Hare breaks Harold Day's record Tigers career points aggregate with his 1,152nd point, kicked on the day that Leicester retained the John Player Cup with a 21-9 victory over London Irish at Twickenham.

Aug 6 – To honour the centenary of the club's foundation, Leicester become the first English club side to embark on a tour to the Southern Hemisphere. They play six games in Australia and Fiji, only losing the opening game to Queensland.

## 1981

May 2 – Tigers win the John Player Cup for a 3rd successive season when they beat Gosforth 22-15 in the final, and are allowed to keep the original trophy which is now on display at the Clubhouse.

## 1984

Feb 18 – A club record seven players appear in England team against Ireland at Twickenham.

## 1985

Sep 14 – New changing room, medical and weights rooms opened under the Crumbie Stand.

## 1986

Sep 17 – Dusty Hare scores a club record 43 points in a game in the 95-6 trouncing of Birmingham at Welford Road.

## 1988

Apr 4 – Leicester are confirmed as the inaugural Courage League champions with a 39-15 victory over Waterloo at Welford Road.

## 1989

Jan 28 – Les Cusworth drops a club record 4 goals at Liverpool St Helens in the 3rd round of the cup.

## 1990

Summer – Tony Russ is appointed the club's first full-time coach.

## 1991

Oct 13 – New Zealand beat Italy 31-21 in the qualifying stages of the World Cup at Welford Road.

## 1992

Apr 11 – Tigers achieve their record points total in a game by demolishing Liverpool St Helens 100-0 at Welford Road.

Sep 5 – Welford Road celebrates its centenary with two special matches. The first sees Leicester lose out 11-18 to an England XV and then overcome a Leicestershire XV 40-20 four days later.

## 1993

May 1 – Leicester win the Pilkington Cup by beating Harlequins 23-16 in the final at Twickenham.

Sep 18 – The new 18 foot electronic scoreboard is unveiled for the match against Orrell.

## 1995

Apr 29 – Tigers win the Courage League for a second time after beating Bristol 17-3 in front of 13,000 at Welford Road.

Sep 23 – The new 3,000 seat Alliance & Leicester stand is used for the first time for the visit of Bath, and officially opened with a game against Transvaal on 20 November.

## 1996

Jan – Peter Wheeler is appointed the club's first Chief Executive.

May 30 – Bob Dwyer is appointed Director of Rugby.

## 1997

Jan 25 – Tigers reach the final of the Heineken European Cup after English teams enter the competition for the first time. In the final at Cardiff Arms Park they are overwhelmed 28-9, by a superb team performance from French side Brive.

Apr 2 – A record six Leicester players are named in the British Lions squad to tour South Africa, including the captain Martin Johnson. Later the same day, Tigers beat Wasps 18-12 in front

of a record English league crowd of 17,000 at Welford Road.

May 10 – Leicester win the Pilkington Cup by beating Sale 9-3 in the final at Twickenham.

Dec 8 – Tigers become a plc after a successful share issue raises vital funds.

## 1998

Feb 17 – Dean Richards takes over as Director of Rugby.

## 1999

May 2 – Tigers clinch a third league title when they take the Allied Dunbar Premiership with a 21-12 victory over Newcastle Falcons at Kingston Park.

Oct 10 – Welford Road hosts a Rugby World Cup game for the second time as Tonga shock Italy 28-25.

## 2000

May 14 – Leicester claim a second successive Premiership crown following a 30-23 win at Bristol's Memorial Stadium.

## 2001

Mar 17 – Take a third Premiership crown in a row when Bath beat Wasps at the Rec, an hour or so after the Tigers had demolished the Falcons 51-7 at Welford Road.

May 13 – Leicester claim the inaugural Zurich Championship crown when they beat Bath 22-10 in the final at Twickenham.

May 19 – Tigers win the European Heineken Cup for the first time, beating Paris based Stade Français in the final at Parc des Princes 34-30.

Summer – Martin Johnson becomes the first player ever to captain the British Lions on two separate tours, when he leads them in Australia.

## 2002

Apr 13 – A fourth consecutive Premiership is wrapped up with a 40-10 victory over Newcastle at Welford Road.

May 25 – Leicester become the first club to retain the European Heineken Cup by beating Irish Province Munster 15-9 in the final at Cardiff's Millennium Stadium.

## 2003

May 31 – Tigers qualify for the 2003/04 European Heineken Cup with a thrilling extra time victory over Saracens at Franklin's Gardens, Northampton to pick up the Zurich Wildcard.

## 2004

May 29 – Tigers book their place in the 2004/05 Heineken Cup season with a comprehensive 48-27 victory over Sale Sharks at Twickenham to claim the Zurich Wildcard.

## 2005

April 30 – Leicester Tigers top the Zurich Premiership after 22 games in the regular season, comfortably beating London

Wasps 45-10 in their last league match, before losing to the self-same Wasps in the final two weeks later. Tigers were the only English team to qualify for the Heineken Cup semi-finals, going out to eventual winners, Toulouse, in the first-ever rugby match played at the Walkers Stadium.

# Leicester Tigers Fixture List 2005-06

LEICESTER
**TIGERS**

| Date | Match | KO | Comp | Date | Match | KO | Comp |
|---|---|---|---|---|---|---|---|
| Sat Aug 13 | Middlesex Sevens | (11:20) | F | Sun Jan 8 | London Irish | (15:00) | GP |
| Fri Aug 19 | Connacht | (18:30) | F | Jan 13-15 | **Stade Français** | | **HC** |
| Fri Aug 26 | **Munster** | **(19:45)** | **F** | Jan 20-22 | Clermont Auvergne | | HC |
| Sat Sep 3 | **Northampton Saints** | **(25:00)** | **GP** | Sat Jan 28 | **Sale Sharks** | **(15:00)** | **GP** |
| Sat Sep 10 | London Wasps | (14:45) | GP | Sat Feb 11 | Gloucester | (14:00) | GP |
| Sat Sep 17 | **Bath** | **(15:00)** | **GP** | Sat Feb 18 | **Worcester Warriors** | **(15:00)** | **GP** |
| Sun Sep 25 | Leeds Tykes | (14:30) | GP | Sun Feb 26 | Newcastle Falcons | (14:30) | GP |
| Sat Oct 1 | Newport-Gwent | (19:10) | PC | Sat Mar 4 | Powergen Cup SF | | PC |
| Sat Oct 8 | **Worcester Warriors** | **(15:00)** | **PC** | Sat Mar 11 | **Leeds Tykes** | **(15:00)** | **GP** |
| Fri Oct 14 | **Newcastle Falcons** | **(19:45)** | **GP** | Sat Mar 25 | Bath | (14:15) | GP |
| Sat Oct 22 | **Clermont Auvergne** | **(14:45)** | **HC** | Mar 31-Apr 2 | Heineken Cup QF | | HC |
| Sat Oct 29 | Stade Français | (14:00) | HC | Sat Apr 8 | **London Wasps** | **(15:00)** | **GP** |
| Fri Nov 4 | Worcester Warriors | (20:00) | GP | Sun Apr 9 | Powergen Cup Final | | PC |
| Sat Nov 12 | **Gloucester** | **(15:00)** | **GP** | Sat Apr 15 | Northampton Saints | (15:00) | GP |
| Fri Nov 18 | Sale Sharks | (20:00) | GP | Apr 22/23 | Heineken Cup SF | | HC |
| Fri Nov 25 | **London Irish** | **(19:45)** | **GP** | Fri Apr 28 | Saracens | (19:45) | GP |
| Sat Dec 3 | **Northampton Saints** | **(14:30)** | **PC** | Sat May 6 | **Bristol** | **(15:00)** | **GP** |
| Sun Dec 11 | **Ospreys Rugby** | **(15:00)** | **HC** | May 12-14 | Premiership Play-Offs | | GP |
| Sun Dec 18 | Ospreys Rugby | (13:00) | HC | | Premiership Semi-finals | | GP |
| Tue Dec 27 | Bristol | (15:00) | GP | May 20-21 | Heineken Cup Final | | HC |
| Mon Jan 2 | **Saracens** | **(15:00)** | **GP** | Sat May 27 | Premiership Final | | GP |

**Bold** – Home Fixtures   GP – Guinness Premiership   HC – Heineken Cup   PC – Powergen Cup   F – Friendly
Please note all fixtures may be subject to change.

## Ticket Hotline: 08701 28 34 30      tickets@tigers.co.uk
## www.leicestertigers.com

# Season Review 2004-05

# Sale Sharks **26**
# Leicester Tigers **19**

**Date:** 5.9.04  **Venue:** Edgeley Park  **Attendance:** 6,952  **Referee:** D.Pearson

## Team Line-Ups

| | | |
|---|---|---|
| J.Robinson (c) | **15** | G.Murphy |
| M.Cueto | **14** | J.Holtby |
| J.Baxendell | **13** | L.Lloyd |
| R.Todd | **12** | D.Gibson |
| S.Hanley | **11** | A.Healey |
| M.Hercus | **10** | A.Goode |
| B.Redpath | **9** | H.Ellis |
| T.Woodman | **1** | G.Rowntree |
| S.Bruno | **2** | G.Chuter |
| B.Stewart | **3** | D.Morris |
| D.Schofield | **4** | (c) M.Johnson |
| C.Day | **5** | B.Kay |
| J.White | **6** | B.Deacon |
| M.Lund | **7** | W.Skinner |
| S.Chabal | **8** | M.Corry |

## Replacements

| | | |
|---|---|---|
| A.Titterrell | **16** | J.Buckland |
| A.Sheridan | **17** | J.White |
| P.Caillet | **18** | L.Abraham |
| C.Jones | **19** | L.Deacon |
| S.Martens | **20** | R.Broadfoot |
| C.Hodgson | **21** | O.Smith |
| C.Mayor | **22** | S.Rabeni |

## Match Stats

| | | |
|---|---|---|
| 88 | Tackles | 65 |
| 6 | Missed Tackles | 15 |
| 60 | Ball Carries | 84 |
| 434 | Metres | 409 |
| 15 | Defenders Beaten | 6 |
| 72 | Passes | 104 |
| 7 | Clean Breaks | 8 |
| 7 | Penalties Conceded | 12 |
| 9 | Turnovers | 15 |
| 51 | Breakdowns Won | 67 |
| 100 | % Scrums Won | 92 |
| 89 | % Line-Outs Won | 94 |

## Premiership Away Record vs Sale Sharks

| Played | Won | Drawn | Lost | Points For | Points Against |
|---|---|---|---|---|---|
| 8 | 3 | 2 | 3 | 202 | 143 |

Sale Sharks carved out a hard-fought 26-19 victory over Leicester Tigers in Zurich Premiership action at Edgeley Park. The home team outscored Tigers by three tries to one in a bruising encounter that had 'season opener' written all over it.

Sale skipper Jason Robinson put his side in the lead in the sixth minute when he got over for the game's first try, but the home team could have held a bigger lead afterwards were it not for some erratic goal-kicking from their American fly-half Mike Hercus.

The home side extended their lead afterwards via an intercept try by scrum-half Bryan Redpath, before Hercus missed a drop-goal attempt – leaving the score at 10-0 in their favour. But that drop-goal attempt seemed to spur Tigers on, with the visitors hitting back via a try by inside centre Daryl Gibson, which fly-half Andy Goode easily converted.

"A lot of good things came out of the game, but it was always going to be tough to win away from home so early in the season." **John Wells**

At 7-10 down Tigers would have been well-pleased with their effort, especially when one considers that Sale were the ones playing all the rugby up till then, and if Hercus had remembered his kicking boots, the home team could have been ahead by more.

Goode rubbed salt into Sale's wounds with a neatly-struck drop-goal to tie the scores at 10-10, but Sale seemed determined to go into half-time with something to show from their first-half effort and they got it shortly before the break when winger Mark Cueto got over for their third five-pointer. Hercus managed his first successful goal kick of the day and Sale were ahead by 17-10, only for Goode to chip away at the lead with another sweetly-struck drop-goal, leaving the score at 17-13 in Sale's favour at the break.

Two Goode penalties in the second half saw Tigers take the lead for the first time at 19-17, before replacement fly-half Charlie Hodgson slotted a drop-goal to put his side back in the lead.

With time running out, Tigers became desperate to get back into Sale's half and they very nearly conceded another intercept try when Chris Jones plucked a long pass out of the air, only to get called back for an earlier infringement. Tigers, however, spilt the ball from the scrum and conceded a penalty which Hodgson slotted for a 23-19 lead, putting them out of the three-point 'comfort zone'.

## Event Line

| Min | | Score | |
|-----|-----|-------|-----|
| 6 | T | 5-0 | Robinson |
| 16 | T | 10-0 | Redpath |
| 31 | TC | 10-7 | **Gibson/Goode** |
| 36 | DG | 10-10 | Goode |
| 38 | TC | 17-10 | Cueto/Hercus |
| 40 | DG | 17-13 | **Goode** |

### Half-Time

| 41 | ⬌ | | Hodgson for Hercus |
|----|-----|-------|-----|
| 44 | P | 17-16 | Goode |
| 46 | ⬌ | | **White for Morris** |
| 46 | ⬌ | | Sheridan for Stewart |
| 55 | P | 17-19 | Goode |
| 56 | ⬌ | | **Rabeni for Healey** |
| 56 | ⬌ | | C.Jones for Schofield |
| 58 | ⬌ | | Titterell for Bruno |
| 58 | ⬌ | | Martens for Redpath |
| 61 | ⬌ | | **Smith for Lloyd** |
| 66 | ⬌ | | **L.Deacon for Kay** |
| 66 | ⬌ | | **Healey for Holtby** |
| 69 | DG | 20-19 | Hodgson |
| 73 | ⬌ | | **Abraham for B.Deacon** |
| 78 | P | 23-19 | Hodgson |
| 81 | P | 26-19 | Hodgson |
| 84 | ⬌ | | Caillet for White |

### Full-Time

### Premiership Table

| Team | P | W | D | L | Pts |
|------|---|---|---|---|-----|
| 9 NEC Harlequins | 1 | 0 | 0 | 1 | 1 |
| **10 Leicester Tigers** | **1** | **0** | **0** | **1** | **1** |
| 11 Bath Rugby | 1 | 0 | 0 | 1 | 0 |

### Tigers Milestone

Fijian star Seru Rabeni made his debut in this game, coming off the bench in the second half. Rabeni went on to play another 13 matches; scoring eight tries, before a knee injury ended his season.

# Leicester Tigers **42**
# Leeds Tykes **20**

**Date:** 11.9.04 **Venue:** Welford Road **Attendance:** 16,533 **Referee:** W.Barnes

## Team Line-Ups

| G.Murphy | 15 | M.Cardey |
| S.Rabeni | 14 | D.Rees |
| O.Smith | 13 | C.Bell |
| D.Gibson | 12 | A.Snyman |
| A.Healey | 11 | T.Biggs |
| A.Goode | 10 | G.Ross |
| H.Ellis | 9 | A.Dickens |
| G.Rowntree | 1 | M.Cusack |
| G.Chuter | 2 | M.Regan |
| J.White | 3 | G.Kerr |
| M.Johnson (c) | 4 | C.Murphy |
| L.Deacon | 5 | (c) T.Palmer |
| B.Deacon | 6 | P.Uys |
| N.Back | 7 | R.Parks |
| M.Corry | 8 | A.Popham |

## Replacements

| J.Buckland | 16 | M.Holt |
| A.Tuilagi | 17 | R.Rawlinson |
| D.Morris | 18 | J.Dunbar |
| H.Tuilagi | 19 | S.Morgan |
| S.Bemand | 20 | P.Christophers |
| R.Broadfoot | 21 | M.McMillan |
| W.Skinner | 22 | D.Albanese |

## Match Stats

| 75 | Tackles | 93 |
| 15 | Missed Tackles | 19 |
| 102 | Ball Carries | 75 |
| 679 | Metres | 335 |
| 19 | Defenders Beaten | 15 |
| 127 | Passes | 101 |
| 10 | Clean Breaks | 4 |
| 11 | Penalties Conceded | 13 |
| 13 | Turnovers | 14 |
| 58 | Breakdowns Won | 57 |
| 100 | % Scrums Won | 100 |
| 81 | % Line-Outs Won | 82 |

## Premiership Home Record vs Leeds Tykes

| Played | Won | Drawn | Lost | Points For | Points Against |
|---|---|---|---|---|---|
| 4 | 4 | 0 | 0 | 130 | 158 |

Leicester Tigers bounced back from their away loss to Sale Sharks with a crushing 42-20 victory over Leeds Tykes in Zurich Premiership action at Welford Road.

The home side outscored Tykes by five tries to two in the end, but they still let a few try-scoring chances go astray, whilst they also conceded the odd penalty on defence when Leeds managed to get behind them.

Tigers got off to the perfect start when they won an early penalty, with fly-half Andy Goode making no mistake as he slotted a monstrous goal from inside his own half – the ball travelling comfortably over the uprights in the end.

Captain Martin Johnson got his team's first try of the day, after incessant pressure from the likes of Geordan Murphy, Austin Healey, Ollie Smith and Seru Rabeni, whilst the latter picked up his first five-pointer in Tigers colours shortly before the break, leaving the home side ahead by 20-3.

Leeds youngster Tom Biggs scored a try against the run of play early in the second half, but a Harry Ellis score, which Goode converted – after Leeds second row Chris Murphy had been sin-binned for repeated infringements – saw Tigers take an unassailable 30-10 lead.

With the game sewn up shortly after the 50-minute mark, Tigers made a few changes, with Ellis coming off for Scott Bemand and Alesana Tuilagi – who scored five tries in a second-team game earlier in the week – replacing Ollie Smith, who impressed in his first start of the season.

Tigers claimed their bonus-point score in the 59th minute through a penalty try, after yet another powerful scrum on Leeds' line, with Goode – who collected 17 points on the day – adding the conversion for a 37-13 lead.

With 20 minutes remaining, head coach John Wells looked to the rest of his bench to rub salt deeper into Tykes' wounds, but all Tigers had to show for their efforts in the final quarter was a Henry Tuilagi score, which Goode was unable to convert from wide out.

"I think a lot of real positives came out of the game, none more so than we actually won the game." **John Wells**

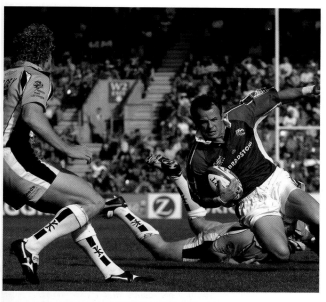

### Event Line

| Min | | Score | |
|-----|---|-------|---|
| 1 | P | 3-0 | Goode |
| 10 | ⟷ | | Dunbar for Uys |
| 12 | TC | 10-0 | M.Johnson/Goode |
| 20 | ⟷ | | Uys for Dunbar |
| 27 | P | 13-0 | Goode |
| 40 | ⟷ | | H.Tuilagi for B.Deacon |
| 40 | TC | 20-0 | Rabeni/Goode |
| 40 | P | 20-3 | Ross |

### Half-Time

| 42 | TC | 20-10 | Biggs/Ross |
|-----|---|-------|---|
| 47 | P | 23-10 | Goode |
| 47 | ⟷ | | Christophers for Bell |
| 52 | ☐ | | Murphy |
| 53 | TC | 30-10 | Ellis/Goode |
| 54 | ⟷ | | Bemand for Ellis |
| 55 | ⟷ | | A.Tuilagi for Smith |
| 57 | P | 30-13 | Ross |
| 59 | TC | 37-13 | Penalty Try/Goode |
| 59 | ⟷ | | Morris for Rowntree |
| 63 | ⟷ | | Morgan for Murphy |
| 63 | ⟷ | | Albanese for Biggs |
| 64 | ⟷ | | Dunbar for Uys |
| 72 | ⟷ | | McMillan for Dickens |
| 73 | T | 42-13 | H.Tuilagi |
| 75 | ⟷ | | Buckland for Chuter |
| 75 | ⟷ | | Broadfoot for Goode |
| 83 | TC | 42-20 | Dunbar/Ross |

### Full-Time

### Premiership Table

| Team | P | W | D | L | Pts |
|------|---|---|---|---|-----|
| 5 Saracens | 2 | 2 | 0 | 0 | 8 |
| **6 Leicester Tigers** | **2** | **1** | **0** | **1** | **6** |
| 7 London Irish | 2 | 1 | 0 | 1 | 5 |

### Tigers Milestone

Prop Graham Rowntree made his 356th appearance for Tigers in this match, taking him past club president Bob Rowell into 15th place on the all-time Leicester appearance list.

# London Irish **22**
# Leicester Tigers **39**

**Date:** 19.9.04  **Venue:** Madejski Stadium  **Attendance:** 9,472  **Referee:** W.Barnes

## Team Line-Ups

| | | |
|---|---|---|
| D.Armitage | **15** | G.Murphy |
| P.Sackey | **14** | S.Rabeni |
| G.Appleford | **13** | O.Smith |
| M.Catt | **12** | D.Gibson |
| S.Staniforth | **11** | A.Healey |
| B.Everitt | **10** | A.Goode |
| D.Edwards | **9** | H.Ellis |
| N.Hatley | **1** | G.Rowntree |
| A.Flavin | **2** | G.Chuter |
| R.Hardwick | **3** | J.White |
| N.Kennedy | **4** | (c) M.Johnson |
| B.Casey | **5** | L.Deacon |
| R.Strudwick (c) | **6** | B.Deacon |
| K.Dawson | **7** | N.Back |
| K.Roche | **8** | M.Corry |

## Replacements

| | | |
|---|---|---|
| P.Durant | **16** | J.Buckland |
| D.Paice | **17** | D.Morris |
| D.Danaher | **18** | B.Kay |
| P.Murphy | **19** | L.Abraham |
| N.Mordt | **20** | H.Tuilagi |
| P.Hodgson | **21** | S.Bemand |
| M.Mapletoft | **22** | A.Tuilagi |

## Match Stats

| | | |
|---|---|---|
| **80** | Tackles | **66** |
| **26** | Missed Tackles | **17** |
| **69** | Ball Carries | **90** |
| **342** | Metres | **480** |
| **17** | Defenders Beaten | **26** |
| **130** | Passes | **101** |
| **6** | Clean Breaks | **14** |
| **10** | Penalties Conceded | **16** |
| **10** | Turnovers | **10** |
| **47** | Breakdowns Won | **61** |
| **80** | % Scrums Won | **78** |
| **90** | % Line-Outs Won | **81** |

## Premiership Away Record vs London Irish

| Played | Won | Drawn | Lost | Points For | Points Against |
|---|---|---|---|---|---|
| **8** | **6** | **0** | **2** | **235** | **152** |

Leicester Tigers roared to a comprehensive 39-22 Zurich Premiership win over London Irish at the Madejski Stadium. Tigers led 19-15 at half-time, before taking control in the second half en route to their first away win of 2004-05, which was, unfortunately, marred by a knee injury to fly-half Andy Goode.

Tigers, courtesy of a stunning Martin Corry try after just 24 seconds and then a Seru Rabeni five-pointer, ran into an early 12-0 lead, only to go behind after a string of first-half penalties – and a Martin Johnson sin-binning – against them. They clicked into gear in the second half, however, scoring two brilliant tries as their support play took a step up and their passes began to stick.

A Barry Everitt penalty finally put the Exiles on the scoreboard, but at 3-12 down after just nine minutes, the home side would have been slightly concerned with the result of the opening exchanges. But London Irish – who looked at their happiest when the game opened up at times during the first period – began chipping away at Tigers' score through Everitt, with their No.10 slotting another four penalties to take the lead away from the visitors.

"We tried to attack their weaknesses and keep away from their strengths and I thought we did just that out there." **John Wells**

But Leicester – who let a few half-chances go a begging, as they did against Leeds the previous week – looked determined to go into the break ahead, with a try from flanker Brett Deacon putting them ahead by 19-15.

A penalty from Goode early in the second half put Tigers ahead by 22-15, before he weighed in with a five-pointer of his own, which he also converted for a 29-15 advantage. Former Wallaby Scott Staniforth scored his team's first try, which fly-half Everitt converted, but an Austin Healey try, with Corry, Neil Back and Harry Ellis all handling, put them out of sight at 36-22.

Goode added a final penalty, before being forced off with his knee injury and Tigers – who employed a five-two split between forwards and backs on the bench – found themselves in a spot of trouble, with Back forced into the backline as a stop-gap measure for two minutes.

### Event Line

| Min | | Score | |
|---|---|---|---|
| 1 | TC | 0-7 | **Corry/Goode** |
| 6 | ▢ | | **M.Johnson** |
| 7 | P | 3-7 | Everitt |
| 9 | T | 3-12 | Rabeni |
| 17 | ⟷ | | **H.Tuilagi for Corry** |
| 19 | P | 6-12 | Everitt |
| 28 | P | | Everitt |
| 31 | ⟷ | | **Corry for H.Tuilagi** |
| 34 | P | | Everitt |
| 39 | P | | Everitt |
| 40 | ⟷ | | **H.Tuilagi for B.Deacon** |
| 40 | TC | | **B.Deacon/Goode** |

### Half-Time

| | | | |
|---|---|---|---|
| 42 | ⟷ | | **B.Deacon for H.Tuilagi** |
| 46 | ⟷ | | Murphy for Roche |
| 51 | P | 15-22 | **Goode** |
| 58 | ⟷ | | **A.Tuilagi for Gibson** |
| 60 | TC | 15-29 | **Goode** |
| 60 | ⟷ | | Hodgson for Edwards |
| 62 | TC | 22-29 | Staniforth/Everitt |
| 66 | ⟷ | | Mapletoft for Armitage |
| 68 | TC | 22-36 | **Healey/Goode** |
| 71 | ⟷ | | **Bemand for Healey** |
| 74 | P | 22-39 | **Goode** |
| 76 | ▢ | | **Chuter** |
| 78 | ⟷ | | **Buckland for Corry** |
| 78 | ⟷ | | **Healey for Goode** |
| 78 | ⟷ | | Mordt for Everitt |
| 79 | ⟷ | | **Kay for L.Deacon** |

### Full-Time

### Premiership Table

| Team | P | W | D | L | Pts |
|---|---|---|---|---|---|
| 4 Northampton | 3 | 2 | 0 | 1 | 11 |
| **5 Leicester Tigers** | **3** | **2** | **0** | **1** | **11** |
| 6 Saracens | 3 | 2 | 0 | 1 | 8 |

### Tigers Milestone

Martin Corry scored the fastest Premiership try of all-time – crossing in just 24 seconds, beating Geordan Murphy's record by two seconds. Corry's record, however, was broken by Wasps' Tom Voyce later in the season.

# Leicester Tigers **32**
# Northampton Saints **13**

**Date:** 25.9.04 **Venue:** Welford Road **Attendance:** 16,815 **Referee:** T.Spreadbury

## Team Line-Ups

| G.Murphy | 15 | B.Reihana |
|---|---|---|
| S.Rabeni | 14 | J.Rudd |
| O.Smith | 13 | M.Tucker |
| D.Gibson | 12 | M.Stcherbina |
| A.Healey | 11 | B.Cohen |
| R.Broadfoot | 10 | S.Drahm |
| H.Ellis | 9 | J.Howard |
| G.Rowntree | 1 | T.Smith |
| G.Chuter | 2 | S.Thompson |
| J.White | 3 | R.Kempson |
| M.Johnson (c) | 4 | S.Boome |
| B.Kay | 5 | D.Browne |
| B.Deacon | 6 | D.Fox |
| N.Back | 7 | (c) C.Krige |
| W.Johnson | 8 | G.Seely |

## Replacements

| J.Buckland | 16 | D.Richmond |
|---|---|---|
| L.Deacon | 17 | C.Budgen |
| P.Cook | 18 | M.Lord |
| H.Tuilagi | 19 | A.Blowers |
| R.Warren | 20 | B.Jones |
| J.Holtby | 21 | W.Human |
| A.Tuilagi | 22 | J.Clarke |

## Match Stats

| | | |
|---|---|---|
| 56 | Tackles | 54 |
| 5 | Missed Tackles | 17 |
| 64 | Ball Carries | 48 |
| 380 | Metres | 159 |
| 17 | Defenders Beaten | 6 |
| 77 | Passes | 62 |
| 9 | Clean Breaks | 2 |
| 11 | Penalties Conceded | 9 |
| 17 | Turnovers | 18 |
| 43 | Breakdowns Won | 40 |
| 100 | % Scrums Won | 91 |
| 78 | % Line-Outs Won | 95 |

## Premiership Home Record vs Northampton Saints

| Played | Won | Drawn | Lost | Points For | Points Against |
|---|---|---|---|---|---|
| 8 | 5 | 1 | 2 | 185 | 156 |

Leicester Tigers overpowered East Midlands rivals, Northampton Saints, by 32-13 with a four-try blitz at a packed Welford Road. Tigers picked up an all-important four-try bonus point, whilst young fly-half Ross Broadfoot – in for the injured Andy Goode – made an impressive first start for Tigers.

Broadfoot scored 12 points, whilst Austin Healey, Neil Back, Harry Ellis and Seru Rabeni ran in tries for the home side, who were also without influential No.8 Martin Corry, who was still bearing the scars from London Irish the week before.

Healey's try came from an Ellis break down the blindside, the latter stabbing ahead and the former benefiting from a kind bounce to beat Bruce Reihana to the ball. Northampton hit back through a Shane Drahm penalty, but Broadfoot cancelled that out with his first successful attempt of the day, before another Drahm three-pointer left the score at 8-6 in Tigers' favour after 29 minutes.

Back, however, claimed a try shortly before half-time, forcing his way over from close-range, with Broadfoot converting, Tigers' No.10 also adding an early second-half penalty goal for a handy 18-6 lead.

"Everyone's delighted and they should be because it's been quite a difficult week."
**John Wells**

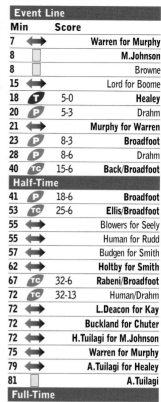

## Event Line

| Min | | Score | |
| --- | --- | --- | --- |
| 7 | ↔ | | Warren for Murphy |
| 8 | ▢ | | M.Johnson |
| 8 | | | Browne |
| 15 | ↔ | | Lord for Boome |
| 18 | T | 5-0 | Healey |
| 20 | P | 5-3 | Drahm |
| 21 | ↔ | | Murphy for Warren |
| 23 | P | 8-3 | Broadfoot |
| 28 | P | 8-6 | Drahm |
| 40 | TC | 15-6 | Back/Broadfoot |
| **Half-Time** | | | |
| 41 | P | 18-6 | Broadfoot |
| 53 | TC | 25-6 | Ellis/Broadfoot |
| 55 | ↔ | | Blowers for Seely |
| 55 | ↔ | | Human for Rudd |
| 57 | ↔ | | Budgen for Smith |
| 62 | ↔ | | Holtby for Smith |
| 67 | TC | 32-6 | Rabeni/Broadfoot |
| 72 | TC | 32-13 | Human/Drahm |
| 72 | ↔ | | L.Deacon for Kay |
| 72 | ↔ | | Buckland for Chuter |
| 72 | ↔ | | H.Tuilagi for M.Johnson |
| 75 | ↔ | | Warren for Murphy |
| 79 | ↔ | | A.Tuilagi for Healey |
| 81 | ▢ | | A.Tuilagi |
| **Full-Time** | | | |

## Premiership Table

| Team | P | W | D | L | Pts |
| --- | --- | --- | --- | --- | --- |
| 2 Gloucester | 4 | 4 | 0 | 0 | 16 |
| **3 Leicester Tigers** | **4** | **3** | **0** | **1** | **16** |
| 4 Newcastle | 4 | 3 | 0 | 1 | 13 |

### Tigers Milestone

This was Tigers' first win over Northampton, at Welford Road, in two previous starts. It was also their first win over Saints in four previous Premiership starts.

Fijian star Seru Rabeni, who was quickly making a name for himself at Welford Road, then found himself held up on Northampton's line, before Ellis scampered over for his team's third try, Rabeni eventually finding himself over the tryline in the 66th minute after good work from replacement winger John Holtby and playmaker Healey.

Broadfoot's conversion made the score 32-6, before Saints hit back in the 72nd minute through replacement winger Wylie Human, who dived over in the right-hand corner for a try that Drahm converted. But there was to be no way back for the well-beaten visitors, even after Tigers replacement Alesana Tuilagi was yellow-carded in the fifth minute of injury-time.

# Newcastle Falcons **15**
# Leicester Tigers **44**

**Date:** 2.10.04 **Venue:** Kingston Park **Attendance:** 8,609 **Referee:** R.Maybank

## Team Line-Ups

| T.May | 15 | G.Murphy |
|---|---|---|
| M.Stephenson | 14 | J.Holtby |
| J.Noon | 13 | O.Smith |
| E.Taione | 12 | S.Rabeni |
| D.Walder | 11 | S.Vesty |
| J.Wilkinson (c) | 10 | R.Broadfoot |
| H.Charlton | 9 | H.Ellis |
| I.Peel | 1 | G.Rowntree |
| A.Long | 2 | G.Chuter |
| M.Hurter | 3 | J.White |
| L.Gross | 4 | (c) M.Johnson |
| M.McCarthy | 5 | L.Deacon |
| C.Charvis | 6 | B.Deacon |
| E.Williamson | 7 | N.Back |
| S.Sititi | 8 | M.Corry |

## Replacements

| M.Ward | 16 | J.Buckland |
|---|---|---|
| J.Isaacson | 17 | B.Kay |
| S.Grimes | 18 | W.Johnson |
| G.Parling | 19 | D.Morris |
| J.Grindal | 20 | S.Bemand |
| T.Flood | 21 | M.Cornwell |
| M.Tait | 22 | A.Tuilagi |

## Match Stats

| 86 | Tackles | 93 |
|---|---|---|
| 19 | Missed Tackles | 11 |
| 75 | Ball Carries | 85 |
| 390 | Metres | 503 |
| 9 | Defenders Beaten | 12 |
| 145 | Passes | 101 |
| 6 | Clean Breaks | 11 |
| 13 | Penalties Conceded | 10 |
| 17 | Turnovers | 11 |
| 56 | Breakdowns Won | 55 |
| 83 | % Scrums Won | 100 |
| 93 | % Line-Outs Won | 92 |

## Premiership Away Record vs Newcastle Falcons

| Played | Won | Drawn | Lost | Points For | Points Against |
|---|---|---|---|---|---|
| 8 | 3 | 2 | 3 | 175 | 156 |

A brace of tries from Leicester Tigers back Seru Rabeni inspired his side to a crushing 44-15 Zurich Premiership victory over Newcastle Falcons at Kingston Park. The visitors rattled up six tries in the end in a commanding performance, with the home side managing just two of their own.

Tigers held a 17-7 half-time lead, but an unanswered 15-point blitz in just seven minutes early in the second half gave them a 32-10 lead – Rabeni's first try and a try from openside flanker Neil Back soon afterwards crushing Newcastle's hopes of a victory over the East Midlanders.

Fittingly, Rabeni scored his side's sixth and final try, but sandwiched in between his tries were further second half scores from back rows Back and Martin Corry – both courtesy of Tigers' powerful pack, which should not have to stand back to any team in the Zurich Premiership.

Tigers got on the scoreboard early in the match when Geordan Murphy – who enjoyed a roving role at the back throughout with Sam Vesty – pounced on a well-weighted chip kick from starting No.10 Ross Broadfoot in the second minute. The young fly-half summed things up well after his side drove ahead from the kick-off, and Murphy's speed got him to the ball first, with Broadfoot slotting the tricky conversion for good measure.

Vesty, who had played a second team match earlier in the week, was a late inclusion in Tigers' starting line-up, with Austin Healey having failed a fitness test, leaving Tigers with a very young looking and inexperienced backline reading: Ellis, Broadfoot, Holtby, Rabeni, Smith, Murphy (who shared the kicking duties with Broadfoot), and Vesty; injuries having claimed the likes of first-team regulars Goode, Gibson and Healey.

It was the visitors' forwards, however, who did the damage, with tighthead prop Julian White leading a dominant scrum and No.8 Corry, despite being sin-binned in the first half, impressing with some barn-storming runs.

"To go away and win two games, with bonus points, is a massive bonus for team morale and confidence." **John Wells**

### Event Line

| Min | | Score | |
|---|---|---|---|
| 1 | TC | 0-7 | **Murphy/Broadfoot** |
| 19 | TC | 7-7 | Stephenson/J.Wilkinson |
| 27 | P | 7-10 | **Broadfoot** |
| 34 | | | **Corry** |
| 34 | | | Charvis |
| 35 | TC | 7-17 | **Penalty Try/Broadfoot** |
| **Half-Time** | | | |
| 41 | ⟷ | | **Cornwell for Broadfoot** |
| 41 | ⟷ | | Ward for Peel |
| 45 | P | 10-17 | J.Wilkinson |
| 47 | P | 10-20 | **Murphy** |
| 53 | T | 10-25 | **Rabeni** |
| 57 | ⟷ | | **Kay for M.Johnson** |
| 57 | ⟷ | | Grimes for McCarthy |
| 57 | ⟷ | | Grindal for Charlton |
| 60 | TC | 10-32 | **Back/Murphy** |
| 64 | ⟷ | | **Morris for Rowntree** |
| 66 | ⟷ | | Tait for Walder |
| 67 | T | 15-32 | Tait |
| 73 | ⟷ | | **W.Johnson for B.Deacon** |
| 74 | T | 15-37 | **Corry** |
| 74 | ⟷ | | Isaacson for Hurter |
| 77 | ⟷ | | A.Tuilagi for Rabeni |
| 78 | TC | 15-44 | **Rabeni/Murphy** |
| 80 | ⟷ | | Parling for Sititi |
| **Full-Time** | | | |

### Premiership Table

| Team | P | W | D | L | Pts |
|---|---|---|---|---|---|
| 1 Sale Sharks | 5 | 5 | 0 | 0 | 21 |
| **2 Leicester Tigers** | **5** | **4** | **0** | **1** | **21** |
| 3 Gloucester | 5 | 4 | 0 | 1 | 16 |

### Tigers Milestone

Seru Rabeni scored two tries
in this match, becoming only the
second Tigers player to score
at least one try in each of his
first four starts.

# Leicester Tigers 16
# Bath Rugby 16

**Date:** 9.10.04 **Venue:** Welford Road **Attendance:** 16,815 **Referee:** C.White

## Team Line-Ups

| | | |
|---|---|---|
| G.Murphy | 15 | L.Best |
| J.Holtby | 14 | A.Higgins |
| O.Smith | 13 | R.Fleck |
| S.Rabeni | 12 | M.Tindall |
| S.Vesty | 11 | B.Daniel |
| R.Broadfoot | 10 | O.Barkley |
| H.Ellis | 9 | M.Wood |
| G.Rowntree | 1 | D.Barnes |
| G.Chuter | 2 | (c)J.Humphreys |
| J.White | 3 | D.Bell |
| M.Johnson (c) | 4 | S.Borthwick |
| B.Kay | 5 | D.Grewcock |
| B.Deacon | 6 | A.Beattie |
| N.Back | 7 | M.Lipman |
| M.Corry | 8 | Z.Fea'unati |

## Replacements

| | | |
|---|---|---|
| J.Buckland | 16 | N.Walshe |
| L.Deacon | 17 | R.Hawkins |
| D.Morris | 18 | M.Stevens |
| W.Johnson | 19 | C.Malone |
| S.Bemand | 20 | S.Davey |
| M.Cornwell | 21 | J.Scaysbrook |
| D.Hipkiss | 22 | R.Fidler |

## Match Stats

| | | |
|---|---|---|
| 101 | Tackles | 89 |
| 15 | Missed Tackles | 9 |
| 75 | Ball Carries | 63 |
| 310 | Metres | 408 |
| 9 | Defenders Beaten | 14 |
| 108 | Passes | 102 |
| 1 | Clean Breaks | 7 |
| 5 | Penalties Conceded | 15 |
| 5 | Turnovers | 7 |
| 60 | Breakdowns Won | 60 |
| 100 | % Scrums Won | 90 |
| 88 | % Line-Outs Won | 91 |

### Premiership Home Record vs Bath Rugby

| Played | Won | Drawn | Lost | Points For | Points Against |
|---|---|---|---|---|---|
| 8 | 6 | 1 | 1 | 237 | 137 |

*"We did a very good job of working our way out of our rut and putting pressure back on them and getting the two points."* **John Wells**

A late score from Leicester Tigers scrum-half Harry Ellis saw his side play to a 16-16 draw against Bath at a packed Welford Road. Tigers, who were behind for most of the match, fought back from a 0-13 half-time deficit to share the points in a hard-fought Zurich Premiership encounter.

Ellis streaked away from yet another powerful Leicester Tigers scrum to sneak in at the left-hand corner – levelling the scores at 16-all. With time running out, young fly-half Ross Broadfoot missed the incredibly tough conversion, but Tigers threw everything at their game opponents hoping to come away with the four points at home.

Tigers did well to hold Bath out after a ferocious start, but former Springbok centre Robbie Fleck set up an early try for openside Michael Lipman – albeit from a forward-looking pass. Bath fly-half Olly Barkley added the conversion for a 7-0 lead and a packed Welford Road went silent, the Leicester faithful going even quieter when Barkley weaved another kick through the uprights for a 10-0 advantage inside the first half-hour of play.

Barkley made it 13-0 before the break, before full back Geordan Murphy put Tigers on the scoreboard six minutes into the second half. A well-taken Murphy try in the right-hand corner saw the home side creep nearer and nearer to Bath, only for the visitors to edge ahead through a Barkley drop-goal.

Broadfoot, who missed a penalty attempt in the 69th minute, chipped away at the lead with a penalty goal to make it 11-16 with time running out, before some late magic from Murphy, and a subsequent hack-ahead and chase by centre Ollie Smith put Tigers back in enemy territory.

Leicester drove ahead from the line-out and won a penalty in the Bath 22, which they kicked to touch. No.8 Martin Corry took the ball at the back of the next line-out; Tigers drove ahead again and won a scrum five metres from the Bath line. Ellis fed, the scrum and it was reset, with the hosts having another scrum feed, before Ellis scampered away, diving over in the corner and drawing things level at 16-16.

## Event Line

| Min | | Score | |
|-----|----|-------|------|
| 5 | TC | 0-7 | Lipman/Barkley |
| 11 | P | 0-10 | Barkley |
| 40 | P | 0-13 | Barkley |
| **Half-Time** | | | |
| 45 | P | 3-13 | Murphy |
| 46 | ⬌ | | Cornwell for Broadfoot |
| 49 | ⬌ | | Morris for White |
| 49 | ⬌ | | W.Johnson for B.Deacon |
| 51 | ⬌ | | Stevens for Barnes |
| 54 | T | 8-13 | Murphy |
| 55 | ⬌ | | Broadfoot for Cornwell |
| 60 | DG | 8-16 | Barkley |
| 77 | P | 11-16 | Broadfoot |
| 78 | ⬌ | | Barnes for Bell |
| 80 | ⬌ | | Scaysbrook for Lipman |
| 80 | ⬌ | | Hipkiss for Rabeni |
| 84 | T | 16-16 | Ellis |
| 86 | ⬌ | | Malone for Barkley |
| **Full-Time** | | | |

## Premiership Table

| Team | P | W | D | L | Pts |
|------|---|---|---|---|-----|
| **1 Leicester Tigers** | **6** | **4** | **1** | **1** | **23** |
| 2 Sale Sharks | 6 | 5 | 0 | 1 | 22 |
| 3 Gloucester | 6 | 5 | 0 | 1 | 21 |

## Tigers Milestone

Tigers were held scoreless in the first half of this match – the first time in a league match since they trailed Gloucester 0-6 at half-time in September 1994.

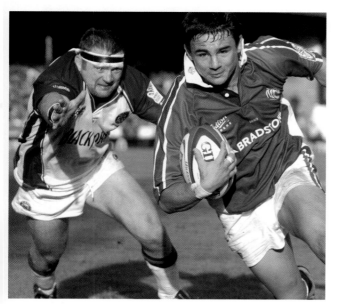

# NEC Harlequins **9**
# Leicester Tigers **15**

**Date:** 16.10.04 **Venue:** The Stoop **Attendance:** 9,954 **Referee:** D.Pearson

## Team Line-Ups

| | | |
|---|---|---|
| G.Duffy | **15** | G.Murphy |
| G.Harder | **14** | S.Vesty |
| W.Greenwood | **13** | O.Smith |
| D.James | **12** | S.Rabeni |
| S.Keogh | **11** | J.Holtby |
| J.Staunton | **10** | A.Goode |
| M.Henjak | **9** | S.Bemand |
| C.Jones | **1** | D.Morris |
| T.Fuga | **2** | G.Chuter |
| M.FitzGerald | **3** | J.White |
| R.Winters | **4** | (c) M.Johnson |
| S.Miall | **5** | B.Kay |
| N.Easter | **6** | M.Corry |
| A.Vos (c) | **7** | N.Back |
| T.Diprose | **8** | W.Johnson |

## Replacements

| | | |
|---|---|---|
| A.Tiatia | **16** | J.Buckland |
| M.Lambert | **17** | G.Rowntree |
| K.Rudzki | **18** | B.Deacon |
| L.Sherriff | **19** | L.Moody |
| S.So'oialo | **20** | H.Ellis |
| A.Jarvis | **21** | M.Cornwell |
| A.Reay | **22** | T.Varndell |

## Match Stats

| | | |
|---|---|---|
| 45 | Tackles | 71 |
| 7 | Missed Tackles | 14 |
| 63 | Ball Carries | 58 |
| 333 | Metres | 267 |
| 14 | Defenders Beaten | 7 |
| 73 | Passes | 64 |
| 5 | Clean Breaks | 7 |
| 12 | Penalties Conceded | 10 |
| 19 | Turnovers | 17 |
| 43 | Breakdowns Won | 42 |
| 94 | % Scrums Won | 92 |
| 56 | % Line-Outs Won | 83 |

### Premiership Away Record vs NEC Harlequins

| Played | Won | Drawn | Lost | Points For | Points Against |
|---|---|---|---|---|---|
| **8** | **7** | **0** | **1** | **212** | **108** |

Fit-again Leicester Tigers fly-half Andy Goode kicked five penalties to give his side a well-deserved 15-9 Zurich Premiership win over NEC Harlequins at The Stoop. In a game that never really reached great heights, Goode's goal-kicking proved decisive in the face of a determined onslaught from the home side.

Harlequins came into this match fighting for survival, having lost their first six Premiership matches of the 2004-05 season, but on the day they gave Tigers – the ZP pace-setters – plenty to think about in awful conditions, which did not suit their expansive approach.

Weather aside, Tigers' attack-orientated game also suffered a blow in the 20th minute when England centre Ollie Smith was forced to leave the field with a serious shoulder injury. Defensively, however, his replacement, young Matt Cornwell, hardly put a foot wrong against his seasoned opponents Dafydd James and Will Greenwood.

"It would've been nice to score tries and play more expansive rugby, but we couldn't do that because of the opposition." **John Wells**

Cornwell entered the fray with his side 6-3 up, Goode having slotted two long-range penalties to Jeremy Staunton's one, but his first touch was assuring enough – winning his side a penalty, which Goode converted for a 9-3 lead after 21 minutes.

Harlequins' re-start put them right back into points-scoring contention, however, and Staunton made no mistake with his third attempt at goal, narrowing the score to 9-6 after 24 minutes, before the home side gained the upperhand when Tigers openside Neil Back was sin-binned for slowing the ball down with the home side on attack.

Quins were not able to take advantage of their one-man overlap, however, and Tigers managed to stay in the game as the rain started coming down, keeping the home team scoreless for 10 minutes and Goode adding another three points before the break after a superb run from Seru Rabeni – easily Tigers' best try-scoring opportunity of the day.

Goode added one more penalty goal in a forgettable second half, which saw Leicester doing the lions' share of defending, but the visitors were deserved winners in the end.

| Event Line | | | |
|---|---|---|---|
| **Min** | | **Score** | |
| 3 | Ⓟ | 0-3 | **Goode** |
| 8 | Ⓟ | 3-3 | Staunton |
| 10 | Ⓟ | 3-6 | **Goode** |
| 20 | ⟷ | | **Cornwell for Smith** |
| 24 | Ⓟ | 3-9 | **Goode** |
| 26 | Ⓟ | 6-9 | Staunton |
| 30 | Ⓟ | 9-9 | Staunton |
| 30 | ☐ | | **Back** |
| 40 | Ⓟ | 9-12 | **Goode** |
| **Half-Time** | | | |
| 51 | Ⓟ | 9-15 | **Goode** |
| 58 | ⟷ | | **Ellis for Bemand** |
| 58 | ⟷ | | Rudzki for Winters |
| 59 | ⟷ | | Tiatia for Easter |
| 61 | ⟷ | | **Rowntree for Morris** |
| 63 | ⟷ | | Lambert for Fitzgerald |
| 72 | ⟷ | | Fitzgerald for Lambert |
| **Full-Time** | | | |

| Premiership Table | | | | | |
|---|---|---|---|---|---|
| **Team** | **P** | **W** | **D** | **L** | **Pts** |
| **1 Leicester Tigers** | **7** | **5** | **1** | **1** | **27** |
| 2 Sale Sharks | 7 | 6 | 0 | 1 | 26 |
| 3 Gloucester | 7 | 6 | 0 | 1 | 25 |

### Tigers Milestone

Andy Goode made his return from a knee injury in this match, scoring all Tigers' points via five penalty goals.

# Leicester Tigers **37**
# Ghial Rugby Calvisano **6**

**Date:** 23.10.04 **Venue:** Welford Road **Attendance:** 16,815 **Referee:** D.Changleng

## Team Line-Ups

| | | |
|---|---|---|
| S.Vesty | **15** | P.Vaccari |
| J.Holtby | **14** | L.Nitoglia |
| S.Rabeni | **13** | G.Raineri |
| D.Gibson | **12** | C.Zanoletti |
| A.Healey | **11** | A.Vodo |
| A.Goode | **10** | G.Fraser |
| H.Ellis | **9** | P.Canavosio |
| G.Rowntree | **1** | G.Bocca |
| J.Buckland | **2** | A.Moretti |
| D.Morris | **3** | S.Perugini |
| M.Johnson (c) | **4** | M.Ngauamo |
| B.Kay | **5** | J.Purll |
| B.Deacon | **6** | R.Mandelli |
| L.Moody | **7** | (c) M.Zaffiri |
| W.Johnson | **8** | V.Bernabo |

## Replacements

| | | |
|---|---|---|
| R.Cockerill | **16** | G.De Carli |
| J.White | **17** | G.Intoppa |
| H.Tuilagi | **18** | M.Castrogiovanni |
| N.Back | **19** | C.Elisara |
| S.Bemand | **20** | M.Murgier |
| M.Cornwell | **21** | P.Griffen |
| A.Tuilagi | **22** | E.Mulieri |

## Match Stats

| | | |
|---|---|---|
| **56** | Tackles | **73** |
| **11** | Missed Tackles | **5** |
| **76** | Ball Carries | **74** |
| **401** | Metres | **406** |
| **5** | Defenders Beaten | **11** |
| **14** | Passes | **15** |
| **3** | Clean Breaks | **5** |
| **7** | Penalties Conceded | **13** |
| **22** | Turnovers | **18** |
| **55** | Breakdowns Won | **46** |
| **92** | % Scrums Won | **91** |
| **95** | % Line-Outs Won | **90** |

Leicester Tigers made a perfect start to their 2004-05 Heineken Cup campaign with a clinical 37-6 victory over Calvisano at a packed Welford Road. The home side scored five tries to nil, with fit-again England flanker Lewis Moody grabbing two five-pointers and scrum-half Harry Ellis also coming away with a brace of tries.

World Cup winner Moody made his return to first-team action after a near 11-month period on the sidelines with a foot injury, and he impressed with his commitment and tackle-count.

The wet conditions were not conducive to a running game and Tigers quickly realised this, opting to keep the ball in hand after the opening exchanges and profiting from it through their powerful pack of forwards, who tore into their Italian opponents.

"I'm pretty chuffed. We were happy to get five points out of a game, which at times was very, very difficult, given the conditions." **John Wells**

## Event Line

| Min | | Score | |
|---|---|---|---|
| 8 | P | 3-0 | Goode |
| 13 | TC | 10-0 | Ellis/Goode |
| 19 | ⬌ | | White for Rowntree |
| 31 | ⬌ | | Rowntree for White |
| 32 | P | 13-0 | Goode |
| 38 | P | 13-3 | Fraser |
| **Half-Time** | | | |
| 41 | ⬌ | | Griffen for Canavosio |
| 41 | ⬌ | | Mulieri for Vaccari |
| 41 | ⬌ | | White for Rowntree |
| 41 | ⬌ | | A.Tuilagi for Healey |
| 44 | T | 18-3 | Rabeni |
| 51 | ⬌ | | Cockerill for Buckland |
| 52 | T | 23-3 | Ellis |
| 55 | ⬌ | | Castrogiovanni for Bocca |
| 56 | P | 23-6 | Fraser |
| 58 | TC | 30-6 | Moody/Goode |
| 61 | ⬌ | | Intoppa for Moretti |
| 62 | TC | 37-6 | Moody/Goode |
| 63 | ⬌ | | De Carli for Perugini |
| 64 | ⬌ | | Buckland for Cockerill |
| 70 | ⬌ | | H.Tuilagi for W.Johnson |
| 72 | ⬌ | | Cornwell for Goode |
| 75 | ⬌ | | Murgier for Raineri |
| **Full-Time** | | | |

## Heineken Cup Table

| Team | P | W | D | L | Pts |
|---|---|---|---|---|---|
| 1 Leicester Tigers | 1 | 1 | 0 | 0 | 5 |
| 2 London Wasps | 1 | 1 | 0 | 0 | 4 |
| 3 Biarritz Olympique | 1 | 0 | 0 | 1 | 0 |
| 4 Ghial Calvisano | 1 | 0 | 0 | 1 | 0 |

## Tigers Milestone

England World Cup winner Lewis Moody made his first start for Tigers since November 29, 2003, having battled a serious foot injury after the RWC. He celebrated his return to first-team action with two tries.

After a drab first half, Tigers were in danger of missing out on that precious four-try bonus point, but a much-improved second-half showing from the home side saw them score four well-worked tries.

Tigers led 13-3 at the break after a try from Ellis in the 14th minute and one conversion and two penalties from fly-half Andy Goode, but they were guilty of not taking their chances afterwards and losing the ball in contact, with the conditions reducing the ball to a bar of soap at times.

Tigers began the second half without winger Austin Healey, who had limped off during the break to be replaced by Alesana Tuilagi, but they wasted no time in putting points on the board through that man Seru Rabeni, who cruised through a gap after a five-minute spell of incessant Leicester pressure on Calvisano's line.

At 18-3 up, Tigers were really sitting pretty, but their level of play took a step up as they set about hunting down more tries to secure that valuable four-try bonus point, with Man of the Match Ellis collecting his second from via a stroll down the blindside after a powerful rolling maul and Moody grabbed his two tries in virtually identical fashion; both of them well-oiled scores, also from rolling mauls. Goode converted two of the three final tries.

# Biarritz Olympique **23**
# Leicester Tigers **8**

**Date:** 30.10.04 **Venue:** Parc des Sports Aguilera **Attendance:** 9,000 **Referee:** D.Courtney

## Team Line-Ups

| | | |
|---|---|---|
| N.Brusque | 15 | G.Murphy |
| P.Bidabe | 14 | J.Holtby |
| F.MartinAramburu | 13 | S.Rabeni |
| D.Traille | 12 | D.Gibson |
| J.Marlu | 11 | S.Vesty |
| J.Peyrelongue | 10 | A.Goode |
| D.Yachvili | 9 | H.Ellis |
| P.Balan | 1 | G.Rowntree |
| B.August | 2 | R.Cockerill |
| D.Avril | 3 | J.White |
| J.Thion (c) | 4 | (c) M.Johnson |
| D.Couzinet | 5 | B.Kay |
| S.Betsen | 6 | L.Moody |
| S.Malonga | 7 | N.Back |
| I.Harinordoquy | 8 | W.Johnson |

## Replacements

| | | |
|---|---|---|
| J.Gonzalez | 16 | J.Buckland |
| B.Lecouls | 17 | D.Morris |
| O.Booyse | 18 | B.Deacon |
| C.Milheres | 19 | H.Tuilagi |
| J.Dupuy | 20 | S.Bemand |
| B.Dambielle | 21 | M.Cornwell |
| T.Lacroix | 22 | A.Tuilagi |

## Match Stats

| | | |
|---|---|---|
| 101 | Tackles | 40 |
| 13 | Missed Tackles | 5 |
| 31 | Ball Carries | 87 |
| 112 | Metres | 368 |
| 5 | Defenders Beaten | 12 |
| 4 | Passes | 10 |
| 1 | Clean Breaks | 5 |
| 16 | Penalties Conceded | 9 |
| 10 | Turnovers | 18 |
| 30 | Breakdowns Won | 80 |
| 60 | % Scrums Won | 89 |
| 69 | % Line-Outs Won | 94 |

French outfit Biarritz handed Leicester Tigers a painful 23-8 thrashing in their Pool 1 Heineken Cup clash at the Stade Aguiléra on a sunny afternoon. Tigers, who trailed 3-20 at the break, outscored their hosts in the second half, but were guilty of conceding too many turnovers in the match, which ultimately cost them.

Biarritz scored only two tries to Tigers' one, but in-form France scrum-half Dimitri Yachvili brought his kicking boots to the ground, slotting both his side's conversions, two penalty goals and a sweetly-struck drop-goal.

Whilst Tigers made too many errors in the first half and were left with a mountain to climb in the second 40 minutes, they made a good fist of it in the final quarter of the match, only for turnovers to come back and haunt them once again. At one stage they were camped in Biarritz's 22 for nearly 20 minutes, but they were unable to get the ball over the whitewash – centre Seru Rabeni getting tackled

"We played well in the second half to get something out of the game. It seemed that we'd struggle to pick up anything at all." **John Wells**

just close, flanker Lewis Moody getting held up short and wing Sam Vesty getting held up over the line. The last attempt was referred to the Television Match Official by referee Donald Courtney, to no avail, however.

Rabeni scored Leicester's only try of the match in the 48th minute – amazingly, those were also the final points of the game – after some quick-thinking from Tigers fly-half Andy Goode and a hack-ahead by John Holtby, but Tigers' normally well-oiled backline was unable to slip into gear and challenge their hosts, whose strong-tackling centres Damien Traille and Féderico Martin Aramburu made life hard for Daryl Gibson and Rabeni.

To top it all off, Andy Goode, usually consistency personified, missed four kicks at goal, coming away with just three points via a fourth-minute penalty after a Biarritz infringement. The rest of the half, however, was all about the home side as they tore in Tigers, disrupting their rhythm and running in two typical French tries in the space of just five minutes.

## Event Line

| Min | | Score | |
|-----|-----|-------|-----|
| 4 | P | 0-3 | Goode |
| 6 | ↔ | | Buckland for Cockerill |
| 13 | P | 3-3 | Yachvili |
| 13 | ↔ | | Cockerill for Buckland |
| 24 | TC | 10-3 | Aramburu/Yachvili |
| 29 | TC | 17-3 | Marlu/Yachvili |
| 40 | DG | 20-3 | Yachvili |
| **Half-Time** | | | |
| 44 | P | 23-3 | Yachvili |
| 45 | ↔ | | H.Tuilagi for W.Johnson |
| 48 | T | 23-8 | Rabeni |
| 48 | ↔ | | Buckland for Cockerill |
| 49 | ↔ | | A.Tuilagi for Holtby |
| 58 | ↔ | | Booyse for Couzinet |
| 61 | ↔ | | Lacroix for Traille |
| 63 | ↔ | | Gonzalez for August |
| 63 | ↔ | | Lecouls for Avril |
| 64 | ↔ | | Morris for Rowntree |
| 68 | ↔ | | Milheres for Malonga |
| 70 | ↔ | | B.Deacon for Back |
| 75 | ↔ | | Avril for Balan |
| 81 | ↔ | | Cornwell for Rabeni |
| **Full-Time** | | | |

## Heineken Cup Table

| Team | P | W | D | L | Pts |
|------|---|---|---|---|-----|
| 1 London Wasps | 2 | 2 | 0 | 0 | 9 |
| **2 Leicester Tigers** | **2** | **1** | **0** | **1** | **5** |
| 3 Biarritz Olympique | 2 | 1 | 0 | 1 | 4 |
| 4 Ghial Calvisano | 2 | 0 | 0 | 2 | 0 |

## Tigers Milestone

This was Leicester's first loss in any competition since September 5, 2004.

# Leicester Tigers **28**
# Gloucester **13**

**Date:** 6.11.04  **Venue:** Welford Road  **Attendance:** 16,815  **Referee:** T.Spreadbury

## Team Line-Ups

| S.Vesty | 15 | J.Goodridge |
|---|---|---|
| D.Hipkiss | 14 | M.Garvey |
| S.Rabeni | 13 | T.Fanolua |
| D.Gibson | 12 | H.Paul |
| T.Varndell | 11 | J.Bailey |
| A.Goode | 10 | B.Davies |
| S.Bemand | 9 | A.Page |
| D.Morris | 1 | C.Bezuidenhout |
| J.Buckland | 2 | C.Fortey |
| J.White | 3 | P.Vickery |
| M.Johnson (c) | 4 | A.Eustace |
| B.Kay | 5 | M.Cornwell |
| H.Tuilagi | 6 | P.Buxton |
| L.Moody | 7 | A.Hazell |
| M.Corry | 8 | (c) J.Boer |

## Replacements

| R.Cockerill | 16 | J.Parkes |
|---|---|---|
| G.Rowntree | 17 | G.Powell |
| B.Deacon | 18 | A.Balding |
| N.Back | 19 | J.Forrester |
| A.Wright | 20 | S.Amor |
| R.Broadfoot | 21 | N.Mauger |
| A.Tuilagi | 22 | S.Kiole |

## Match Stats

| 57 | Tackles | 102 |
|---|---|---|
| 14 | Missed Tackles | 18 |
| 92 | Ball Carries | 48 |
| 572 | Metres | 202 |
| 14 | Defenders Beaten | 11 |
| 89 | Passes | 68 |
| 14 | Clean Breaks | 8 |
| 11 | Penalties Conceded | 9 |
| 20 | Turnovers | 16 |
| 62 | Breakdowns Won | 42 |
| 90 | % Scrums Won | 100 |
| 88 | % Line-Outs Won | 92 |

## Premiership Home Record vs Gloucester

| Played | Won | Drawn | Lost | Points For | Points Against |
|---|---|---|---|---|---|
| 8 | 7 | 0 | 1 | 204 | 139 |

Leicester Tigers bounced back from their disappointing Heineken Cup loss to Biarritz, recording a resounding 28-13 Zurich Premiership victory over Gloucester in front of a sell-out crowd at Welford Road, with two superb second-half tries from Alesana Tuilagi giving the home team a significant cushion in the end.

Whilst 'super sub' Tuilagi was the obvious standout on the day in the try-scoring stakes; Seru Rabeni won the official man of the match award, back row Henry Tuilagi had a colossal impact as a ball-carrier, Martin Corry made a massive difference upon his return from suspension and second row Martin Johnson, as always, led from the front.

Whilst Tuilagi's two tries were just what the doctor ordered, Fijian backline ace Seru Rabeni, scored a stunning try in the 11th minute after Gloucester had begun the game with all guns blazing, inside centre Henry Paul — who was meant to start the game at fly-half, but changed to No.12 before kick-off — opening the scoring in the second minute with a penalty goal.

"It wasn't for me or for Pat to tell them how they played against Biarritz. Today they actually stood up out there." **John Wells**

Paul's move to inside centre was one of three late changes to Gloucester's backline, the most notable being the last-minute injury to their star scrum-half Andy Gomarsall because of a back spasm, which saw young Alex Page forced into a starting role alongside fellow novice, fly-half Brad Davies.

Tigers preyed on the Cherry and Whites' lack of experience in that crucial nine-ten channel in the first half, but for all the ball that they had, and the crowd support, to boot, they were unable to turn their dominance into points.

Leicester led 10-6 at half-time, before replacement winger Tuilagi put the game beyond doubt. Alesana's first try came from a typically powerful run from his brother, Henry, before Martin Johnson, who found himself on the wing, put the younger Tuilagi away for the score. His second try came directly from a Gloucester mistake, the big winger racing almost 50 metres, before skating over after being tap-tackled by a desperate defender.

### Event Line

| Min | | Score | |
|---|---|---|---|
| 4 | P | 0-3 | Paul |
| 11 | TC | 7-3 | Rabeni/Goode |
| 17 | P | 10-3 | Goode |
| 26 | ↔ | | B.Deacon for M.Johnson |
| 36 | ↔ | | M.Johnson for B.Deacon |
| 40 | P | 10-6 | Paul |
| **Half-Time** | | | |
| 44 | P | 13-6 | Goode |
| 52 | ↔ | | Forrester for Hazell |
| 52 | ↔ | | A.Tuilagi for Hipkiss |
| 54 | T | 18-6 | A.Tuilagi |
| 56 | ↔ | | Balding for Cornwell |
| 59 | ↔ | | Rowntree for Morris |
| 62 | ↔ | | B.Deacon for H.Tuilagi |
| 66 | ↔ | | Mauger for Fanolua |
| 66 | ↔ | | Back for Moody |
| 71 | P | 21-6 | Goode |
| 73 | ↔ | | Powell for Vickery |
| 73 | ↔ | | Cockerill for Buckland |
| 74 | TC | 28-6 | A.Tuilagi/Goode |
| 75 | ↔ | | Broadfoot for Vesty |
| 78 | ↔ | | Moody for M.Johnson |
| 81 | TC | 28-13 | Paul |
| **Full-Time** | | | |

### Premiership Table

| Team | P | W | D | L | Pts |
|---|---|---|---|---|---|
| 1 Sale Sharks | 8 | 7 | 0 | 1 | 31 |
| **2 Leicester Tigers** | **8** | **6** | **1** | **1** | **31** |
| 3 London Wasps | 8 | 6 | 0 | 2 | 27 |

### Tigers Milestone

Assistant forwards coach Richard Cockerill came off the bench to replace James Buckland late in the second half – his first Premiership appearance at Welford Road since the 2001-02 season.

# Worcester Warriors **11**
# Leicester Tigers **38**

**Date:** 13.11.04  **Venue:** Sixways  **Attendance:** 8,477  **Referee:** G.Ashton-Jones

## Team Line-Ups

| | | |
|---|---|---|
| T.Delport | **15** | S.Vesty |
| D.O'Leary | **14** | T.Varndell |
| D.Rasmussen | **13** | S.Rabeni |
| G.Trueman | **12** | D.Gibson |
| B.Gollings | **11** | A.Healey |
| T.Hayes | **10** | A.Goode |
| C.Stuart-Smith | **9** | S.Bemand |
| T.Windo | **1** | M.Holford |
| B.Daly | **2** | J.Buckland |
| C.Horsman | **3** | D.Morris |
| T.Collier | **4** | (c) M.Johnson |
| C.Gillies | **5** | L.Deacon |
| L.Greeff | **6** | B.Deacon |
| P.Sanderson (c) | **7** | N.Back |
| D.Hickey | **8** | H.Tuilagi |

## Replacements

| | | |
|---|---|---|
| N.Lyman | **16** | R.Cockerill |
| A.Van Niekerk | **17** | C.Noon |
| P.Murphy | **18** | J.Hamilton |
| M.Gabey | **19** | W.Johnson |
| M.Powell | **20** | W.Skinner |
| D.Roke | **21** | M.Cornwell |
| P.Sampson | **22** | R.Broadfoot |

## Match Stats

| | | |
|---|---|---|
| 72 | Tackles | 118 |
| 15 | Missed Tackles | 9 |
| 92 | Ball Carries | 86 |
| 349 | Metres | 501 |
| 8 | Defenders Beaten | 16 |
| 124 | Passes | 113 |
| 8 | Clean Breaks | 23 |
| 6 | Penalties Conceded | 19 |
| 12 | Turnovers | 9 |
| 86 | Breakdowns Won | 46 |
| 100 | % Scrums Won | 88 |
| 77 | % Line-Outs Won | 84 |

## Premiership Away Record vs Worcester Warriors

| Played | Won | Drawn | Lost | Points For | Points Against |
|---|---|---|---|---|---|
| 1 | 1 | 0 | 0 | 38 | 11 |

Leicester Tigers negotiated their potentially tricky Zurich Premiership fixture against the Worcester Warriors with aplomb, recording a crushing 38-11 win over the Premiership new-boys at Sixways. The visitors scored six tries to one, with winger Tom Varndell running in a brilliant second-half hat-trick.

First-half tries from scrum-half Scott Bemand, openside flanker Neil Back and right-wing Austin Healey gave Tigers a 17-6 half-time lead, with Varndell – in only his second match for Leicester – running in his three tries in the space of 13 minutes (a record for Tigers in the Premiership, beating the previous fastest mark of 19 minutes set by Back against Bath in 2000), showing great strength and exceptional pace in the process.

Varndell's first try came from a scrum in --'s 22 – after fit-again second row Louis Deacon had disrupted the home team's line-out ball, forcing a knock-on and then the scrum – whilst his second score came from a superb bit of interplay between backs and forwards, with hooker James Buckland giving him the perfect try-scoring pass.

But Varndell saved his best for last, with his third try a wonderful effort after Healey elected to send the ball wide from his own 22 once again. Fly-half Andy Goode and inside centre Daryl Gibson also handled, but Varndell's pace saw him skin the Worcester defence, Gibson's pass having come shortly before Tigers' 10-metre line.

"I think it was a professional performance, but what pleased me most was what Varndell and Cornwell did out there." **John Wells**

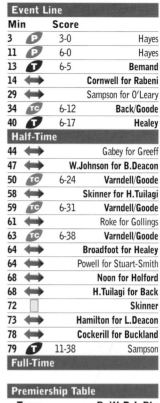

### Event Line

| Min | | Score | |
|-----|---|-------|---|
| 3 | P | 3-0 | Hayes |
| 11 | P | 6-0 | Hayes |
| 13 | T | 6-5 | Bemand |
| 14 | ⬌ | | Cornwell for Rabeni |
| 29 | ⬌ | | Sampson for O'Leary |
| 34 | TC | 6-12 | Back/Goode |
| 40 | T | 6-17 | Healey |

### Half-Time

| | | | |
|-----|---|-------|---|
| 44 | ⬌ | | Gabey for Greeff |
| 47 | ⬌ | | W.Johnson for B.Deacon |
| 50 | TC | 6-24 | Varndell/Goode |
| 58 | ⬌ | | Skinner for H.Tuilagi |
| 59 | TC | 6-31 | Varndell/Goode |
| 61 | ⬌ | | Roke for Gollings |
| 63 | TC | 6-38 | Varndell/Goode |
| 64 | ⬌ | | Broadfoot for Healey |
| 64 | ⬌ | | Powell for Stuart-Smith |
| 68 | ⬌ | | Noon for Holford |
| 68 | ⬌ | | H.Tuilagi for Back |
| 72 | ▯ | | Skinner |
| 73 | ⬌ | | Hamilton for L.Deacon |
| 78 | ⬌ | | Cockerill for Buckland |
| 79 | T | 11-38 | Sampson |

### Full-Time

### Premiership Table

| Team | P | W | D | L | Pts |
|------|---|---|---|---|-----|
| 1 Leicester Tigers | 9 | 7 | 1 | 1 | 36 |
| 2 Sale Sharks | 9 | 7 | 0 | 2 | 31 |
| 3 London Wasps | 9 | 7 | 0 | 2 | 31 |

### Tigers Milestone

Tom Varndell became the youngest-ever hat-trick try-scorer in the history of the Premiership, breaking the record previously held by Gloucester winger Marcel Garvey.

Despite Tigers' second-half blitzkrieg, however, it was all Worcester Warriors for the first 12 minutes of the match and the home team held a deserved 6-0 lead. Coach John Wells had warned all and sundry about Worcester's "brawling and nasty" pack and they certainly got stuck into Leicester, with fly-half Tommy Hayes slotting two penalty goals after all their early pressure.

But Gibson marshalled Tigers' defence superbly, whilst Healey made a welcome return to the Leicester line-up, having played just 40 minutes (against Calvisano) in the previous six weeks, with a host of niggling injuries contriving to keep him off the field.

On a disappointing note, Fijian star Rabeni suffered a knee injury early on, which was to come back and haunt him later in the season, with 19-year-old Matt Cornwell ably standing in for the Tigers' try-scoring machine.

# London Wasps 17
# Leicester Tigers 17

**Date:** 21.11.04 **Venue:** Causeway Stadium **Attendance:** 10,000 **Referee:** A.Rowden

## Team Line-Ups

| M.Van Gisbergen | 15 | S.Vesty |
|---|---|---|
| E.Thrower | 14 | T.Varndell |
| P.Richards | 13 | M.Cornwell |
| A.Erinle | 12 | D.Gibson |
| T.Voyce | 11 | A.Healey |
| J.Brooks | 10 | A.Goode |
| M.Dawson | 9 | S.Bemand |
| C.Dowd | 1 | M.Holford |
| P.Greening | 2 | J.Buckland |
| W.Green | 3 | D.Morris |
| S.Shaw | 4 | (c) M.Johnson |
| R.Birkett | 5 | L.Deacon |
| J.Hart | 6 | W.Johnson |
| T.Rees | 7 | N.Back |
| L.Dallaglio (c) | 8 | H.Tuilagi |

## Replacements

| T.Leota | 16 | E.Taukafa |
|---|---|---|
| A.McKenzie | 17 | M.Hampson |
| M.Lock | 18 | J.Hamilton |
| J.Haskell | 19 | D.Montagu |
| H.Biljon | 20 | A.Dodge |
| M.Priscott | 21 | R.Broadfoot |
| R.Hoadley | 22 | W.Skinner |

## Match Stats

| 59 | Tackles | 65 |
|---|---|---|
| 10 | Missed Tackles | 17 |
| 54 | Ball Carries | 62 |
| 272 | Metres | 357 |
| 17 | Defenders Beaten | 10 |
| 58 | Passes | 88 |
| 4 | Clean Breaks | 3 |
| 7 | Penalties Conceded | 12 |
| 14 | Turnovers | 16 |
| 46 | Breakdowns Won | 47 |
| 100 | % Scrums Won | 100 |
| 77 | % Line-Outs Won | 83 |

### Premiership Away Record vs London Wasps

| Played | Won | Drawn | Lost | Points For | Points Against |
|---|---|---|---|---|---|
| **8** | **3** | **1** | **4** | **185** | **200** |

A late try from winger Austin Healey and a superb conversion in difficult conditions from fly-half Andy Goode gave Leicester Tigers a 17-17 draw against London Wasps in an entertaining Zurich Premiership clash at the Causeway Stadium in High Wycombe.

Tigers finished the match strongly after fighting back from a 7-17 deficit in the final quarter, with Goode slotting a long-range penalty and then converting Healey's score.

The build-up to Healey's try was vintage Tigers as they battered a tiring Wasps pack with a host of line-outs on their line, before Healey sliced through the Wasps defence like a hot knife through butter. The 10,000-strong crowd went silent and one could hear a pin drop as Goode lined up and successfully slotted the conversion virtually from the touchline, with the Tigers supporters in the crowd showing their approval.

Goode very nearly won the match for his side with a long-range drop-goal attempt in virtually the final act of play in the match, but Leicester can feel satisfied with the result – a draw at the defending champions' home ground without six England internationals, one Irish test player and nine injured players, one of whom is Fijian sensation Seru Rabeni, the leading try-scorer in the Zurich Premiership.

During the game itself, Tigers took the lead for the one and only time midway through the first half when young winger Tom Varndell finished off a superb backline move, which saw the flyer dummy Wasps full back Mark Van Gisbergen before gliding over for his fourth try in two weeks.

Tigers' try, and Goode's subsequent conversion, gave the visitors a 7-6 lead after two long-range penalties from London Wasps right-wing Edd Thrower within the first 15 minutes had given them an early 6-0 advantage.

Aside from Varndell's score, both sides' defences held out for most of the first half, with Tigers opting for clever cross-kicks in a bid to unlock the Wasps defence, with Goode and Healey, in particular, doing their utmost to give Varndell a run on the outside.

"I'm pleased we got something out of it as it looked like were only going to get one point out of this match at one stage." **John Wells**

| Event Line | | | |
|---|---|---|---|
| **Min** | | **Score** | |
| 8 | P | 3-0 | Thrower |
| 15 | P | 6-0 | Thrower |
| 18 | TC | 6-7 | **Varndell/Goode** |
| 34 | T | 11-7 | Van Gisbergen |
| Half-Time | | | |
| 58 | P | 14-7 | Thrower |
| 61 | ⟷ | | **Montagu for H.Tuilagi** |
| 63 | P | 17-7 | Thrower |
| 63 | ⟷ | | Leota for Greening |
| 66 | ⟷ | | **Taukafa for Buckland** |
| 68 | P | 17-10 | Goode |
| 77 | TC | 17-17 | **Healey/Goode** |
| 78 | ⟷ | | Lock for Hart |
| 80 | ⟷ | | Biljon for Dawson |
| Full-Time | | | |

| Premiership Table | | | | | |
|---|---|---|---|---|---|
| **Team** | **P** | **W** | **D** | **L** | **Pts** |
| **1 Leicester Tigers** | **10** | **7** | **2** | **1** | **38** |
| 2 London Wasps | 10 | 7 | 1 | 2 | 33 |
| 3 Sale Sharks | 10 | 7 | 0 | 3 | 32 |

### Tigers Milestone

Austin Healey's match-saving try was his 56th score for Tigers in his 200th match for the club.

# Leicester Tigers 21
# Saracens 9

**Date:** 27.11.04 **Venue:** Welford Road **Attendance:** 16,815 **Referee:** D.Pearson

## Team Line-Ups

| S.Vesty | 15 | R.Kydd |
|---|---|---|
| T.Varndell | 14 | R.Haughton |
| D.Hipkiss | 13 | B.Johnston |
| D.Gibson | 12 | K.Sorrell |
| A.Healey | 11 | T.Castaignede |
| A.Goode | 10 | M.Bartholomeusz |
| S.Bemand | 9 | M.Williams |
| M.Holford | 1 | K.Yates |
| R.Cockerill | 2 | M.Cairns |
| D.Morris | 3 | C.Visagie |
| M.Johnson (c) | 4 | S.Raiwalui |
| L.Deacon | 5 | I.Fullarton |
| B.Deacon | 6 | T.Randell |
| N.Back | 7 | B.Skirving |
| H.Tuilagi | 8 | (c) H.Vyvyan |

## Replacements

| J.Buckland | 16 | A.Kyriacou |
|---|---|---|
| M.Hampson | 17 | N.Lloyd |
| J.Hamilton | 18 | K.Chesney |
| W.Johnson | 19 | D.Seymour |
| R.Broadfoot | 20 | M.Rauluni |
| O.Smith | 21 | G.Jackson |
| L.Lloyd | 22 | T.Vaikona |

## Match Stats

| 71 | Tackles | 105 |
|---|---|---|
| 10 | Missed Tackles | 21 |
| 100 | Ball Carries | 57 |
| 472 | Metres | 240 |
| 21 | Defenders Beaten | 10 |
| 145 | Passes | 78 |
| 23 | Clean Breaks | 10 |
| 9 | Penalties Conceded | 8 |
| 19 | Turnovers | 16 |
| 73 | Breakdowns Won | 48 |
| 85 | % Scrums Won | 90 |
| 89 | % Line-Outs Won | 82 |

## Premiership Home Record vs Saracens

| Played | Won | Drawn | Lost | Points For | Points Against |
|---|---|---|---|---|---|
| 8 | 7 | 1 | 0 | 257 | 110 |

A late try from replacement centre Ollie Smith – in his comeback game after a five-game lay-off because of a shoulder injury sustained against NEC Harlequins – gave Leicester Tigers a hard-fought 21-9 win over Saracens in Zurich Premiership action at Welford Road.

Smith's try – his first of the season – and fly-half Andy Goode's subsequent conversion, stretched the final score from 14-9 to 21-9, giving Leicester their third successive triumph in the absence of their England stars and Ireland's Geordan Murphy, whilst the return from injury of Smith and Leon Lloyd and the superb showings from No.8 Henry Tuilagi and scrum-half Scott Bemand would also have pleased head coach John Wells.

Bemand ended up with the official Man of the Match Award, but it could easily have gone to Tuilagi, whose powerful running and punishing defence kept his side on the front foot. Skipper Martin Johnson was his usual dependable self, whilst Goode, despite not having the best day kicking-wise, was a constant thorn in Sarries' flesh on attack, combing superbly with inside centre Daryl Gibson.

"I'm very proud of what they've achieved over the last three weeks considering the amount of changes we've been through. **John Wells**

Tigers outscored their visitors by two tries to nil in the end, with a first-half effort from try-scoring machine Tom Varndell handing his side an 8-6 half-time advantage, after Saracens had taken a surprise 6-3 lead after 31 minutes of play.

Two more Goode penalties took his team into a 14-6 lead in the second half, before Smith raced over from a five-metre scrum in the 78th minute; Bemand flinging out a pass which Smith ran onto, eventually coasting over for the crucial five-pointer, which Goode converted.

Gibson came very close to notching up his team's third try, after a committed chip and charge from wily veteran Austin Healey, but it was not to be for the visitors as referee Dave Pearson sounded his final whistle – the scoreboard reading Leicester Tigers 21 Saracens 9.

## Event Line

| Min | | Score | |
|-----|-----|-------|-----|
| 3 | P | 3-0 | Goode |
| 11 | P | 3-3 | Kydd |
| 32 | P | 3-6 | Kydd |
| 36 | T | 8-6 | Varndell |
| **Half-Time** | | | |
| 41 | ↔ | | Seymour for Skirving |
| 45 | ↔ | | **Smith for Hipkiss** |
| 56 | P | 11-6 | Goode |
| 58 | P | 14-6 | Goode |
| 59 | ↔ | | Chesney for Raiwalui |
| 59 | ↔ | | Jackson for Kydd |
| 61 | P | 14-9 | Jackson |
| 63 | ↔ | | **Lloyd for Varndell** |
| 65 | ↔ | | Lloyd for Yates |
| 65 | ↔ | | Rauluni for Williams |
| 69 | ↔ | | **W.Johnson for H.Tuilagi** |
| 77 | TC | 21-9 | **Smith/Goode** |
| 81 | ↔ | | Vaikona for Bartholomeusz |
| 83 | ↔ | | **Buckland for B.Deacon** |
| **Full-Time** | | | |

## Premiership Table

| Team | P | W | D | L | Pts |
|------|---|---|---|---|-----|
| **1 Leicester Tigers** | **11** | **8** | **2** | **1** | **42** |
| 2 London Wasps | 11 | 7 | 1 | 3 | 34 |
| 3 Sale Sharks | 11 | 7 | 0 | 4 | 32 |

## Tigers Milestone

Saracens have now never won in 28 previous visits to Welford Road. The closest they ever came was a 10-all draw in the Premiership in April 1998

# London Wasps **31**
# Leicester Tigers **37**

**Date:** 5.12.04 **Venue:** Causeway Stadium **Attendance:** 10,000 **Referee:** N.Williams

## Team Line-Ups

| | | |
|---|---|---|
| M.V-Gisbergen | **15** | G.Murphy |
| J.Lewsey | **14** | L.Lloyd |
| A.Erinle | **13** | O.Smith |
| S.Abbott | **12** | D.Gibson |
| T.Voyce | **11** | A.Healey |
| A.King | **10** | A.Goode |
| M.Dawson | **9** | H.Ellis |
| C.Dowd | **1** | G.Rowntree |
| P.Greening | **2** | G.Chuter |
| W.Green | **3** | J.White |
| S.Shaw | **4** | (c) M.Johnson |
| R.Birkett | **5** | L.Deacon |
| J.Worsley | **6** | L.Moody |
| J.O'Connor | **7** | N.Back |
| L.Dallaglio (c) | **8** | M.Corry |

## Replacements

| | | |
|---|---|---|
| B.Gotting | **16** | R.Cockerill |
| A.McKenzie | **17** | B.Kay |
| J.Haskell | **18** | D.Morris |
| J.Hart | **19** | W.Johnson |
| H.Biljon | **20** | S.Bemand |
| J.Brooks | **21** | S.Vesty |
| R.Hoadley | **22** | A.Tuilagi |

## Match Stats

| | | |
|---|---|---|
| 35 | Tackles | 95 |
| 6 | Missed Tackles | 11 |
| 81 | Ball Carries | 45 |
| 358 | Metres | 283 |
| 11 | Defenders Beaten | 6 |
| 8 | Passes | 15 |
| 5 | Clean Breaks | 4 |
| 10 | Penalties Conceded | 19 |
| 14 | Turnovers | 13 |
| 62 | Breakdowns Won | 30 |
| 55 | % Scrums Won | 100 |
| 93 | % Line-Outs Won | 86 |

Leicester Tigers recorded a nail-biting 37-31 Heineken Cup victory over London Wasps in an absorbing encounter at the Causeway Stadium in High Wycombe. The result, which was set up by an outstanding first-half showing by Leicester, and fly-half Andy Goode's goal-kicking in the latter stages of the match, sets up Pool 1 of the competition for an exciting finale.

Goode missed just one kick at goal, slotting a crucial late penalty goal and also adding a drop-goal from close-range in the 78th minute, for a personal haul of 22 points on the day.

"It was an emotional last few moments, pegged down on our own line and a penalty try going to come if anything else went amiss. I'm very proud of the lads." **John Wells**

| Event Line | | | |
|---|---|---|---|
| **Min** | | **Score** | |
| 1 | TC | 0-7 | Moody/Goode |
| 8 | P | 0-10 | Goode |
| 12 | T | 0-15 | Murphy |
| 14 | P | 3-15 | Van Gisbergen |
| 17 | P | 6-15 | Van Gisbergen |
| 18 | TC | 6-22 | Corry/Goode |
| 23 | | | Ellis |
| 26 | TC | 13-22 | Lewsey/Van Gisbergen |
| 37 | P | 16-22 | Van Gisbergen |
| 39 | P | 16-25 | Goode |
| 40 | P | 19-25 | Van Gisbergen |
| **Half-Time** | | | |
| 45 | P | 22-25 | Van Gisbergen |
| 52 | P | 25-25 | Van Gisbergen |
| 59 | P | 25-28 | Goode |
| 59 | ↔ | | Gotting for Greening |
| 61 | P | 25-31 | Goode |
| 65 | ↔ | | McKenzie for Green |
| 67 | P | 28-31 | Van Gisbergen |
| 68 | ↔ | | A.Tuilagi for Lloyd |
| 69 | P | 31-31 | Van Gisbergen |
| 78 | P | 31-34 | Goode |
| 81 | DG | 31-37 | Goode |
| **Full Time** | | | |

But Leicester's powerful front row will be quick to point out that they also had a role to play in the lead-up to Goode's penalty goal in the 77th minute, with referee Nigel Williams awarding the visitors with a penalty after yet another dominant scrum, Goode making no mistake – putting his side ahead by 34-31. The match, however, was far from over and Goode's snap-drop gave them a handy six-point advantage at a crucial stage, although Leicester's brave defensive effort on their own line in the closing stages of the game also deserves a mention.

Whilst the ending to this game had the crowd on its feet, the match started out at a frantic pace, with Leicester Tigers running in three stunning tries as they racked up a 22-6 lead after 18 minutes.

Flanker Lewis Moody crossed after just one minute and 13 seconds of play, shortly followed by a try to full back Geordan Murphy. At 0-15 down, Wasps clawed their way back through two well-struck Mark Van Gisbergen penalties, but the visitors hit back with a Martin Corry try – a phase of play that could easily have come right out of an Australian Rules playbook, leaving Tigers in control at 22-6.

A try by Josh Lewsey and Van Gisbergen's accurate kicking boot kept Wasps in the match, Tigers holding a 25-19 half-time lead, before levelling the scores at 25-25 and then 31-31 in the second half. Goode, however, kept his cool, slotting the tricky penalty, as well as a drop-goal, for a crucial away win over the defending champions.

### Heineken Cup Table

| Team | P | W | D | L | Pts |
|---|---|---|---|---|---|
| 1 London Wasps | 3 | 2 | 0 | 1 | 10 |
| 2 Biarritz Olympique | 3 | 2 | 0 | 1 | 9 |
| **3 Leicester Tigers** | 3 | 2 | 0 | 1 | 9 |
| 4 Ghial Calvisano | 3 | 0 | 0 | 3 | 0 |

### Tigers Milestone

Prop Graham Rowntree, who scored Leicester's first Heineken Cup try back in 1996 – became the first-ever Englishman to clock up 50 appearances in the Heineken Cup.

# Leicester Tigers **35**
# London Wasps **27**

Date: 12.12.04  Venue: Welford Road  Attendance: 16,815  Referee: A.Rolland

## Team Line-Ups

| | | |
|---|---|---|
| G.Murphy | 15 | M.V-Gisbergen |
| L.Lloyd | 14 | J.Lewsey |
| O.Smith | 13 | A.Erinle |
| D.Gibson | 12 | S.Abbott |
| A.Healey | 11 | T.Voyce |
| A.Goode | 10 | A.King |
| H.Ellis | 9 | M.Dawson |
| G.Rowntree | 1 | C.Dowd |
| G.Chuter | 2 | B.Gotting |
| J.White | 3 | W.Green |
| M.Johnson (c) | 4 | S.Shaw |
| B.Kay | 5 | R.Birkett |
| L.Moody | 6 | J.Worsley |
| N.Back | 7 | J.O'Connor |
| M.Corry | 8 | (c) L.Dallaglio |

## Replacements

| | | |
|---|---|---|
| R.Cockerill | 16 | J.Barrett |
| L.Deacon | 17 | A.McKenzie |
| D.Morris | 18 | J.Haskell |
| W.Johnson | 19 | J.Hart |
| S.Bemand | 20 | H.Biljon |
| S.Vesty | 21 | J.Brooks |
| A.Tuilagi | 22 | R.Hoadley |

## Match Stats

| | | |
|---|---|---|
| 122 | Tackles | 87 |
| 14 | Missed Tackles | 14 |
| 99 | Ball Carries | 105 |
| 605 | Metres | 384 |
| 14 | Defenders Beaten | 14 |
| 16 | Passes | 14 |
| 8 | Clean Breaks | 4 |
| 9 | Penalties Conceded | 11 |
| 18 | Turnovers | 13 |
| 75 | Breakdowns Won | 86 |
| 85 | % Scrums Won | 92 |
| 89 | % Line-Outs Won | 70 |

There was more drama and plenty of excitement after yet another superb Heineken Cup Pool 1 clash between Leicester Tigers and London Wasps, with the home side coming away with a well-deserved 35-27 win over the reigning champions.

For the second week in a row these two quality outfits produced a contest of the highest quality and with last Sunday's 37-31 win for Leicester Tigers aptly termed the 'Battle of Britain, Part One', we were treated to 'Part Two' at Welford Road, with tries, scrums, drama and moments of individual brilliance the order of the day.

In fact, those watching could have been forgiven for thinking it was Groundhog Day, with the start of this fixture mirroring the beginning to last week's helter-skelter 80-odd minutes at High Wycombe. Tigers scored early on, when fly-half Andy Goode chipped over a penalty from short-range after a dominant Tigers scrum, and they kept the scoreboard

"I thought both teams were tremendous today. I think the best team won, but Wasps contributed to another game which was excellent in terms of its intensity and quality."
**John Wells**

rolling, before it was the turn of Wasps to give the scoreboard operators something to do as they hit back with a 13-point blitz of their own.

Wasps' burst left the score at 19-13 in Leicester's favour with half-time fast approaching, but the home team showed that ruthless streak that was missing last week as they added two more opportunistic five-pointers before the break.

Scrum-half Harry Ellis dashed away for his team's first try of the day, followed by a further three Andy Goode penalties and at 0-19, Wasps staged an immediate comeback through a Tom Voyce try. Further first-half tries from Leon Lloyd and George Chuter, however, left the home team ahead by 29-13 at half-time.

A Joe Worsley try cut the score to 20-29 early in the second half, but two Goode penalties put Tigers more than two converted tries ahead, despite prop Will Green rumbling over for the visitors. Tigers battled gamely for that all-important fourth try. It did not come in the end, but few would have guessed just how crucial it would eventually become in the final Heineken Cup analysis.

### Event Line

| Min | | Score | |
|---|---|---|---|
| 3 | P | 3-0 | Goode |
| 5 | TC | 10-0 | Ellis/Goode |
| 9 | P | 13-0 | Goode |
| 17 | P | 16-0 | Goode |
| 20 | P | 19-0 | Goode |
| 25 | P | 19-3 | Van Gisbergen |
| 26 | ⬌ | | Morris for Rowntree |
| 29 | P | 19-6 | Van Gisbergen |
| 31 | TC | 19-13 | Voyce/Van Gisbergen |
| 36 | ⬌ | | Rowntree for Morris |
| 38 | T | 24-13 | Chuter |
| 40 | T | 29-13 | Lloyd |

### Half-Time

| 49 | TC | 29-20 | Worsley/Van Gibergen |
|---|---|---|---|
| 56 | P | 32-20 | Goode |
| 62 | ⬌ | | Hoadley for Erinle |
| 66 | ⬌ | | Biljon for Dawson |
| 67 | P | 35-20 | Goode |
| 69 | TC | 35-27 | Green/Van Gisbergen |
| 74 | ⬌ | | Brooks for King |
| 75 | ⬌ | | Bemand for Ellis |
| 79 | ⬌ | | Hart for Abbott |
| 80 | ⬌ | | Abbott for Hart |

### Full-Time

### Heineken Cup Table

| Team | P | W | D | L | Pts |
|---|---|---|---|---|---|
| 1 Biarritz Olympique | 4 | 3 | 0 | 1 | 14 |
| **2 Leicester Tigers** | **4** | **3** | **0** | **1** | **13** |
| 3 London Wasps | 4 | 2 | 0 | 2 | 10 |
| 4 Ghial Calvisano | 4 | 0 | 0 | 4 | 0 |

### Tigers Milestone

Flanker Lewis Moody joined an illustrious Leicester club in making his 100th first-team appearance, having made his debut in August 1996.

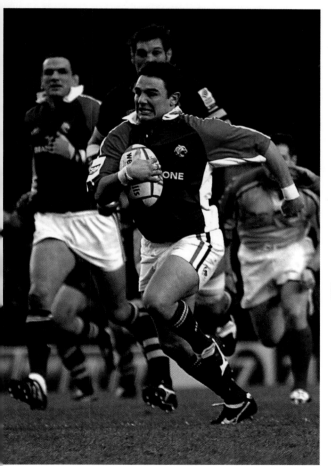

# Leicester Tigers **13**
# Gloucester **20**

**Date:** 18.12.04 **Venue:** Welford Road **Attendance:** 9,902 **Referee:** A.Rowden

## Team Line-Ups

| | | |
|---|---|---|
| S.Vesty | **15** | J.Goodridge |
| A.Tuilagi | **14** | M.Garvey |
| L.Lloyd | **13** | N.Mauger |
| O.Smith | **12** | H.Paul |
| T.Varndell | **11** | S.Kiole |
| R.Broadfoot | **10** | B.Davies |
| S.Bemand | **9** | A.Gomarsall |
| M.Holford | **1** | C.Bezuidenhout |
| G.Chuter | **2** | M.Davies |
| D.Morris | **3** | G.Powell |
| J.Hamilton | **4** | A.Eustace |
| B.Kay (c) | **5** | A.Brown |
| B.Deacon | **6** | (c) J.Boer |
| L.Moody | **7** | A.Hazell |
| W.Johnson | **8** | A.Balding |

## Replacements

| | | |
|---|---|---|
| E.Taukafa | **16** | N.Curnier |
| G.Rowntree | **17** | N.Wood |
| L.Deacon | **18** | P.Buxton |
| N.Back | **19** | J.Forrester |
| A.Wright | **20** | A.Page |
| D.Hipkiss | **21** | T.Fanolua |
| R.Warren | **22** | J.Bailey |

Leicester Tigers' 2004-05 Powergen Cup campaign was to be short-lived, with the young home side falling 13-20 to Gloucester in Round Six action at Welford Road. Tigers, who led 7-3 at half-time thanks to an opportunistic Tom Varndell try, were rocked by a sin-binning and a penalty try shortly afterwards in the second half, which ultimately cost them the match.

The 'Cherry and Whites' took the game away from Tigers in a dramatic spell between the 58th and 61st minutes when the home side lost flanker Brett Deacon to the sin bin – for hands in the ruck – and afterwards referee Ashley Rowden firmly removed himself from the Welford Road Christmas card list when he awarded the visitors a penalty try after an incessant amount of pressure on Leicester's line.

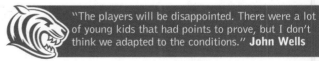

"The players will be disappointed. There were a lot of young kids that had points to prove, but I don't think we adapted to the conditions." **John Wells**

Gloucester's spell of pressure began in the 51st minute when they opted to kick a penalty to touch in Leicester's 22. They won another two penalties, before being rewarded with a five-metre scrum when they were held up over Tigers' tryline. Deacon was then yellow-carded, Gloucester won another three penalties and then Rowden trotted under the uprights, signalling the penalty try amongst a loud chorus of boos from the crowd.

Then, just two minutes later, a fairly innocent looking high bomb from a Gloucester player eluded Tigers replacement Roger Warren and it seemed to go forward off a Cherry and White player. The referee continued with play and the ball bounced into inside centre Henry Paul's hands. Paul did some fancy footwork, before the ball found its way to outside centre Nathan Mauger for the run-in, Paul making no mistake with the conversion for the 14-point swing, which knocked the stuffing out of the Tigers.

The home side, to their credit, did fight back strongly, and the likes of forwards George Chuter, James Hamilton, Ben Kay and Lewis Moody featured prominently – as they did in the first half – but all they had to show from the second half was an early penalty from fly-half Ross Broadfoot and a three-pointer from full back Sam Vesty in the 73rd minute, which took the score to 13-20 and put the home side just a goal away.

## Event Line

| Min | | Score | |
|-----|-----|-------|-----|
| 11 | P | 0-3 | Paul |
| 36 | TC | 7-3 | Varndell/Broadfoot |
| **Half-Time** | | | |
| 45 | T | 7-6 | Paul |
| 49 | P | 10-6 | Broadfoot |
| 49 | ⟷ | | Buxton for Eustace |
| 56 | ▯ | | B.Deacon |
| 58 | TC | 10-13 | Paul |
| 59 | ⟷ | | Warren for Broadfoot |
| 61 | TC | 10-20 | Mauger/Paul |
| 61 | ⟷ | | Forrester for Hazell |
| 73 | P | 13-20 | Vesty |
| 75 | ⟷ | | Taukafa for Chuter |
| 82 | ⟷ | | Hipkiss for A.Tuilagi |
| **Full-Time** | | | |

## Tigers Milestone

This game marked utility back Sam Vesty's 50th appearance for Tigers – 34 starts and 16 appearances off the bench.

# Leicester Tigers **50**
# Worcester Warriors **7**

**Date:** 27.12.04  **Venue:** Welford Road  **Attendance:** 16,815  **Referee:** R.Debney

## Team Line-Ups

| | | |
|---|---|---|
| G.Murphy | **15** | T.Delport |
| S.Rabeni | **14** | G.Pieters |
| O.Smith | **13** | B.Hinshelwood |
| D.Gibson | **12** | G.Trueman |
| S.Vesty | **11** | P.Sampson |
| A.Goode | **10** | J.Brown |
| S.Bemand | **9** | N.Cole |
| G.Rowntree | **1** | T.Windo |
| G.Chuter | **2** | A.Van Niekerk |
| J.White | **3** | C.Horsman |
| M.Johnson (c) | **4** | T.Collier |
| L.Deacon | **5** | C.Gillies |
| W.Johnson | **6** | D.Hickey |
| N.Back | **7** | (c) P.Sanderson |
| M.Corry | **8** | B.MacLeod-Henderson |

## Replacements

| | | |
|---|---|---|
| J.Buckland | **16** | L.Fortey |
| B.Deacon | **17** | C.Hall |
| D.Morris | **18** | S.Vaili |
| B.Kay | **19** | P.Murphy |
| H.Ellis | **20** | M.Powell |
| M.Cornwell | **21** | T.Hayes |
| D.Hipkiss | **22** | D.Roke |

## Match Stats

| | | |
|---|---|---|
| 68 | Tackles | 68 |
| 10 | Missed Tackles | 15 |
| 80 | Ball Carries | 56 |
| 575 | Metres | 295 |
| 17 | Defenders Beaten | 11 |
| 134 | Passes | 85 |
| 14 | Clean Breaks | 6 |
| 9 | Penalties Conceded | 9 |
| 18 | Turnovers | 17 |
| 48 | Breakdowns Won | 47 |
| 95 | % Scrums Won | 89 |
| 90 | % Line-Outs Won | 84 |

## Premiership Home Record vs Worcester Warriors

| Played | Won | Drawn | Lost | Points For | Points Against |
|---|---|---|---|---|---|
| 1 | 1 | 0 | 0 | 50 | 7 |

There was plenty of Christmas cheer at Welford Road post-Boxing Day, but Martin Johnson and his team limited the pleasantries to the sidelines, with Leicester Tigers racking up a clinical 50-7 win over Worcester Warriors. Leicester ran in seven superb tries as they cemented their place at the top of the Zurich Premiership standings at the end of 2004 with yet another commanding victory.

There were plenty of heroes for Tigers, none more so than fly-half Andy Goode, who contributed 20 points – through one try, six conversions and one penalty goal – whilst utility backs Sam Vesty and Dan Hipkiss, two late replacements on the day, slotted in superbly well.

Vesty came into the starting line-up for the injured Austin Healey, whilst Hipkiss replaced Fijian star Seru Rabeni – who was still battling with his knee – in the 12th minute after the latter was forced into a starting role at the 11th hour when flyer Tom Varndell withdrew after falling ill.

"We went into the game knowing full well that we needed to scrummage well, which is why I think White got Man of the Match." **John Wells**

## Event Line

| Min | | Score | |
|-----|---|-------|---|
| 6 | P | 3-0 | Goode |
| 13 | ⟷ | | Hipkiss for Rabeni |
| 15 | TC | 10-0 | Back/Goode |
| 20 | ⟷ | | Morris for Rowntree |
| 39 | TC | 17-0 | Penalty Try/Goode |
| 40 | TC | 24-0 | Gibson/Goode |
| 40 | T | 29-0 | Goode |
| **Half-Time** | | | |
| 41 | ⟷ | | Fortey for Windo |
| 41 | ⟷ | | Hayes for Brown |
| 48 | TC | 36-0 | Murphy/Goode |
| 49 | ⟷ | | Ellis for Bemand |
| 52 | ⟷ | | Cornwell for Smith |
| 60 | ⟷ | | Murphy for Collier |
| 63 | TC | 36-7 | Trueman/Hayes |
| 63 | ⟷ | | Buckland for Chuter |
| 63 | ⟷ | | Kay for M.Johnson |
| 66 | ⟷ | | Hall for Van Niekerk |
| 67 | TC | 43-7 | Ellis/Goode |
| 76 | TC | 50-7 | Hipkiss/Goode |
| 76 | ⟷ | | B.Deacon for Back |
| **Full-Time** | | | |

## Premiership Table

| Team | P | W | D | L | Pts |
|------|---|---|---|---|-----|
| 1 Leicester Tigers | 12 | 9 | 2 | 1 | 47 |
| 2 London Wasps | 12 | 8 | 1 | 3 | 38 |
| 3 Sale Sharks | 12 | 8 | 0 | 4 | 36 |

## Tigers Milestone

Twenty-two-year-old Ollie Smith played his 100th match for Tigers (84 starts, 15 off the bench). Only seven players in the history of Tigers have reached the 100-game milestone, including the likes of Paul Dodge, Barry Evans and Steve Kenney.

Leicester's first-half tries were scored by flanker Neil Back, a penalty try, inside centre Daryl Gibson and fly-half Andy Goode, the latter also striking three conversions and one penalty for good measure.

Leicester's fifth try came in the 47th minute, via some Geordan Murphy magic, which saw him collect his own kick ahead, followed by tries to scrum-half Harry Ellis – who came on as a replacement for Scott Bemand – and Hipkiss; the latter's try bringing the crowd to its feet after wonderful interplay between backs and forwards.

# Gloucester **13**
# Leicester Tigers **28**

**Date:** 2.1.05 **Venue:** Kingsholm **Attendance:** 13,000 **Referee:** D.Pearson

## Team Line-Ups

| | | |
|---|---|---|
| J.Goodridge | **15** | G.Murphy |
| M.Garvey | **14** | O.Smith |
| N.Mauger | **13** | L.Lloyd |
| T.Fanolua | **12** | D.Gibson |
| S.Kiole | **11** | T.Varndell |
| H.Paul | **10** | A.Goode |
| A.Gomarsall | **9** | H.Ellis |
| C.Bezuidenhout | **1** | D.Morris |
| M.Davies | **2** | G.Chuter |
| P.Vickery | **3** | J.White |
| A.Eustace | **4** | (c) M.Johnson |
| A.Brown | **5** | B.Kay |
| J.Boer (c) | **6** | L.Moody |
| A.Hazell | **7** | N.Back |
| A.Balding | **8** | M.Corry |

## Replacements

| | | |
|---|---|---|
| N.Currier | **16** | J.Buckland |
| T.Sigley | **17** | M.Holford |
| N.Wood | **18** | L.Deacon |
| P.Buxton | **19** | W.Johnson |
| J.Forrester | **20** | S.Bemand |
| A.Page | **21** | S.Vesty |
| J.Bailey | **22** | M.Cornwell |

## Match Stats

| | | |
|---|---|---|
| 49 | Tackles | 91 |
| 1 | Missed Tackles | 6 |
| 79 | Ball Carries | 42 |
| 272 | Metres | 230 |
| 6 | Defenders Beaten | 1 |
| 142 | Passes | 62 |
| 0 | Clean Breaks | 0 |
| 9 | Penalties Conceded | 12 |
| 15 | Turnovers | 7 |
| 77 | Breakdowns Won | 44 |
| 91 | % Scrums Won | 70 |
| 91 | % Line-Outs Won | 80 |

## Premiership Away Record vs Gloucester

| Played | Won | Drawn | Lost | Points For | Points Against |
|---|---|---|---|---|---|
| **8** | **3** | **0** | **5** | **151** | **192** |

Leicester Tigers got 2005 off to the best possible start when they recorded a 28-13 victory over Gloucester at Kingsholm. Tigers, who do not boast the best record in front of the notorious Shed, racked up three tries in a heart-stopping encounter of the highest order, which produced the exact same final score as these two teams' previous Zurich Premiership encounter, at Welford Road in November, 2004.

Fly-half Andy Goode, who contributed 20 points in Leicester's 50-7 post-Christmas win over Worcester, came away with 13 crucial points on the day – two conversions, two penalties and one drop-goal, whilst Tigers' defence in the second half was simply outstanding, with the visitors repelling a series of Gloucester raids on their goalline in the final quarter.

The only downer was the nasty elbow injury suffered by No.8 Martin Corry in the 22nd minute. Corry, who made the England No.8 shirt his own during November after a series of brilliant performances for Leicester this season, looked in some discomfort as he trudged from the field, but at least the visitors were able to call upon someone of the calibre of Will Johnson to replace him.

Tigers soon found themselves 0-10 down against a fired-up home team, but Ollie Smith, who was playing on the wing, combined with Geordan Murphy to put Leon Lloyd away for Leicester's first try of the night. Goode converted and added a penalty to tie the scores at 10-10, before slotting his second penalty to put the visitors ahead at 13-10.

Smith then showed terrific speed to race over for his team's second try, with Goode missing the conversion, but slotting a drop-goal shortly before half-time for a commanding 21-10 lead.

Gloucester's Henry Paul came up with the first points of the second half, taking Gloucester to 13-21 with just over half an hour remaining, but Leicester moved up a gear just short of the 50-minute mark when they broke out of their 22 when they sent some scrum-ball wide. Goode slipped a neat grubber through for his backline to chase from a subsequent line-out, with inside centre Daryl Gibson reacting the quickest after the ball rebounded off the uprights.

"I think the players are delighted to have won this game. I made the point to them earlier that I won here only twice in 17 years." **John Wells**

### Event Line

| Min | | Score | |
|-----|---|-------|---|
| 3 | T | 5-0 | Mauger |
| 11 | T | 10-0 | Eustace |
| 15 | TC | 10-7 | Lloyd/Goode |
| 19 | P | 10-10 | Goode |
| 23 | ⟷ | | W.Johnson for Corry |
| 30 | ⟷ | | Buckland for Chuter |
| 35 | P | 10-13 | Goode |
| 39 | T | 10-18 | Smith |
| 40 | ⟷ | | Chuter for Buckland |
| 40 | DG | 10-21 | Goode |

### Half-Time

| | | | |
|-----|---|-------|---|
| 41 | ⟷ | | Buckland for Chuter |
| 45 | P | 13-21 | Paul |
| 50 | TC | 13-28 | Gibson/Goode |
| 51 | ⟷ | | Sigley for Bezuidenhout |
| 51 | ⟷ | | Forrester for Balding |
| 56 | ▢ | | Lloyd |
| 58 | ⟷ | | Vesty for Murphy |
| 66 | ⟷ | | Buxton for Eustace |
| 68 | ⟷ | | Bailey for Garvey |
| 80 | ⟷ | | Cornwell for Goode |

### Full-Time

### Premiership Table

| Team | P | W | D | L | Pts |
|------|---|---|---|---|-----|
| 1 Leicester Tigers | 13 | 10 | 2 | 1 | 51 |
| 2 London Wasps | 13 | 9 | 1 | 3 | 43 |
| 3 Sale Sharks | 13 | 8 | 0 | 5 | 37 |

### Tigers Milestone

This match produced exactly the same scoreline as the previous Zurich Premiership encounters between these two sides.

# Leicester Tigers **17**
# Biarritz Olympique **21**

**Date:** 9.1.05 **Venue:** Welford Road **Attendance:** 16,815 **Referee:** A.Lewis

## Team Line-Ups

| G.Murphy | 15 | N.Brusque |
|---|---|---|
| O.Smith | 14 | P.Bidabe |
| L.Lloyd | 13 | F.M'tin Aramburu |
| D.Gibson | 12 | T.Lacroix |
| A.Healey | 11 | J.Marlu |
| A.Goode | 10 | D.Traille |
| H.Ellis | 9 | D.Yachvili |
| D.Morris | 1 | P.Balan |
| G.Chuter | 2 | B.August |
| J.White | 3 | D.Avril |
| M.Johnson (c) | 4 | J.Thion |
| L.Deacon | 5 | O.Olibeau |
| L.Moody | 6 | S.Betsen Tchoua |
| N.Back | 7 | I.Harinordoquy |
| W.Johnson | 8 | (c)T.Lievremont |

## Replacements

| J.Buckland | 16 | J.Gonzalez |
|---|---|---|
| G.Rowntree | 17 | B.Lecouls |
| B.Kay | 18 | K.Lealamanu'a |
| L.Abraham | 19 | C.Milheres |
| S.Bemand | 20 | D.Couzinet |
| S.Vesty | 21 | B.Dambielle |
| A.Tuilagi | 22 | J.Dupuy |

## Match Stats

| 49 | Tackles | 72 |
|---|---|---|
| 11 | Missed Tackles | 10 |
| 100 | Ball Carries | 45 |
| 830 | Metres | 230 |
| 10 | Defenders Beaten | 11 |
| 45 | Passes | 12 |
| 22 | Clean Breaks | 13 |
| 12 | Penalties Conceded | 19 |
| 30 | Turnovers | 17 |
| 67 | Breakdowns Won | 41 |
| 94 | % Scrums Won | 100 |
| 100 | % Line-Outs Won | 68 |

Leicester Tigers' title chances in the 2004-05 Heineken Cup took a severe knock when they suffered a disappointing 17-21 defeat to French side Biarritz in front of a sell-out crowd at Welford Road. Tigers trailed 0-18 at half-time, with two late second-half tries giving them an all-important bonus point.

Tries from replacement winger Alesana Tuilagi and livewire scrum-half Harry Ellis also gave the final scoreline some semblance of respectability, with Tigers not enjoying their best 80 minutes of the season against a determined and well-drilled Biarritz outfit.

"I thought we played some tremendous football in the second half, but we just didn't finish our half-chances, as we did in our other games." **John Wells**

Fly-half Andy Goode converted both tries, both of which came in the final 10 minutes of the match, and it resulted in an all-important bonus point for Tigers, who now have a mountain to climb if they are to qualify for the 2004-05 Heineken Cup quarter-finals. First and foremost they have to win well against Calvisano, but they also have to hope other results go their way – most notably in the Biarritz-Wasps match at the Stade Aguiléra at the same time.

The visitors came out with intent, crossing Tigers' tryline twice in the first 40 minutes and stamping their authority on proceedings with a performance one would normally associate with the hosts.

Biarritz coped with everything Tigers threw at them, although, in fairness, it was not a helluva lot – as the visitors disrupted Leicester's normally powerful scrum and their consistent line-out, not allowing the home side a stable platform to attack from, whilst at the same time sticking to the basics; making their tackles, attacking the advantage line and finding touch, most notably through the booming boots of makeshift fly-half Damien Traille and classy full back Nicolas Brusque.

Ellis' second-half sin-binning did not help matters either – after a scuffle with his opposite number Dimitri Yachvili – leaving Tigers a man and 3-21 down with time running out. Their two tries, however, gave them some hope, whilst also keeping their slim Heineken Cup hopes alive ahead of their final Pool 1 clash with Calvisano.

| Event Line | | | |
|---|---|---|---|
| **Min** | | **Score** | |
| 4 | TC | 0-7 | Thion/Yachvili |
| 13 | P | 0-10 | Yachvili |
| 17 | DG | 0-13 | Traille |
| 25 | T | 0-18 | Marlu |
| **Half-Time** | | | |
| 42 | P | 3-18 | **Goode** |
| 46 | ⬌ | | Couzinet for Olibeau |
| 51 | ⬌ | | Lealamanu'a for Balan |
| 51 | ⬌ | | Lecouls for Avril |
| 51 | ⬌ | | **Rowntree for Morris** |
| 53 | ▢ | | **Ellis** |
| 54 | P | 3-21 | Yachvili |
| 61 | ⬌ | | Gonzalez for August |
| 68 | ⬌ | | **Kay for W.Johnson** |
| 68 | ⬌ | | **A.Tuilagi for Healey** |
| 75 | TC | 10-21 | **A.Tuilagi/Goode** |
| 75 | ⬌ | | **Buckland for Chuter** |
| 78 | ⬌ | | Milheres for Lievremont |
| 80 | TC | 17-21 | **Ellis/Goode** |
| **Full-Time** | | | |

| Heineken Cup Table | | | | | |
|---|---|---|---|---|---|
| **Team** | **P** | **W** | **D** | **L** | **Pts** |
| 1 Biarritz Olympique | 5 | 4 | 0 | 1 | 18 |
| 2 London Wasps | 5 | 3 | 0 | 2 | 15 |
| **3 Leicester Tigers** | **5** | **3** | **0** | **2** | **14** |
| 4 Ghial Calvisano | 5 | 0 | 0 | 5 | 0 |

**Tigers Milestone**

Biarritz were the only side that managed to beat Tigers both home and away this season.

# Ghial Rugby Calvisano **10**
# Leicester Tigers **62**

**Date:** 15.1.05 **Venue:** Campo Comunale, Rovato **Attendance:** 2,500 **Referee:** R.Dickson

## Team Line-Ups

| M.Ravazzolo | **15** | S.Vesty |
|---|---|---|
| L.Nitoglia | **14** | G.Murphy |
| M.Murgier | **13** | O.Smith |
| C.Zanoletti | **12** | D.Gibson |
| N.Maz'cato (c) | **11** | A.Tuilagi |
| G.Fraser | **10** | A.Goode |
| P.Canavosio | **9** | H.Ellis |
| G.Bocca | **1** | G.Rowntree |
| A.Moretti | **2** | G.Chuter |
| M.Castrogiovanni | **3** | D.Morris |
| V.Bernabo | **4** | (c) M.Johnson |
| M.Ngauamo | **5** | B.Kay |
| R.Mandelli | **6** | W.Johnson |
| G.Intoppa | **7** | L.Moody |
| E.Candiago | **8** | L.Deacon |

## Replacements

| D.Davo | **16** | J.Buckland |
|---|---|---|
| S.Perugini | **17** | J.White |
| N.Cattina | **18** | L.Abraham |
| P.Griffen | **19** | N.Back |
| G.Raineri | **20** | S.Bemand |
| A.Vodo | **21** | A.Healey |
| P.Vaccari | **22** | M.Cornwell |

## Match Stats

| 135 | Tackles | 37 |
|---|---|---|
| 17 | Missed Tackles | 5 |
| 41 | Ball Carries | 133 |
| 216 | Metres | 521 |
| 5 | Defenders Beaten | 17 |
| 11 | Passes | 20 |
| 2 | Clean Breaks | 6 |
| 8 | Penalties Conceded | 9 |
| 8 | Turnovers | 15 |
| 30 | Breakdowns Won | 91 |
| 83 | % Scrums Won | 94 |
| 71 | % Line-Outs Won | 84 |

Leicester Tigers kept their Heineken Cup hopes alive with a crushing 62-10 win over Calvisano in Rovato, leaving them with a nervous wait ahead of the final pool matches of the weekend, which would ultimately decide their fate in Europe this season.

The visitors scored 10 tries in the end, but for most of the match, after they collected their fourth try – towards the end of the first half – everyone's attention was turned towards the other Pool 1 match of the day between Biarritz and London Wasps. Biarritz eventually managed an 18-15 victory at the Stade Aguiléra, ruling out Tigers' chances of topping the pool, but they still remain in with a chance of qualifying for the quarter-finals as one of the tournament's two lucky losers.

Northampton Saints claimed the first lucky losers spot with their win over Glasgow, with Tigers left to wait on the last two Pool 5 matches – between Newcastle Falcons and the Dragons (at Kingston Park) and Edinburgh and Perpignan (at Murrayfield). Leicester will be hoping that Perpignan do not beat Edinburgh with a bonus point or that the Dragons beat Newcastle; also without a bonus point. Even if Newcastle and Perpignan both win, Tigers can still go through – provided the latter do not score four tries against Edinburgh.

"I think we'll look back at the end of this season and see that there were moments of individual brilliance, but also some rubbish in there as well." **John Wells**

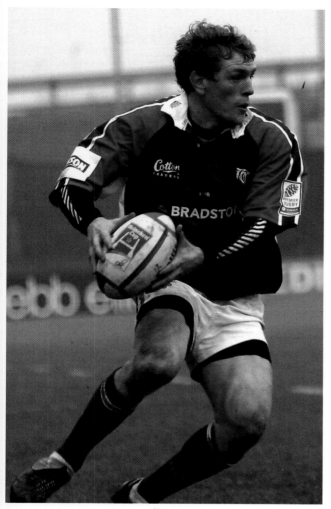

## Event Line

| Min | | Score | |
|---|---|---|---|
| 13 | TC | 0-7 | **Ellis/Goode** |
| 16 | TC | 0-14 | **A.Tuilagi/Goode** |
| 20 | P | 3-14 | Fraser |
| 25 | TC | 8-14 | Nitoglia |
| 33 | TC | 10-21 | **Chuter/Goode** |
| 37 | TC | 10-28 | **A.Tuilagi/Goode** |
| 40 | T | 10-33 | **Murphy** |
| **Half-Time** | | | |
| 41 | ⟷ | | Vodo for Mazzucato |
| 41 | ⟷ | | Griffen for Fraser |
| 47 | TC | 10-40 | **Chuter/Goode** |
| 56 | ⟷ | | **Healey for Vesty** |
| 56 | ⟷ | | **White for Rowntree** |
| 57 | ⟷ | | **Back for W.Johnson** |
| 59 | ⟷ | | **Bemand for Ellis** |
| 59 | ⟷ | | **Buckland for Chuter** |
| 60 | ⟷ | | Perugini for Castrogiovanni |
| 62 | T | 10-45 | **Murphy** |
| 67 | ⟷ | | Cattina for Candiago |
| 68 | TC | 10-52 | **Murphy/Goode** |
| 70 | T | 10-57 | **Goode** |
| 70 | ⟷ | | Vaccari for Ravazzolo |
| 72 | ⟷ | | **Cornwell for Gibson** |
| 73 | ⟷ | | Raineri for Zanoletti |
| 77 | ▢ | | Ngauamo |
| 77 | ▢ | | **Moody** |
| 78 | ⟷ | | Davo for Bocca |
| 80 | T | 10-62 | **White** |
| 80 | ⟷ | | **Abraham for L.Deacon** |
| **Full-Time** | | | |

## Heineken Cup Table

| Team | P | W | D | L | Pts |
|---|---|---|---|---|---|
| 1 Biarritz Olympique | 6 | 5 | 0 | 1 | 22 |
| **2 Leicester Tigers** | **6** | **4** | **0** | **2** | **19** |
| 3 London Wasps | 6 | 3 | 0 | 3 | 16 |
| 4 Ghial Calvisano | 6 | 0 | 0 | 6 | 0 |

## Tigers Milestone

Tigers needed to score at least four tries in this fixture to stay alive in the Heineken Cup, their 10 tries eventually seeing them into the quarter-finals as one of the two lucky losers.

Ireland star Geordan Murphy claimed a hat-trick of tries, as well as the official Heineken Cup Man of the Match Award, but it was scrum-half Harry Ellis who set the ball rolling with a superb kick and chase, fly-half Andy Goode converting for a 7-0 lead.

Goode also crossed for a try, giving him a points' haul of 17, whilst hooker George Chuter and winger Alesana Tuilagi both claimed a brace of tries, with replacement prop Julian White doing his best impression of a three-quarter to get himself on the scoreboard in the closing stages of the rout.

This result sees Tigers finish the regular season on 19 points, just three points behind Pool 1 winners Biarritz, and still in with a shout of qualifying for the quarter-finals. As it turns out, Edinburgh thrashed Perpignan on the Sunday, with Tigers having found out their fate whilst in the air – en route to Leicester – a day after this match.

# Leicester Tigers **32**
# NEC Harlequins **17**

**Date:** 29.1.05  **Venue:** Welford Road  **Attendance:** 16,815  **Referee:** R.Maybank

## Team Line-Ups

| | | |
|---|---|---|
| G.Murphy | **15** | G.Duffy |
| J.Holtby | **14** | S.Keogh |
| L.Lloyd | **13** | D.James |
| O.Smith | **12** | M.Deane |
| A.Healey | **11** | U.Monye |
| A.Goode | **10** | J.Staunton |
| H.Ellis | **9** | S.So'oialo |
| G.Rowntree (c) | **1** | C.Jones |
| G.Chuter | **2** | A.Tiatia |
| D.Morris | **3** | J.Dawson |
| L.Deacon | **4** | R.Winters |
| B.Kay | **5** | S.Maling |
| W.Johnson | **6** | N.Easter |
| N.Back | **7** | L.Sherriff |
| B.Deacon | **8** | (c) T.Diprose |

## Replacements

| | | |
|---|---|---|
| E.Taukafa | **16** | J.Hayter |
| J.White | **17** | M.Worsley |
| L.Abraham | **18** | S.Miall |
| H.Tuilagi | **19** | K.Horstmann |
| S.Bemand | **20** | A.Reay |
| D.Gibson | **21** | H.Barratt |
| A.Tuilagi | **22** | T.Williams |

## Premiership Home Record vs NEC Harlequins

| Played | Won | Drawn | Lost | Points For | Points Against |
|---|---|---|---|---|---|
| 8 | 8 | 0 | 0 | 257 | 102 |

## Match Stats

| | | |
|---|---|---|
| **53** | Tackles | **61** |
| **5** | Missed Tackles | **13** |
| **69** | Ball Carries | **45** |
| **351** | Metres | **157** |
| **13** | Defenders Beaten | **5** |
| **97** | Passes | **48** |
| **4** | Clean Breaks | **1** |
| **10** | Penalties Conceded | **15** |
| **14** | Turnovers | **11** |
| **51** | Breakdowns Won | **39** |
| **100** | % Scrums Won | **88** |
| **79** | % Line-Outs Won | **88** |

"It wasn't pretty to be honest, but fair dues to the guys out there. We played badly at times, but still managed to get a good result." **John Wells**

Leicester Tigers strengthened their position at the top of the Zurich Premiership standings with a 32-17 victory over NEC Harlequins at Welford Road. Tigers fly-half Andy Goode contributed 22 points, in the process becoming only the 10th player in Leicester's history to pass 700 career points for the club.

The biggest news of the day, however, was the non-participation of regular skipper Martin Johnson, who withdrew from the side on the morning of the game. Louis Deacon shifted from No.8 to the second row to partner England lock Ben Kay, with loosehead prop Graham Rowntree taking over the leadership duties.

The back row originally named by head coach John Wells also underwent something of an overhaul, with Will Johnson coming off the bench to fill the No.8 position and Brett Deacon, who had originally been promoted to the bench when Lewis Moody limped out of the game at Friday's training run (Johnson had already been set to start in Moody's place), filling the No.6 spot.

Quins ran into an early 10-3 lead, thanks to a try by prop Jon Dawson, before winger Ugo Monye crossed, giving his side a handy 17-9 lead after 20 minutes. Tigers, however, hardly seemed to notice; fly-half Andy Goode added his fourth penalty before Austin Healey dotted down courtesy of a Goode cross-kick and some basketball-like athleticism from Kay.

Tigers led 19-17 at half-time, with Goode extending that to 22-17 in the 50th minute with his fifth successful penalty goal, whilst Quins lost blindside flanker Nick Easter to the sin-bin. Goode's sixth penalty, followed by a Henry Tuilagi try, and Goode's subsequent conversion, completed the scoring.

Tuilagi replaced Brett Deacon in the 54th minute – his first first-team match since November 27, 2004 – making an immediate impact with some powerful surges, whilst points-machine Goode maintained a 100 per cent record en route to his Bradstone Man of the Match Award.

## Event Line

| Min | | Score | |
|-----|-----|-------|-----|
| 1 | TC | 0-7 | Dawson/Staunton |
| 4 | P | 3-7 | **Goode** |
| 10 | P | 3-10 | Staunton |
| 13 | P | 6-10 | **Goode** |
| 18 | P | 9-10 | **Goode** |
| 20 | TC | 9-17 | Monye/Staunton |
| 30 | P | 12-17 | **Goode** |
| 32 | TC | 19-17 | **Healey/Goode** |

### Half-Time

| | | | |
|-----|-----|-------|-----|
| 50 | | | Easter |
| 52 | P | 22-17 | **Goode** |
| 52 | ↔ | | **H.Tuilagi for B.Deacon** |
| 58 | ↔ | | **White for Rowntree** |
| 58 | ↔ | | **Gibson for Healey** |
| 62 | P | 25-17 | **Goode** |
| 62 | ↔ | | Worsley for Dawson |
| 62 | ↔ | | Miall for Winters |
| 62 | ↔ | | Williams for Duffy |
| 87 | TC | 32-17 | **H.Tuilagi/Goode** |

### Full-Time

## Premiership Table

| Team | P | W | D | L | Pts |
|------|---|---|---|---|-----|
| **1 Leicester Tigers** | **14** | **11** | **2** | **1** | **55** |
| 2 London Wasps | 14 | 9 | 1 | 4 | 44 |
| 3 Sale Sharks | 14 | 9 | 0 | 5 | 42 |

## Tigers Milestone

Andy Goode scored 22 of Tigers' 32 points – becoming just the 10th player to have scored 700 career points for Leicester.

# Bath Rugby **6**
# Leicester Tigers **6**

**Date:** 5.2.05 **Venue:** Recreation Ground **Attendance:** 10,500 **Referee:** D.Rose

## Team Line-Ups

| M.Perry | 15 | S.Vesty |
|---|---|---|
| A.Williams | 14 | J.Holtby |
| A.Higgins | 13 | O.Smith |
| A.Crockett | 12 | D.Gibson |
| J.Maddock | 11 | A.Healey |
| C.Malone | 10 | A.Goode |
| N.Walshe | 9 | S.Bemand |
| M.Stevens | 1 | M.Holford |
| L.Mears | 2 | G.Chuter |
| D.Bell | 3 | D.Morris |
| J.Hudson | 4 | (c) M.Johnson |
| R.Fidler | 5 | L.Deacon |
| A.Beattie (c) | 6 | H.Tuilagi |
| M.Lipman | 7 | N.Back |
| Z.Fea'unati | 8 | W.Johnson |

## Replacements

| J.Humphreys | 16 | E.Taukafa |
|---|---|---|
| C.Loader | 17 | J.Rawson |
| J.Scaysbrook | 18 | B.Deacon |
| G.Lewis | 19 | D.Montagu |
| M.Wood | 20 | L.Abraham |
| K.Lewitt | 21 | L.Lloyd |
| T.Cheeseman | 22 | A.Tuilagi |

## Match Stats

| 80 | Tackles | 71 |
|---|---|---|
| 11 | Missed Tackles | 8 |
| 50 | Ball Carries | 63 |
| 185 | Metres | 305 |
| 8 | Defenders Beaten | 11 |
| 66 | Passes | 105 |
| 0 | Clean Breaks | 2 |
| 9 | Penalties Conceded | 11 |
| 12 | Turnovers | 17 |
| 58 | Breakdowns Won | 73 |
| 100 | % Scrums Won | 71 |
| 71 | % Line-Outs Won | 78 |

## Premiership Away Record vs Bath Rugby

| Played | Won | Drawn | Lost | Points For | Points Against |
|---|---|---|---|---|---|
| 8 | 4 | 1 | 3 | 116 | 113 |

Leicester Tigers and Bath could not be separated after 80 minutes in the mud at The Rec as they played out a 6-6 draw – the first time in Zurich Premiership history that two teams have drawn both games against each other in the same season.

Fly-half Andy Goode kicked a penalty and claimed the Man of the Match honours, whilst winger Austin Healey weighed in with a crucial drop-goal.

Goode fell inches short with a penalty from right of the posts as his non-kicking foot stayed steady on the muddy surface, but on 15 minutes opposite number Chris Malone managed to go one better when his effort from just left went between the posts for a 3-0 lead.

Leicester almost scored the only try of the game when Healey went over in the right corner after a line-out on halfway, a break from No.8 Henry Tuilagi and then a backs move from left to right put him in, but centre Ollie Smith's scoring pass was judged to have gone forward.

"We only just had enough fit players at the club to put out a full 22 for this match, so we're reasonably happy." **John Wells**

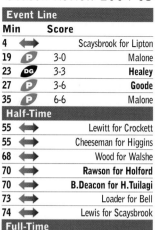

### Event Line

| Min | | Score | |
|---|---|---|---|
| 4 | ⟷ | | Scaysbrook for Lipton |
| 19 | P | 3-0 | Malone |
| 23 | DG | 3-3 | **Healey** |
| 27 | P | 3-6 | **Goode** |
| 35 | P | 6-6 | Malone |

### Half-Time

| | | | |
|---|---|---|---|
| 55 | ⟷ | | Lewitt for Crockett |
| 55 | ⟷ | | Cheeseman for Higgins |
| 68 | ⟷ | | Wood for Walshe |
| 70 | ⟷ | | **Rawson for Holford** |
| 70 | ⟷ | | **B.Deacon for H.Tuilagi** |
| 73 | ⟷ | | Loader for Bell |
| 74 | ⟷ | | Lewis for Scaysbrook |

### Full-Time

### Premiership Table

| Team | P | W | D | L | Pts |
|---|---|---|---|---|---|
| 1 **Leicester Tigers** | 15 | 11 | 3 | 1 | 57 |
| 2 Sale Sharks | 15 | 10 | 0 | 5 | 46 |
| 3 London Wasps | 15 | 9 | 1 | 5 | 45 |

### Tigers Milestone

Tigers and Bath played to another draw, having drawn 16-16 in their previous Zurich Premiership encounter this season – the first time in ZP history that two teams have drawn both games against each other in the same year.

Bath scrummed well and relieved the pressure, but Healey was back to haunt them on 23 minutes as he made the most of slow ball, dropped into the pocket and kept sufficient footing to nail a drop-goal right down the middle to level the scores.

Healey was one of a number of players not to be thrown off their game by the atrocious conditions and he pressurised Bath with a superb kick-and-chase, which ultimately led to the award of a penalty 45 metres out, which Man of the Match Goode converted magnificently with the aid of the left upright.

Tuilagi was again in the thick of things with some big carries, but with Bath hacking ahead in the mud, a Tigers hand dragged back one of the chasers, with Malone converting the penalty from just left in what turned out to be the final score of the match as the sides went into the break tied at 6-6.

# Leicester Tigers **83**
# Newcastle Falcons **10**

**Date:** 19.2.05  **Venue:** Welford Road  **Attendance:** 16,815  **Referee:** T.Spreadbury

## Team Line-Ups

| | | |
|---|---|---|
| S.Vesty | **15** | T.Flood |
| L.Lloyd | **14** | T.May |
| O.Smith | **13** | M.Tait |
| D.Gibson | **12** | M.Mayerhofler |
| A.Healey | **11** | M.Stephenson |
| A.Goode | **10** | M.Wilkinson |
| S.Bemand | **9** | J.Grindal |
| G.Rowntree | **1** | (c) I.Peel |
| G.Chuter | **2** | M.Thompson |
| D.Morris | **3** | M.Ward |
| M.Johnson (c) | **4** | L.Gross |
| L.Deacon | **5** | G.Parling |
| H.Tuilagi | **6** | M.McCarthy |
| N.Back | **7** | C.Harris |
| M.Corry | **8** | S.Sititi |

## Replacements

| | | |
|---|---|---|
| J.Buckland | **16** | J.Isaacson |
| J.Rawson | **17** | A.Long |
| L.Moody | **18** | C.Hamilton |
| W.Johnson | **19** | P.Dowson |
| H.Ellis | **20** | O.Phillips |
| G.Murphy | **21** | L.Dickson |
| S.Rabeni | **22** | D.Walder |

## Match Stats

| | | |
|---|---|---|
| **56** | Tackles | **83** |
| **3** | Missed Tackles | **20** |
| **106** | Ball Carries | **46** |
| **602** | Metres | **152** |
| **20** | Defenders Beaten | **3** |
| **167** | Passes | **86** |
| **12** | Clean Breaks | **0** |
| **12** | Penalties Conceded | **8** |
| **15** | Turnovers | **17** |
| **70** | Breakdowns Won | **46** |
| **100** | % Scrums Won | **100** |
| **87** | % Line-Outs Won | **70** |

## Premiership Home Record vs Newcastle Falcons

| Played | Won | Drawn | Lost | Points For | Points Against |
|---|---|---|---|---|---|
| **8** | **7** | **0** | **1** | **318** | **128** |

Leicester Tigers cruised to an emphatic 83-10 win over a shell-shocked Newcastle Falcons at Welford Road, beating their 75-13 Zurich Premiership victory over Rotherham at the same venue last season. Tigers scored a massive 11 tries on the day, with fly-half Andy Goode sporting a 100 per cent kicking record and Ollie Smith, Neil Back and Leon Lloyd all scoring two tries.

Goode slotted 13 from 13 kicks at goal – a record in the ZP – as he continued to press his England selection claims, whilst fellow England wannabe, outside centre Ollie Smith, picked up a double in the first half after a fine performance on both attack and defence.

Goode, Smith and the rest of Tigers' backs were once again well-served by a rampant forward unit, which tore into the Falcons – even after the early loss of lock Louis Deacon, who limped off in the fifth minute. Deacon was replaced by No.8 Martin Corry in the second row, with Will Johnson coming into the back row and not missing a beat.

Tigers went ahead by 3-0 early on, but Newcastle centre Mark Mayerhofler crept over for a score when Tigers coughed up possession on their own line in the 13th minute – that after the visitors had done well to pin their hosts in their own 22. Winger Tom May converted and Newcastle were ahead by 7-3.

There would have been a few nervous flutters in the Tigers camp at that stage, but they remained composed, with an Austin Healey box-kick eventually bringing them back into enemy territory.

Healey sped through a gap in the midfield from the subsequent five-metre scrum for his team's first try of the day and the flood-gates soon opened, with Daryl Gibson scoring and Smith grabbing his double; Tigers claiming the four-try bonus point before half-time.

Newcastle would have been hoping to hit back early in the second half, only to concede a fifth try when Lloyd went over in the right-hand corner after just two minutes, before Henry Tuilagi, Back (twice), Will Johnson, Geordan Murphy and Lloyd applied the finishing touches.

Johnson rid himself of an unwanted record when he crossed for his try in the 63rd minute – his first try for Tigers in 102 matches!

"I thought at times we were outstanding. Even though Newcastle gave us space, we still had to execute it and we did it well." **John Wells**

## Event Line

| Min | | Score | |
|-----|-----|-------|-----|
| 3 | P | 3-0 | Goode |
| 5 | ⟷ | | W.Johnson for L.Deacon |
| 12 | TC | 3-7 | Mayerhofler/May |
| 21 | ⟷ | | Isaacson for Peel |
| 23 | TC | 10-7 | Healey/Goode |
| 24 | ⟷ | | Peel for Isaacson |
| 28 | TC | 17-7 | Smith/Goode |
| 31 | TC | 24-7 | Gibson/Goode |
| 35 | P | 24-10 | May |
| 37 | TC | 31-10 | Smith/Goode |
| 40 | P | 34-10 | Goode |
| **Half-Time** | | | |
| 41 | ⟷ | | Rabeni for Smith |
| 41 | ⟷ | | Isaacson for Peel |
| 41 | ⟷ | | Long for Thompson |
| 43 | TC | 41-10 | Lloyd/Goode |
| 47 | TC | 48-10 | H.Tuilagi/Goode |
| 50 | ⟷ | | Dickson for Grindal |
| 51 | ⟷ | | Buckland for Chuter |
| 51 | ⟷ | | Rawson for Rowntree |
| 51 | ⟷ | | Hamilton for Gross |
| 51 | ⟷ | | Dowson for Sititi |
| 55 | TC | 55-10 | Back/Goode |
| 55 | ⟷ | | Moody for H.Tuilagi |
| 61 | ⟷ | | Phillips for Stephenson |
| 63 | TC | 62-10 | W.Johnson/Goode |
| 68 | TC | 69-10 | Back/Goode |
| 69 | ⟷ | | Ellis for Bemand |
| 69 | ⟷ | | Murphy for Vesty |
| 70 | TC | 76-10 | Murphy/Goode |
| 76 | TC | 83-10 | Lloyd/Goode |
| **Full-Time** | | | |

## Premiership Table

| Team | P | W | D | L | Pts |
|------|---|---|---|---|-----|
| **1 Leicester Tigers** | **16** | **12** | **3** | **1** | **62** |
| 2 Sale Sharks | 16 | 11 | 0 | 5 | 50 |
| 3 London Wasps | 16 | 10 | 1 | 5 | 50 |

# Northampton Saints **26**
# Leicester Tigers **11**

**Date:** 26.2.05  **Venue:** Franklin's Gardens  **Attendance:** 12,084  **Referee:** A.Rowden

## Team Line-Ups

| B.Reihana | 15 | S.Rabeni |
|---|---|---|
| J.Rudd | 14 | J.Holtby |
| N.Starling | 13 | L.Lloyd |
| M.Stcherbina | 12 | D.Gibson |
| B.Cohen | 11 | A.Healey |
| S.Drahm | 10 | S.Vesty |
| J.Howard | 9 | S.Bemand |
| S.Emms | 1 | M.Holford |
| D.Richmond | 2 | G.Chuter |
| R.Morris | 3 | D.Morris |
| M.Lord | 4 | (c) M.Johnson |
| D.Browne | 5 | J.Hamilton |
| D.Fox | 6 | W.Johnson |
| C.Krige (c) | 7 | N.Back |
| A.Blowers | 8 | H.Tuilagi |

## Replacements

| C.Budgen | 16 | J.Buckland |
|---|---|---|
| B.Sturgess | 17 | J.Rawson |
| G.Seely | 18 | L.Abraham |
| M.Soden | 19 | B.Deacon |
| B.Fulton | 20 | R.Warren |
| L.Myring | 21 | D.Hipkiss |
| W.Human | 22 | A.Tuilagi |

## Match Stats

| 58 | Tackles | 104 |
|---|---|---|
| 8 | Missed Tackles | 20 |
| 84 | Ball Carries | 66 |
| 427 | Metres | 360 |
| 20 | Defenders Beaten | 8 |
| 124 | Passes | 109 |
| 9 | Clean Breaks | 5 |
| 12 | Penalties Conceded | 12 |
| 20 | Turnovers | 17 |
| 65 | Breakdowns Won | 42 |
| 100 | % Scrums Won | 100 |
| 79 | % Line-Outs Won | 61 |

## Premiership Away Record vs Northampton Saints

| Played | Won | Drawn | Lost | Points For | Points Against |
|---|---|---|---|---|---|
| 8 | 4 | 0 | 4 | 112 | 149 |

Leicester Tigers suffered a rare Zurich Premiership loss, going down 11-26 to East Midlands rivals Northampton Saints in the 100th meeting at Franklin's Gardens between these two teams. A severely depleted Tigers line-up – without 15 of its top players, all of whom were on international duty at senior and junior level – was outscored by three tries to one by a side occupying the bottom position in the ZP standings before this match.

This was Leicester's first loss in the Premiership since their opening day 19-26 defeat to Sale Sharks at Edgeley Park back in September 2004. It was also the first time this season that the men from Welford Road have failed to collect at least one point in a ZP match, Tigers having claimed a losing bonus point that day against Sale, as well as having played to three draws this season.

"They played with the intensity and passion we expected from them, but we were just unable to match them on the day." **John Wells**

**Event Line**

| Min | | Score | |
|---|---|---|---|
| 3 | T | 5-0 | Drahm |
| 13 | | | Back |
| 14 | P | 8-0 | Drahm |
| 20 | DG | 11-0 | Drahm |
| 22 | P | 11-3 | Vesty |
| 23 | TC | 18-3 | Rudd/Drahm |
| 29 | | | M.Johnson |
| 29 | ↔ | | Sturgess for Fox |
| 29 | | | Emms |
| 36 | P | 21-3 | Drahm |
| 39 | ↔ | | Fox for Sturgess |
| 40 | T | 21-8 | Lloyd |
| 40 | P | 21-11 | Vesty |

**Half-Time**

| | | | |
|---|---|---|---|
| 50 | ↔ | | B.Deacon for W.Johnson |
| 53 | ↔ | | Seeley for Browne |
| 55 | ↔ | | Human for N.Starling |
| 67 | ↔ | | Buckland for Chuter |
| 67 | ↔ | | Abraham for H.Tuilagi |
| 67 | ↔ | | A.Tuilagi for Rabeni |
| 74 | T | 26-11 | Cohen |
| 75 | ↔ | | Hipkiss for Holtby |
| 75 | ↔ | | Soden for Blowers |
| 76 | ↔ | | Rawson for Morris |
| 78 | ↔ | | Sturgess for Morris |
| 81 | ↔ | | Budgen for Lord |

**Full-Time**

**Premiership Table**

| Team | P | W | D | L | Pts |
|---|---|---|---|---|---|
| 1 Leicester Tigers | 17 | 12 | 3 | 2 | 62 |
| 2 London Wasps | 17 | 11 | 1 | 5 | 54 |
| 3 Sale Sharks | 17 | 11 | 0 | 6 | 50 |

In the end, a disappointing first-half performance, which saw them concede 21 points, cost them dearly, but their second half showing was perhaps more to blame, with the visitors dominant everywhere — except on the scoreboard where, of course, it matters most.

Tigers would no doubt have still had their heads in the clouds after their 11-try demolition of Newcastle Falcons, but they were promptly brought down to earth in the opening exchanges at Franklin's Gardens, with a fired-up Saints team getting stuck into their visitors.

Yellow cards to World Cup stars Neil Back and Martin Johnson did not help Tigers' cause either, with Northampton's Shane Drahm scoring a try and adding a penalty and a left-footed drop-goal for an 11-0 lead.

Makeshift fly-half and goal-kicker Sam Vesty chipped over a penalty for Tigers, but a John Rudd try put the home team ahead by 18-3, before Leon Lloyd hit back for Tigers — the teams changing ends at 21-11 in Northampton's favour.

Tigers had their chances in the second half, but were unable to convert their territorial advantage into points, before conceding a late try to out-of-favour England winger Ben Cohen when they tried to run the ball out of their own 22.

**Tigers Milestone**

This was Leicester's 100th visit to Franklin's Gardens to play Northampton since 1894; the two sides had clashed at a different ground in the city some six years earlier, whilst Tigers have met both Gloucester and Saracens at the venue in recent years.

# Leicester Tigers **15**
# London Irish **6**

**Date:** 11.3.05 **Venue:** Welford Road **Attendance:** 16,815 **Referee:** C.White

## Team Line-Ups

| S.Vesty | 15 | M.Horak |
|---|---|---|
| D.Hipkiss | 14 | D.Shabbo |
| L.Lloyd | 13 | R.Penney |
| D.Gibson | 12 | M.Catt |
| A.Tuilagi | 11 | J.Bishop |
| A.Healey | 10 | B.Everitt |
| S.Bemand | 9 | P.Hodgson |
| M.Holford | 1 | N.Hatley |
| J.Buckland | 2 | A.Flavin |
| D.Morris | 3 | R.Hardwick |
| M.Johnson (c) | 4 | (c) R.Strudwick |
| L.Deacon | 5 | N.Kennedy |
| H.Tuilagi | 6 | P.Gustard |
| N.Back | 7 | K.Dawson |
| W.Johnson | 8 | R.Reid |

## Replacements

| G.Chuter | 16 | D.Wheatley |
|---|---|---|
| J.Rawson | 17 | D.Paice |
| J.Hamilton | 18 | K.Roche |
| B.Deacon | 19 | D.Danaher |
| R.Broadfoot | 20 | N.Mordt |
| A.Dodge | 21 | R.Laidlaw |
| L.Abraham | 22 | K.Barrett |

## Match Stats

| 68 | Tackles | 71 |
|---|---|---|
| 8 | Missed Tackles | 7 |
| 75 | Ball Carries | 63 |
| 412 | Metres | 349 |
| 7 | Defenders Beaten | 8 |
| 124 | Passes | 97 |
| 3 | Clean Breaks | 3 |
| 9 | Penalties Conceded | 8 |
| 19 | Turnovers | 9 |
| 71 | Breakdowns Won | 57 |
| 100 | % Scrums Won | 92 |
| 75 | % Line-Outs Won | 77 |

## Premiership Home Record vs London Irish

| Played | Won | Drawn | Lost | Points For | Points Against |
|---|---|---|---|---|---|
| **8** | **7** | **0** | **1** | **236** | **126** |

A severely depleted Leicester Tigers team had to pull out all the stops en route to recording a 15-6 win over a determined London Irish outfit at Welford Road. Tigers, wearing their new tight-fitting shirts for the first time, were without 16 players on various forms of international duty, but they dug deep, eventually outscoring the Exiles by two tries to nil.

Tigers held a narrow 8-3 half-time lead, having scored the only try of the first half when powerhouse left-wing Alesana Tuilagi crashed over in the left-hand corner in the 39th minute, after fly-half Austin Healey had sliced through the first line of London Irish's defence. Healey had tried those darts from close-range throughout the opening gambit, this time it worked, although his pass to Tuilagi was not as accurate as he would have hoped. It mattered little; however, Tigers were ahead by 8-3 at the break.

"I'm pretty chuffed to be honest. To get a win says a lot about the squad and spirit, despite what happened at Northampton last time out." **John Wells**

The second half began with a flurry or two from London Irish, with centre Rodd Penney coming close in the first minute, before being rightfully denied by the Television Match Official, whilst scrum-half Paul Hodgson caused a few flutters when he sniped ahead from the next movement.

But Leicester's defence held out on both occasions, as it would for the duration of the match, although they were made to work hard, at times, to keep a clean sheet. Everitt missed a long-range attempt in the 50th minute, before knocking over his next shot at goal in the 54th minute – leaving the score at 8-6 in Tigers' favour.

The rest of the match was in severe danger of petering out, until a frantic final few minutes, which saw the home side claim a late try through replacement back row Luke Abraham, who impressed when coming on for veteran openside Neil Back, who limped off with a dead leg in the 35th minute.

A super-charged Abraham finished the game strongly, following up Alesana Tuilagi's charge-down from an attempted Michael Horak clearance for the touchdown. Replacement fly-half Ross Broadfoot, who did some good things when he came on in the 62nd minute, slotted the simple conversion, putting his team more than seven points ahead at a crucial stage.

| Event Line | | |
|---|---|---|
| **Min** | **Score** | |
| 15 🅿 | 3-0 | Vesty |
| 32 ↔ | | Mordt for Penney |
| 34 🅿 | 3-3 | Everitt |
| 34 ↔ | | **Abraham for Back** |
| 38 🇹 | 8-3 | **A.Tuilagi** |
| **Half-Time** | | |
| 48 ↔ | | Wheatley for Hardwick |
| 51 🅿 | 8-6 | Everitt |
| 53 ↔ | | Roche for Reid |
| 58 ↔ | | **Chuter for Buckland** |
| 60 ↔ | | Reid for Roche |
| 60 ↔ | | Danaher for Gustard |
| 61 ↔ | | **B.Deacon for A.Tuilagi** |
| 63 ↔ | | **Broadfoot for Hipkiss** |
| 75 🆃🅲 | 15-6 | **Abraham/Broadfoot** |
| 81 ↔ | | Paice for Flavin |
| 82 ↔ | | Roche for Reid |
| **Full-Time** | | |

| Premiership Table | | | | | |
|---|---|---|---|---|---|
| **Team** | **P** | **W** | **D** | **L** | **Pts** |
| **1 Leicester Tigers** | **18** | **13** | **3** | **2** | **66** |
| 2 London Wasps | 18 | 12 | 1 | 5 | 59 |
| 3 Sale Sharks | 18 | 11 | 0 | 7 | 50 |

### Tigers Milestone

Replacement flanker Luke Abraham scored one of Tigers' two tries on the night - just a few days before departing for a playing stint in New Zealand

# Leicester Tigers **42**
# Barbarians **19**

**Date:** 18.3.05  **Venue:** Welford Road  **Attendance:** 10,198  **Referee:** M.Fox

## Team Line-Ups

| | | |
|---|---|---|
| R.Warren | **15** | J.Swart |
| L.Lloyd | **14** | P.Bernat-Salles |
| D.Hipkiss | **13** | A.Snyman |
| P.Howard | **12** | R.Dourthe |
| A.Tuilagi | **11** | K.Logan |
| S.Vesty | **10** | G.Townsend |
| S.Bemand (c) | **9** | M.Williams |
| M.Holford | **1** | G.Faliva |
| E.Taukafa | **2** | J.Gonzalez |
| J.Rawson | **3** | C.Califano |
| J.Hamilton | **4** | R.Strudwick |
| L.Deacon | **5** | K.Chesney |
| B.Deacon | **6** | P.Gustard |
| D.Montagu | **7** | (c) P.Volley |
| W.Johnson | **8** | F.Ntamack |

## Replacements

| | | |
|---|---|---|
| J.Buckland | **16** | R.Rawlinson |
| P.Cook | **17** | M.Holt |
| H.Tuilagi | **18** | A.Codling |
| J.Wheeler | **19** | E.Pavanello |
| A.Wright | **20** | M.Powell |
| A.Dodge | **21** | F.Gelez |
| F.Tuilagi | **22** | D.Doherty |
| M.Johnson | **23** | N/A |
| A.Healey | **24** | N/A |

A stunning 20-point blitz in just five minutes in the second half put Tigers on course for a 42-19 victory over the Barbarians in their entertaining NIG Challenge match at Welford Road. Tigers outscored their visitors by seven tries to three, with left-wing Alesana Tuilagi grabbing a hat-trick.

Tuilagi scored two of his tries deep into injury-time, both of them using his trademark pace and power, despite the fact that he operated in confined spaces, but it was his brother, back row Henry, who featured in Leicester's points spree, scoring his side's third try, after No.8 Will Johnson crashed over in the 58th minute.

Tigers held a narrow 7-5 half-time lead, with full back Roger Warren opening their account in the second half with a penalty in the 54th minute. Johnson's try was next, followed by Henry's spectacular effort – which included a huge hand-off on winger Kenny Logan – from a fantastic Pat Howard cut-out pass, before Alesana, put the icing on top in the 63rd minute from a Will Johnson chip kick, the former outpacing the cover-defence for the touchdown after birthday boy Johnson's superb break and kick-ahead.

"They've got quite a few test caps in their line-up, we didn't have quite as many, and so the lads came off quite chuffed." **John Wells**

That took the score out to 27-5 and it was game over – even after a late fightback from the Barbarians.

It certainly was a tough week in Leicester with news of Wells' departure next season and Matt Hampson's awful neck injury, but all off-field happenings were put to one side when both teams took to Welford Road at 7.45pm for the annual NIG Challenge. And Howard, who will take over the coaching reigns from the departing Wells, showed that he has lost none of his old skills, with the former Wallaby sending the ball down the backline with his first touch.

Howard even managed to get on the scoreboard, before giving way in the 64th minute to another former Tiger, utility back Freddie Tuilagi, who returned to Welford Road for one last time, coach Wells giving the three Samoan brothers a run together, much to their delight. Even Tigers skipper Martin Johnson joined in the fun, replacing Will in the 78th minute, much to the 10,198-strong crowd's approval.

| Event Line | | | |
| --- | --- | --- | --- |
| **Min** | | **Score** | |
| 4 | TC | 7-0 | Howard/Warren |
| 33 | T | 7-5 | Califano |
| **Half-time** | | | |
| 41 | ↔ | | Gelez for Snyman |
| 41 | ↔ | | Doherty for Dourthe |
| 50 | ↔ | | Pavanello for Ntamack |
| 52 | ↔ | | **Buckland for Taukafa** |
| 52 | ↔ | | **Cook for Holford** |
| 52 | ↔ | | **H.Tuilagi for Hamilton** |
| 52 | ↔ | | **Wheeler for B.Deacon** |
| 52 | ↔ | | **Dodge for Lloyd** |
| 54 | P | 10-5 | Warren |
| 58 | T | 15-5 | W.Johnson |
| 60 | TC | 22-5 | H.Tuilagi/Warren |
| 63 | T | 27-5 | A.Tuilagi |
| 64 | ↔ | | **F.Tuilagi for Howard** |
| 65 | ↔ | | Codling for Chesney |
| 65 | ↔ | | Powell for Williams |
| 69 | ↔ | | **Healey for Warren** |
| 73 | ↔ | | Rawlinson for Gonzalez |
| 73 | ↔ | | Holt for Faliva |
| 74 | TC | 27-12 | Bernat-Salles/Gelez |
| 77 | TC | 27-19 | Volley/Gelez |
| 78 | ↔ | | **M.Johnson for W.Johnson** |
| 79 | T | 32-19 | Vesty |
| 81 | T | 37-19 | A.Tuilagi |
| 82 | ↔ | | Wright for Montagu |
| 84 | T | 42-19 | A.Tuilagi |
| **Full-Time** | | | |

## Tigers Milestone

This game was a family affair of note - with three sets of brothers, the Johnsons, Tuilagis and Deacons, all playing a role and two sons of former Tigers, Joe Wheeler and Alex Dodge (sons of Peter Wheeler and Paul Dodge respectively), making their first-team debuts.

# Leeds Tykes **23**
# Leicester Tigers **22**

**Date:** 27.3.05 **Venue:** Headingley **Attendance:** 6,723 **Referee:** S.Davey

## Team Line-Ups

| | | |
|---|---|---|
| T.Biggs | 15 | G.Murphy |
| A.Snyman | 14 | L.Lloyd |
| P.Christophers | 13 | O.Smith |
| C.Bell | 12 | D.Gibson |
| D.Rees | 11 | A.Healey |
| G.Ross | 10 | A.Goode |
| A.Dickens | 9 | H.Ellis |
| M.Shelley | 1 | D.Morris |
| M.Regan | 2 | G.Chuter |
| G.Kerr | 3 | J.White |
| S.Hooper (c) | 4 | (c) M.Johnson |
| T.Palmer | 5 | L.Deacon |
| S.Morgan | 6 | W.Johnson |
| R.Parks | 7 | N.Back |
| A.Popham | 8 | M.Corry |

## Replacements

| | | |
|---|---|---|
| M.Holt | 16 | J.Buckland |
| R.Rawlinson | 17 | M.Holford |
| J.Dunbar | 18 | H.Tuilagi |
| D.Hyde | 19 | L.Moody |
| M.McMillan | 20 | S.Bemand |
| C.McMullen | 21 | S.Vesty |
| D.Albanese | 22 | A.Tuilagi |

## Match Stats

| | | |
|---|---|---|
| 85 | Tackles | 56 |
| 13 | Missed Tackles | 14 |
| 58 | Ball Carries | 83 |
| 408 | Metres | 455 |
| 14 | Defenders Beaten | 13 |
| 74 | Passes | 134 |
| 7 | Clean Breaks | 10 |
| 14 | Penalties Conceded | 14 |
| 11 | Turnovers | 19 |
| 48 | Breakdowns Won | 59 |
| 70 | % Scrums Won | 100 |
| 86 | % Line-Outs Won | 54 |

## Premiership Away Record vs Leeds Tykes

| Played | Won | Drawn | Lost | Points For | Points Against |
|---|---|---|---|---|---|
| 4 | 0 | 0 | 4 | 69 | 125 |

Leicester Tigers suffered a shock 22-23 Zurich Premiership loss to Leeds Tykes at Headingley – their fourth successive Premiership defeat at this venue. Both teams scored one try each in a nail-biting encounter, but the boot of Leeds fly-half Gordon Ross just eclipsed that of Andy Goode's as the fired-up home side, desperate to avoid relegation at the end of this season, tackled their way to a famous victory.

This match always loomed as a banana-skin of some proportions for Tigers, despite the fact that Leeds found themselves at the bottom of the standings before kick-off. Desperation, however, can bring the best out of most sides and Leeds proved that again, as Tigers' Headlingley bogey continued into the 2004-05 season. In four matches held at this ground between these two teams, Tigers have managed just one league point.

Five penalties from Ross gave the home team a handy 15-9 half-time lead, with fly-half Goode, recently capped at test level for England, having contributed all his team's first-half points through two penalties and a well-taken drop-goal.

"Whether Leeds deserved to win or we deserved to win is immaterial. I guess they deserved it, scoring more points in the end." **John Wells**

| Event Line | | | |
|---|---|---|---|
| **Min** | | **Score** | |
| 3 | ☐ | | White |
| 4 | P | 3-0 | Ross |
| 4 | ⟷ | | Holford for W.Johnson |
| 8 | P | 3-3 | Goode |
| 10 | P | 6-3 | Ross |
| 12 | P | 6-6 | Goode |
| 13 | ⟷ | | W.Johnson for Holford |
| 21 | ⟷ | | Moody for Corry |
| 29 | P | 9-6 | Ross |
| 29 | ⟷ | | Corry for Moody |
| 39 | P | 12-6 | Ross |
| 40 | DG | 12-9 | Goode |
| 40 | P | 15-9 | Ross |
| **Half-Time** | | | |
| 45 | P | 15-12 | Goode |
| 51 | TC | 15-19 | Lloyd/Goode |
| 51 | ⟷ | | Dunbar for Morgan |
| 51 | ⟷ | | Moody for W.Johnson |
| 60 | T | 20-19 | Biggs |
| 60 | ⟷ | | McMillan for Dickens |
| 60 | ⟷ | | Albanese for Christophers |
| 62 | ⟷ | | Buckland for Chuter |
| 62 | ⟷ | | A.Tuilagi for Smith |
| 65 | P | 23-19 | Ross |
| 67 | ⟷ | | H.Tuilagi for Back |
| 71 | P | 23-22 | Goode |
| 79 | ⟷ | | Holt for Kerr |
| 83 | ⟷ | | Bemand for Ellis |
| **Full-Time** | | | |

| Premiership Table | | | | | |
|---|---|---|---|---|---|
| **Team** | **P** | **W** | **D** | **L** | **Pts** |
| **1 Leicester Tigers** | **19** | **13** | **3** | **3** | **67** |
| 2 London Wasps | 19 | 13 | 1 | 5 | 63 |
| 3 Sale Sharks | 19 | 11 | 0 | 8 | 51 |

## Tigers Milestone

All eight Premiership encounters between Leeds and Leicester have still been won by the home team on the day.

It was a disjointed first half for the visitors, who had fit-again tighthead prop Julian White sin-binned in the opening exchanges. Ross slotted the subsequent three points after White's yellow card, before Goode equalised in the eighth minute, multi-skilled Ireland full back Geordan Murphy having done well in the build-up.

Goode slotted a penalty, cutting the score to 12-15 after 45 minutes, before a Leon Lloyd try – courtesy of a good build-up from his team-mates – put the visitors ahead for the first time at 19-15 after 52 minutes. Leeds, however, refused to lie down, with young full back Tom Biggs scoring after a daring run from just inside Leicester's half and Ross adding his sixth penalty for a 23-19 lead.

Goode cut the deficit to just one point in the 70th minute, before coming agonisingly close to winning the game for his team with a long-range penalty attempt in the 83rd minute.

# Leinster **13**
# Leicester Tigers **29**

**Date:** 2.4.05  **Venue:** Lansdowne Road  **Attendance:** 48,500  **Referee:** J.Jutge

## Team Line-Ups

| | | |
|---|---|---|
| G.Dempsey | 15 | S.Vesty |
| S.Horgan | 14 | G.Murphy |
| B.O'Driscoll | 13 | O.Smith |
| F.Contepomi | 12 | D.Gibson |
| D.Hickie | 11 | L.Lloyd |
| D.Holwell | 10 | A.Goode |
| G.Easterby | 9 | H.Ellis |
| R.Corrigan (c) | 1 | G.Rowntree |
| S.Byrne | 2 | G.Chuter |
| R.Nebbett | 3 | D.Morris |
| M.O'Kelly | 4 | (c) M.Johnson |
| L.Cullen | 5 | L.Deacon |
| C.Potts | 6 | L.Moody |
| K.Gleeson | 7 | N.Back |
| E.Miller | 8 | M.Corry |

## Replacements

| | | |
|---|---|---|
| E.Byrne | 16 | J.Buckland |
| D.Blaney | 17 | J.Rawson |
| D.Dillon | 18 | W.Johnson |
| V.Costello | 19 | H.Tuilagi |
| B.O'Meara | 20 | S.Bemand |
| S.Jennings | 21 | A.Healey |
| G.D'Arcy | 22 | A.Tuilagi |

## Match Stats

| | | |
|---|---|---|
| 69 | Tackles | 62 |
| 10 | Missed Tackles | 7 |
| 58 | Ball Carries | 62 |
| 263 | Metres | 355 |
| 7 | Defenders Beaten | 9 |
| 4 | Passes | 6 |
| 0 | Clean Breaks | 4 |
| 13 | Penalties Conceded | 10 |
| 12 | Turnovers | 15 |
| 45 | Breakdowns Won | 57 |
| 83 | % Scrums Won | 100 |
| 83 | % Line-Outs Won | 90 |

Leicester Tigers booked their place in the 2004-05 Heineken Cup semi-finals with a stunning 29-13 triumph over Leinster at a packed Lansdowne Road. Tigers scored two tries to one, with England fly-half Andy Goode proving his value to the team once again with a match-winning 19-point haul.

Goode kicked two conversions, four penalties and one drop-goal, with centres Ollie Smith and Daryl Gibson getting their team's tries and sending them into the semi-finals, with French powerhouse, Toulouse, next in wait for the rampant Tigers; the first-ever English side to win a Heineken Cup quarter-final away from home.

It was an emotional victory for the visitors – who began the match without star tighthead prop Julian White, who picked up a stinger at training earlier in the week – but it was a deserved one.

"We kept up the pressure throughout. I think it was down to our defensive line-outs, scrums and pressure that we kept on turning the ball over." **John Wells**

| Min | | Score | |
|---|---|---|---|
| 12 | P | 0-3 | **Goode** |
| 18 | P | 3-3 | Holwell |
| 34 | P | 3-6 | **Goode** |
| 34 | ↔ | | **Bemand for Ellis** |
| 38 | TC | 3-13 | **Smith/Goode** |
| 40 | ☐ | | Potts |
| 40 | P | 3-16 | **Goode** |
| **Half-Time** | | | |
| 41 | ↔ | | **Ellis for Bemand** |
| 50 | ↔ | | Costello for Potts |
| 52 | ↔ | | D'Arcy for Contepomi |
| 57 | P | 6-16 | Holwell |
| 58 | TC | 6-23 | **Gibson/Goode** |
| 60 | ↔ | | Jennings for Gleeson |
| 65 | P | 6-26 | **Goode** |
| 69 | DG | 6-29 | **Goode** |
| 75 | TC | 13-29 | Horgan/Holwell |
| 78 | ↔ | | **Healey for Vesty** |
| **Full-Time** | | | |

### Tigers Milestone

Captain Martin Johnson played his 50th Heineken Cup match – becoming the second Tiger, and second-ever Englishman, to achieve this feat.

Captain Martin Johnson, as always, was a colossus for his side, but each and every Tigers player deserves a pat on the back for what was achieved, with the likes of Graham Rowntree, Darren Morris – who replaced White and scrummed powerfully in unison with Rowntree and hooker George Chuter – Lewis Moody (the Heineken Cup Man of the Match), Martin Corry, Goode, Smith, Geordan Murphy and Sam Vesty deserving special mention.

At 6-3 up, Smith's dazzling try, which was made possible by a Louis Deacon line-out steal, put the visitors ahead by 13-3, with Tigers eventually going into half-time 16-3 ahead.

The second half began with a ferocious onslaught from Leinster, but the cool and calm visitors kept them at bay. Leinster No.10 David Holwell got the first points of the second 40 minutes, but Tigers flanker Lewis Moody plucked the kick-off out of the air, before off-loading brilliantly in the tackle to Gibson, who finished superbly, with Goode converting for unassailable 23-6 lead.

Goode added a fourth penalty in the 63rd minute, for a 26-6 advantage, before slotting a superb drop-goal just four minutes later, despite being dumped onto his behind in the process. A late Shane Horgan try, which Holwell converted, gave the home side a final glimmer of hope, but nothing was ever going to stop the Tigers juggernaut – and their lively supporters – from sweeping all before them in sensational fashion.

# Leicester Tigers **45**
# Sale Sharks **15**

**Date:** 9.4.05  **Venue:** Welford Road  **Attendance:** 16,815  **Referee:** D.Rose

## Team Line-Ups

| | | | |
|---|---|---|---|
| G.Murphy | **15** | (c) | J.Robinson |
| T.Varndell | **14** | | M.Cueto |
| L.Lloyd | **13** | | C.Jones |
| D.Gibson | **12** | | R.Todd |
| A.Tuilagi | **11** | | S.Hanley |
| A.Goode | **10** | | M.Hercus |
| S.Bemand | **9** | | B.Redpath |
| G.Rowntree | **1** | | A.Sheridan |
| G.Chuter | **2** | | A.Titterrell |
| D.Morris | **3** | | B.Stewart |
| M.Johnson (c) | **4** | | C.Jones |
| L.Deacon | **5** | | D.Schofield |
| W.Johnson | **6** | | J.White |
| L.Moody | **7** | | M.Lund |
| M.Corry | **8** | | S.Chabal |

## Replacements

| | | |
|---|---|---|
| J.Buckland | **16** | S.Bruno |
| J.Rawson | **17** | S.Turner |
| H.Tuilagi | **18** | I.F'dez Lobbe |
| N.Back | **19** | P.Anglesea |
| H.Ellis | **20** | D.Blair |
| S.Vesty | **21** | J.Payne |
| O.Smith | **22** | S.Martens |

## Match Stats

| | | |
|---|---|---|
| 69 | Tackles | 70 |
| 9 | Missed Tackles | 14 |
| 66 | Ball Carries | 66 |
| 455 | Metres | 465 |
| 13 | Defenders Beaten | 8 |
| 125 | Passes | 58 |
| 10 | Clean Breaks | 5 |
| 15 | Penalties Conceded | 14 |
| 15 | Turnovers | 9 |
| 51 | Breakdowns Won | 44 |
| 90 | % Scrums Won | 92 |
| 95 | % Line-Outs Won | 76 |

## Premiership Home Record vs Sale Sharks

| Played | Won | Drawn | Lost | Points For | Points Against |
|---|---|---|---|---|---|
| 8 | 7 | 0 | 1 | 255 | 112 |

Leicester Tigers racked up an impressive 45-15 win over Sale Sharks in Zurich Premiership action at Welford Road, cementing their position at the top of the standings with just two league matches remaining in the 2004-05 season. It was top-class rugby from a top-notch outfit, who despite facing an early 0-7 deficit, which later became 3-10, wrapped up the four-try bonus point before half-time.

Fly-half Andy Goode once again contributed a bucket-load of points, whilst there were irresistible performances from the likes of Lewis Moody, Martin Corry and Geordan Murphy.

Sale went ahead through an early Mark Cueto try – after just six minutes of play – which was converted by American fly-half Mike Hercus, but once Tigers reeled their opponents in, there was to be no respite.

First-half tries were scored by openside flanker Lewis Moody, outside centre Leon Lloyd, Goode – from an intercept – and skipper Martin Johnson, a popular try-scorer if ever!

The second half began in similar fashion for Tigers, with Goode opening up the Sale defence with a text-book break, before linking up with Murphy, who put big winger Alesana Tuilagi away in the right-hand corner for try number five. Goode struck the conversion sweetly and Leicester were ahead by 38-10.

But Sale refused to give up at that stage, with Cueto getting his second try in the 54th minute after a prolonged spell of pressure. Tigers, however, ran in their sixth try of the day through speedy winger Tom Varndell; keeping up his 100 per cent try-scoring record in the first team. The build-up to Varndell's try was team work at its very best, with the tight five doing exceptionally well and Bradstone Man of the Match, inside centre Daryl Gibson, also handling superbly.

Goode, who sported a 100 per cent kicking record on the day, slotted the touchline conversion with aplomb, for the 45-15 lead, with a flurry of substitutions and two yellow cards – one to Graham Rowntree and one to Chris Jones – contributing to a timid end to a game that reached great heights when Leicester were in full cry.

"Through the week I know the lads have found it very difficult to get their minds round this weekend, but it was a pleasing result." **John Wells**

| Event Line | | |
|---|---|---|
| **Min** | **Score** | |
| 6 🏉 | 0-7 | Cueto/Hercus |
| 15 🏉 | 3-7 | **Goode** |
| 17 🏉 | 3-10 | Hercus |
| 24 🏉 | 10-10 | **Moody/Goode** |
| 30 🏉 | 17-10 | **Lloyd/Goode** |
| 33 🏉 | 24-10 | **Goode** |
| 39 🏉 | 31-10 | **M.Johnson/Goode** |
| **Half-Time** | | |
| 47 ⬌ | | **H.Tuilagi for W.Johnson** |
| 50 🏉 | 38-10 | **A.Tuilagi/Goode** |
| 52 ⬌ | | Turner for Stewart |
| 54 🏉 | 38-15 | Cueto |
| 56 ⬌ | | **Smith for Lloyd** |
| 56 ⬌ | | Bruno for Titterell |
| 57 🏉 | 45-15 | **Varndell/Goode** |
| 59 ⬌ | | Fernandez Lobbe for Chabal |
| 59 ⬌ | | Blair for Hercus |
| 59 ⬌ | | Martens for Redpath |
| 62 ▢ | | **Rowntree** |
| 64 ⬌ | | **Rawson for H.Tuilagi** |
| 67 ▢ | | C.Jones |
| 68 ⬌ | | Payne for Todd |
| 74 ⬌ | | **Ellis for Bemand** |
| 74 ⬌ | | **Vesty for Gibson** |
| 74 ⬌ | | **H.Tuilagi for Rowntree** |
| 78 ⬌ | | **Buckland for Chuter** |
| 78 ⬌ | | Anglesea for C.Jones |
| **Full-Time** | | |

### Premiership Table

| Team | P | W | D | L | Pts |
|---|---|---|---|---|---|
| **1 Leicester Tigers** | **20** | **14** | **3** | **3** | **72** |
| 2 London Wasps | 20 | 14 | 1 | 5 | 68 |
| 3 Bath Rugby | 20 | 11 | 2 | 7 | 53 |

### Tigers Milestone

Andy Goode's points-haul of 20 saw him join John Liley, Joel Stransky and Tim Stimpson in scoring 500 or more league points for Leicester.

# Saracens **19**
# Leicester Tigers **17**

**Date:** 17.4.05  **Venue:** Vicarage Road  **Attendance:** 16,812  **Referee:** C.White

## Team Line-Ups

| | | |
|---|---|---|
| M.Bartholomeusz | **15** | S.Vesty |
| B.Johnston | **14** | G.Murphy |
| K.Sorrell | **13** | M.Cornwell |
| D.Harris | **12** | D.Gibson |
| T.Vaikona | **11** | A.Tuilagi |
| T.Castaignede | **10** | A.Goode |
| K.Bracken | **9** | H.Ellis |
| K.Yates | **1** | G.Rowntree |
| R.Ibanez | **2** | G.Chuter |
| B.Broster | **3** | J.White |
| K.Chesney | **4** | (c) M.Johnson |
| S.Raiwalui | **5** | L.Deacon |
| R.Hill | **6** | W.Johnson |
| D.Seymour | **7** | N.Back |
| H.Vyvyan (c) | **8** | M.Corry |

## Replacements

| | | |
|---|---|---|
| M.Cairns | **16** | J.Buckland |
| N.Lloyd | **17** | L.Moody |
| I.Fullarton | **18** | D.Morris |
| B.Russell | **19** | H.Tuilagi |
| M.Rauluni | **20** | S.Bemand |
| N.Little | **21** | R.Broadfoot |
| P.Bailey | **22** | T.Varndell |

## Premiership Away Record vs Saracens

| Played | Won | Drawn | Lost | Points For | Points Against |
|---|---|---|---|---|---|
| 8 | 3 | 1 | 4 | 171 | 159 |

## Match Stats

| | | |
|---|---|---|
| **54** | Tackles | **72** |
| **5** | Missed Tackles | **5** |
| **70** | Ball Carries | **46** |
| **402** | Metres | **164** |
| **5** | Defenders Beaten | **5** |
| **102** | Passes | **113** |
| **2** | Clean Breaks | **2** |
| **7** | Penalties Conceded | **15** |
| **9** | Turnovers | **10** |
| **63** | Breakdowns Won | **50** |
| **100** | % Scrums Won | **100** |
| **100** | % Line-Outs Won | **85** |

"The loss of Deacon and Corry had a massive effect on our line-out and without control we weren't able to get into our stride." **John Wells**

## Event Line

| Min | | Score | |
|---|---|---|---|
| 7 | P | 3-0 | Castaignède |
| 10 | ⟷ | | **Moody for L.Deacon** |
| 19 | TC | 10-0 | Castaignède |
| 22 | T | 10-5 | **Chuter** |
| 25 | ▌ | | **Corry** |
| 25 | ⟷ | | Russell for Hill |
| 27 | P | 10-8 | **Goode** |
| 32 | ⟷ | | Hill for Russell |
| 36 | P | 10-11 | **Goode** |
| 40 | P | 10-14 | **Goode** |
| **Half-Time** | | | |
| 41 | ⟷ | | Lloyd for Yates |
| 44 | P | 13-14 | Castaignède |
| 45 | ⟷ | | Russell for Seymour |
| 55 | ⟷ | | Cairns for Ibanez |
| 55 | ⟷ | | Rauluni for Bracken |
| 57 | ⟷ | | Little for Bartholomeusz |
| 58 | P | 13-17 | **Goode** |
| 60 | P | 16-17 | Castaignède |
| 63 | ▌ | | **M.Johnson** |
| 63 | ▌ | | Russell |
| 64 | P | 19-17 | Castaignède |
| 64 | ⟷ | | **Bemand for Ellis** |
| 64 | ⟷ | | **Varndell for A.Tuilagi** |
| 67 | ⟷ | | Fullarton for Raiwalui |
| 68 | ⟷ | | **Buckland for Chuter** |
| 73 | ⟷ | | **H.Tuilagi for Back** |
| **Full-Time** | | | |

## Premiership Table

| | Team | P | W | D | L | Pts |
|---|---|---|---|---|---|---|
| 1 | London Wasps | 21 | 15 | 1 | 5 | 73 |
| **2** | **Leicester Tigers** | **21** | **14** | **3** | **4** | **73** |
| 3 | Sale Sharks | 21 | 12 | 0 | 9 | 56 |

## Tigers Milestone

Andy Goode became the 193rd player to make his 100th first-team start for Tigers, whilst his 12 points took him past the 800-point mark, joining eight other players.

A 14-man Leicester Tigers outfit suffered a narrow 17-19 defeat to Saracens at Vicarage Road, setting up an exciting winner-takes-all Zurich Premiership finale against London Wasps at Welford Road in Round 22. Both sides scored one try each, with Tigers very nearly pulling off the victory, despite losing influential No.8 Martin Corry to a red card – which later became a three-week ban – in the first half.

Corry was red-carded by referee Chris White in the 28th minute for foul play, but Tigers actually outscored their opponents by 12-9 without their powerhouse No.8, and they very nearly came away with a win after a helter-skelter ending to a tempestuous match.

Without Corry, the visitors were forced to battle without their premier jumper at the tail of Leicester's usually well-oiled line-out – that after a facial injury to second row Louis Deacon, in the 11th minute, had left them without a No.4 jumper, leaving Johnson as their sole line-out specialist and replacement flanker Lewis Moody as their second option.

But Johnson seemed to take a step up with his team under the cosh, carrying the ball up strongly and calling the shots at the line-outs. At crucial times, however, Tigers needed that extra line-out option and without Deacon and Corry they lacked enough variety to secure enough clean ball when it mattered most.

Frenchman Thomas Castaignède did all the scoring for the Men in Black, collecting a try, one conversion and four penalties on the day. Hooker George Chuter scored a superb try for Tigers, after Sarries had taken an early 10-0 lead, with fly-half Andy Goode eventually turning that into a 17-13 advantage via four penalty goals – three in the first half and one in the second half.

But it was not going to be Leicester's day, with a Castaignède penalty narrowing the scoreline to 16-17, before Tigers skipper Martin Johnson and Saracens flanker Ben Russell were yellow-carded for fighting; Russell having landed a multitude of punches on Johnno's brow, whilst the latter did not even react.

Referee White thought otherwise, however, reducing Tigers to 13 men and Saracens to 14, whilst Castaignède slotted the match-winning penalty from close-range, condemning Leicester to their second loss in their last three ZP starts.

# Leicester Tigers **19**
# Toulouse **27**

**Date:** 24.4.05 **Venue:** Walkers Stadium **Attendance:** 31,883 **Referee:** A.Rolland

## Team Line-Ups

| G.Murphy | 15 | C.Poitrenaud |
|---|---|---|
| L.Lloyd | 14 | V.Clerc |
| O.Smith | 13 | Y.Jauzion |
| D.Gibson | 12 | F.Fritz |
| A.Healey | 11 | C.Heymans |
| A.Goode | 10 | (c) F.Michalak |
| H.Ellis | 9 | J.Elissalde |
| G.Rowntree | 1 | J.Poux |
| G.Chuter | 2 | W.Servat |
| J.White | 3 | O.Hasan Jalil |
| M.Johnson (c) | 4 | R.Millo-Chlusky |
| L.Deacon | 5 | T.Brennan |
| L.Moody | 6 | J.Bouilhou |
| N.Back | 7 | F.Maka |
| H.Tuilagi | 8 | G.Lamboley |

## Replacements

| J.Buckland | 16 | Y.Bru |
|---|---|---|
| D.Morris | 17 | D.Human |
| B.Kay | 18 | I.Maka |
| W.Johnson | 19 | C.Labit |
| S.Bemand | 20 | J.Dubois |
| S.Vesty | 21 | B.Baby |
| T.Varndell | 22 | G.Thomas |

## Match Stats

| | | |
|---|---|---|
| 48 | Tackles | 85 |
| 9 | Missed Tackles | 8 |
| 88 | Ball Carries | 53 |
| 441 | Metres | 482 |
| 8 | Defenders Beaten | 9 |
| 126 | Passes | 76 |
| 2 | Clean Breaks | 11 |
| 11 | Penalties Conceded | 10 |
| 15 | Turnovers | 9 |
| 66 | Breakdowns Won | 30 |
| 89 | % Scrums Won | 100 |
| 94 | % Line-Outs Won | 83 |

Toulouse ended Leicester Tigers' 2004-05 Heineken Cup dream, with the French aristocrats recording a 27-19 win at the Walkers Stadium, having outscored their hosts by three tries to one after enjoying a slender 10-9 half-time lead. Tigers enjoyed superiority for much of the first half, despite going into the break one point down, but an early second-half try gave the visitors an eight-point cushion, which Leicester were just unable to bounce back from.

As a result, the 'hosts' – playing at a neutral venue, but with some 29,000 supporters dressed in green backing them – were forced to play catch-up for most of the second half through the boot of fly-half Andy Goode. Toulouse scored a late try through fly-half and captain Frédéric Michalak, before Leicester eventually responded with a five-pointer by replacement winger Tom Varndell.

The match could not have started on a better note for Toulouse, albeit rather fortuitously when referee Alain Rolland missed a forward pass in the build-up to flanker Finau Maka's try in the second minute. Goode opened his team's account with a penalty in the ninth minute, but scrum-half Jean-Baptiste Elissalde quickly cancelled that out with a penalty goal of his own.

Two more Goode penalties saw Toulouse lead by just 10-9 at half-time, but Tigers had earlier lost their star England prop Graham Rowntree with a knee injury, whilst flanker Lewis Moody battled gamely for most of the first half, having also taken a knock to his knee after a bright start.

Moody was unable to return to the fray at the start of the second half, but worse was to follow when Toulouse benefited from yet another forward pass, Elissalde scampering over after a counter-attack by full back Clément Poitrenaud and centre Yannick Jauzion.

Goode chipped away at the 9-17 scoreline with his fourth penalty goal of the day, but Elissalde cancelled it out with his fifth successful strike, before Wales skipper Gareth Thomas showed great composure to put Michalak away for the match-clinching score.

Varndell's try gave the scoreline some respectability, once again highlighting the youngster's nose for the tryline, but it was too little too late for Tigers.

"I know there were some dubious decisions, but I think they were just that much smarter than us on the day." **John Wells**

| Event Line | | |
|---|---|---|
| **Min** | **Score** | |
| 3 🏉TC | 0-7 | F.Maka/Elissalde |
| 8 ⬌ | | I.Maka for Bouilhou |
| 10 🅟 | 3-7 | **Goode** |
| 15 🅟 | 3-10 | Elissalde |
| 20 ⬌ | | **Morris for Rowntree** |
| 26 🅟 | 6-10 | **Goode** |
| 33 🅟 | 9-10 | **Goode** |
| 40 ⬌ | | **Kay for Moody** |
| **Half-Time** | | |
| 43 ⬌ | | Bru for Servat |
| 51 🏉TC | 9-17 | Elissalde |
| 55 ⬌ | | Human for Poux |
| 60 🅟 | 12-17 | **Goode** |
| 65 🅟 | 12-20 | Elissalde |
| 68 ⬌ | | **W.Johnson for H.Tuilagi** |
| 68 ⬌ | | **Bemand for Ellis** |
| 68 ⬌ | | Thomas for Poitrenaud |
| 72 ⬌ | | Labit for F.Maka |
| 74 🏉TC | 12-27 | Michalak/Elissalde |
| 77 ⬌ | | Baby for Jauzion |
| 80 ⬌ | | **Varndell for Lloyd** |
| 80 🏉TC | 19-27 | **Varndell/Goode** |
| 81 ⬌ | | Dubois for Elissalde |
| **Full-Time** | | |

## Tigers Milestone

Walkers Stadium is the fifth different ground in Leicester that Tigers have played on, after the Belgrave Cricket & Cycle Ground, Victoria Park, Welford Road and Welford Road Rec.

# Leicester Tigers **45**
# London Wasps **10**

Date: 30.4.05  Venue: Welford Road  Attendance: 16,815  Referee: T.Spreadbury

## Team Line-Ups

| | | |
|---|---|---|
| S.Vesty | **15** | M.V-Gisbergen |
| G.Murphy | **14** | P.Sackey |
| O.Smith | **13** | A.Erinle |
| D.Gibson | **12** | J.Lewsey |
| A.Healey | **11** | T.Voyce |
| A.Goode | **10** | A.King |
| H.Ellis | **9** | M.Dawson |
| D.Morris | **1** | T.Payne |
| G.Chuter | **2** | P.Greening |
| J.White | **3** | W.Green |
| M.Johnson (c) | **4** | S.Shaw |
| B.Kay | **5** | R.Birkett |
| H.Tuilagi | **6** | J.Worsley |
| N.Back | **7** | T.Rees |
| L.Deacon | **8** | (c) L.Dallaglio |

## Replacements

| | | |
|---|---|---|
| J.Buckland | **16** | T.Leota |
| M.Holford | **17** | A.McKenzie |
| B.Deacon | **18** | J.Hart |
| W.Johnson | **19** | M.Purdy |
| S.Bemand | **20** | W.Fury |
| D.Hipkiss | **21** | J.Brooks |
| A.Tuilagi | **22** | J.Mbu |

## Match Stats

| | | |
|---|---|---|
| 127 | Tackles | 55 |
| 15 | Missed Tackles | 9 |
| 62 | Ball Carries | 115 |
| 703 | Metres | 539 |
| 9 | Defenders Beaten | 14 |
| 100 | Passes | 148 |
| 13 | Clean Breaks | 2 |
| 18 | Penalties Conceded | 8 |
| 11 | Turnovers | 26 |
| 51 | Breakdowns Won | 96 |
| 100 | % Scrums Won | 100 |
| 86 | % Line-Outs Won | 80 |

## Premiership Home Record vs London Wasps

| Played | Won | Drawn | Lost | Points For | Points Against |
|---|---|---|---|---|---|
| 8 | 8 | 0 | 0 | 248 | 102 |

Leicester Tigers stalwarts Martin Johnson and Neil Back, and head coach John Wells, were given an emotional send-off at a packed Welford Road, with Leicester booking their place in the 2004-05 Zurich Premiership Final courtesy of an emphatic 45-10 triumph over London Wasps. Tigers scored five tries to one, but the three farewells were what captured everyone's imagination on a fantastic afternoon.

Even Johnson had a strain in his voice when addressing the sell-out crowd afterwards, chairman Peter Tom and chief executive Peter Wheeler having presented the trio with their coat pegs from the Welford Road changing rooms, which they have used, collectively, for the last 54 years.

Said Johnno: "I'd just like to say that I'm totally overwhelmed by today; it's been a brilliant 16 years and I couldn't have wished for anything else. I'd like to thank all the players I've played with, not just this season, and also to the supporters; thank you, it's been wonderful."

"You couldn't have written the script any better, but I think the result led the emotional side of things." **John Wells**

Captain Johnson was, as always a colossus – in the line-outs, in defence and attack – Back capped off his last appearance, as a player, at Welford Road with a try, his 125th for Leicester Tigers, whilst Wells – who has worked wonders since taking over as head coach in January 2004 – seemed content with watching his two former team-mates hog all the attention afterwards.

Tigers scored five tries, the first from England scrum-half Harry Ellis after a typically powerful surge from No.8 Henry Tuilagi, who swatted defenders away like flies. Tuilagi was at it again less than five minutes later when he stormed ahead from a scrum just in Tigers' half, only to get dragged down inches from the line in a brave tackle from Wasps winger Tom Voyce. Cruelly, Tuilagi suffered a compound fracture of his right leg, robbing the home side of their most potent strike weapon at that stage.

A Daryl Gibson try, which Goode converted from the touchline, followed by a drop-goal from the latter, took the half-time score to 23-3, before second-half tries by Geordan Murphy, Neil Back and Dan Hipkiss put the icing on the cake and sent Tigers into the 2005 Zurich Premiership Final and still firmly on track for some silverware.

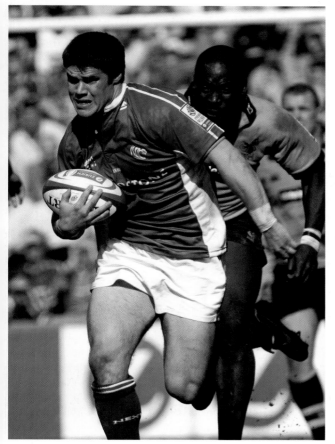

## Event Line

| Min | | Score | |
|-----|--|-------|--|
| 6 | P | 3-0 | Goode |
| 13 | P | 3-3 | Van Gisbergen |
| 15 | P | 6-3 | Goode |
| 23 | TC | 13-3 | Ellis/Goode |
| 31 | ⬌ | | W.Johnson for H.Tuilagi |
| 32 | TC | 20-3 | Gibson/Goode |
| 40 | DG | 23-3 | Goode |
| **Half-Time** | | | |
| 41 | P | 26-3 | Goode |
| 43 | TC | 33-3 | Murphy/Goode |
| 55 | ⬌ | | Purdy for Birkett |
| 55 | ⬌ | | Brooks for King |
| 58 | ⬌ | | Leota for Greening |
| 58 | ⬌ | | Hart for Worsley |
| 59 | T | 38-3 | Back |
| 61 | ⬌ | | Buckland for Chuter |
| 61 | ⬌ | | Holford for Morris |
| 61 | ⬌ | | A.Tuilagi for Healey |
| 63 | ⬌ | | Hipkiss for Gibson |
| 67 | TC | 45-3 | Hipkiss/Goode |
| 67 | ☐ | | Buckland |
| 69 | ⬌ | | Bemand for Murphy |
| 69 | ⬌ | | Gibson for Hipkiss |
| 69 | ⬌ | | Hipkiss for Smith |
| 71 | ⬌ | | Chuter for M.Johnson |
| 72 | ⬌ | | Fury for Dawson |
| 77 | TC | 45-10 | Voyce/Van Gisbergen |
| 79 | ⬌ | | B.Deacon for Kay |
| 79 | ⬌ | | M.Johnson for Chuter |
| **Full-Time** | | | |

## Premiership Table

| Team | P | W | D | L | Pts |
|------|---|---|---|---|-----|
| 1 Leicester Tigers | 22 | 15 | 3 | 4 | 78 |
| 2 London Wasps | 22 | 15 | 1 | 6 | 73 |
| 3 Sale Sharks | 22 | 13 | 0 | 9 | 60 |

## Tigers Milestone

This win, Tigers' 15th of the Zurich Premiership season, saw Leicester remain unbeaten at Welford Road in the ZP. They have not lost in their last 13 Premiership matches at Welford Road.

# Leicester Tigers **14**
# London Wasps **39**

**Date:** 14.5.05 **Venue:** Twickenham **Attendance:** 66,000 **Referee:** C.White

## Team Line-Ups

| | | |
|---|---|---|
| S.Vesty | **15** | M.V-Gisbergen |
| G.Murphy | **14** | P.Sackey |
| O.Smith | **13** | A.Erinle |
| D.Gibson | **12** | J.Lewsey |
| L.Lloyd | **11** | T.Voyce |
| A.Goode | **10** | A.King |
| H.Ellis | **9** | M.Dawson |
| D.Morris | **1** | T.Payne |
| G.Chuter | **2** | P.Greening |
| J.White | **3** | W.Green |
| M.Johnson (c) | **4** | S.Shaw |
| B.Kay | **5** | R.Birkett |
| L.Deacon | **6** | J.Hart |
| N.Back | **7** | J.Worsley |
| M.Corry | **8** | (c) L.Dallaglio |

## Replacements

| | | |
|---|---|---|
| J.Buckland | **16** | T.Leota |
| M.Holford | **17** | A.McKenzie |
| B.Deacon | **18** | J.Hart |
| W.Johnson | **19** | M.Purdy |
| S.Bemand | **20** | W.Fury |
| D.Hipkiss | **21** | J.Brooks |
| A.Tuilagi | **22** | J.Mbu |

## Match Stats

| | | |
|---|---|---|
| 83 | Tackles | 82 |
| 10 | Missed Tackles | 11 |
| 83 | Ball Carries | 79 |
| 359 | Metres | 462 |
| 9 | Defenders Beaten | 10 |
| 112 | Passes | 124 |
| 4 | Clean Breaks | 8 |
| 13 | Penalties Conceded | 15 |
| 16 | Turnovers | 9 |
| 62 | Breakdowns Won | 62 |
| 100 | % Scrums Won | 100 |
| 100 | % Line-Outs Won | 84 |

London Wasps shattered Leicester Tigers' Zurich Premiership dream, recording a 39-14 victory in the 2005 final at Twickenham. It was a disappointing end to the Tigers playing careers of Martin Johnson and Neil Back, and also the coaching career of John Wells, but the men from the East Midlands were unable to find that edge they were looking for on the day.

The start of the match had memories of Toulouse – when Tigers went down 19-27 in their Heineken Cup semi-final at the Walkers Stadium – with Wasps capitalising on Leicester's early mistakes. Those early errors saw the defending champions run into a 13-0 lead, Van Gisbergen taking all his chances at goal and winger Tom Voyce scoring a try.

But Tigers did not panic; they battered away at Wasps, with fly-half Andy Goode – the leading points-scorer in the Zurich Premiership for the second successive season – slotting a penalty, having being impeded whilst chasing his own kick ahead.

"Well, they didn't let us play...and they did to us what we did to them in the last three games." **John Wells**

### Event Line

| Min | | Score | |
|---|---|---|---|
| 3 | P | 0-3 | Van Gisbergen |
| 5 | TC | 0-10 | Voyce/Van Gisbergen |
| 8 | DG | 0-13 | King |
| 12 | P | 3-13 | Goode |
| 19 | ↔ | | Bemand for Ellis |
| 27 | P | 6-13 | Goode |
| 33 | P | 6-16 | Van Gisbergen |
| 37 | P | 6-19 | Van Gisbergen |
| **Half-Time** | | | |
| 44 | P | 6-22 | Van Gisbergen |
| 54 | P | 9-22 | Goode |
| 70 | TC | 9-29 | V-Gsbgen/V-Gsbgen |
| 75 | P | 9-32 | Van Gisbergen |
| 75 | ↔ | | Buckland for Chuter |
| 75 | ↔ | | W.Johnson for Kay |
| 77 | T | 14-32 | Bemand |
| 77 | ↔ | | Fury for Dawson |
| 77 | ↔ | | Hoadley for Voyce |
| 77 | ↔ | | Brooks for King |
| 77 | ↔ | | Lock for Hart |
| 77 | ↔ | | Purdy for Worsley |
| 78 | TC | 14-39 | Hoadley/V-Gsbgen |
| **Full-Time** | | | |

### Tigers Milestone

Martin Johnson and Neil Back ended their Tigers careers in 13th and 22nd place respectively in the all-time Leicester appearance chart, with Back also finishing in 8th place on the all-time try-scoring list.

A second Goode penalty, in the 27th minute, saw Tigers come within seven points of Wasps, but Van Gisbergen soon extended their lead to 16-6, and then 19-6 – the eventual half-time score.

Tigers coach John Wells, predictably, rang the changes at the break, with Graham Rowntree and Lewis Moody replacing Darren Morris and Louis Deacon respectively, but their presence did not quite have the desired effect, Van Gisbergen stretching Wasps' lead after just two minutes with his fourth successful penalty of the day.

Goode got one back in the 49th minute, but at 9-22 down Leicester were always going to be up against it, with Wasps' flat defensive lines pinning them back and limiting their options on attack.

Van Gisbergen's try, which he converted, followed by a penalty, preceded a Scott Bemand try in the 76th minute, before Wasps replacement Rob Hoadley put the icing on the cake for his side with a late try.

It was a disappointing end for Johnson and Back, and indeed for coach John Wells; taking the gloss off a wonderful season, which saw them win 15 of their 23 Premiership matches and 21 of their 33 fixtures overall. The contribution of Johnson, Back and Wells will never be forgotten – even if they were unable to sign off with a win.

# Season Summary 2004-05

For Leicester Tigers, the 2004-05 season was one of near misses. Under head coach John Wells, Tigers played 33 matches; winning 21, losing nine and drawing three, whilst they also qualified for the Heineken Cup semi-finals (the only English team to do so), they contested the Zurich Premiership Final, and their development team won the 2004-05 Zurich A League title.

Loyal Tigers servant Wells — who left Leicester to join the RFU's Academy — probably summed things up best after his side's Premiership Final loss to Wasps at Twickenham, saying: "Don't forget where we were this time last year. I think a lot of teams would be pleased with the season we've had.

"We, at Leicester, obviously demand more than that and that is understandable. Yes, it's disappointing we have to come away without something tangible, other than the second team championship. But I don't write the script, I don't write the fairytales. Professional sport is ruthless and the most attractive teams don't always win."

In all, the first team scored 111 tries; 76 of them in the Zurich Premiership, where they claimed nine four-try bonuses, three more than their nearest rivals, eventual champions, London Wasps. Tigers scored 978 points in all matches in '04-05, conceding just 559 in the process.

As far as international honours were concerned; once again no team was able to match Tigers, who in '04-05 provided eight British & Irish Lions tourists, eight England players during the autumn internationals and Six Nations, four Churchill Cup squad members, one England Sevens player, one Irish international, five England U21 regulars (and three World Cup squad members), one Scotland U21 regular, four England U19 World Cup squad members and another four England U18 players.

The season itself started on a disappointing note, with Tigers losing away to Sale Sharks on the opening weekend of the Premiership. That, however, was quickly remedied by a big win over Leeds Tykes, at home, which saw the team go unbeaten right up until the end of October — when a rampant Biarritz side beat Leicester 23-8 at Stade Aguiléra.

Tigers returned to the Premiership with a 28-13 win over Gloucester, at Welford Road, before spending three weeks without their autumn international stars; Graham Rowntree, Julian White, Ben Kay, Lewis Moody, Martin Corry and Harry Ellis (the latter making his test debut against South Africa) all playing for England and Geordan Murphy turning out for Ireland, who beat Tri-Nations champions, South Africa, at Lansdowne Road. In their absence, Tigers beat Worcester Warriors away — with Tom Varndell claiming a hat-trick in the space of 13

minutes – before drawing with Wasps (away) and beating Saracens at home.

The return of Tigers' galaxy of test stars coincided with a Heineken Cup double-header against defending champions London Wasps, matches which produced rugby of the highest order, but more importantly; Tigers winning both matches and keeping their European chances alive ahead of the New Year. Gloucester knocked Tigers out of the Powergen Cup the following week, but 2004 ended on a high with a 50-7 win over Premiership new-boys, Worcester, at Welford Road.

The New Year started well with a 28-13 win over Gloucester at The Shed. The victory, however, came at a cost, with Tigers losing their star No.8 Martin Corry to a freak elbow injury; ruling him out of action for six weeks and once again keeping him out of a Heineken Cup tie. (He missed the October Heineken Cup matches because of suspension.) But Leicester would still have been confident of success at home, only to suffer a gut-wrenching 17-21 loss to Biarritz at Welford Road, a late Harry Ellis try giving them the consolation of a bonus point. As it turns out, that bonus point managed to keep Tigers in contention for a lucky losers spot, the men in green, red and white racking up an emphatic 62-10 victory over Calvisano the following week and scraping into the play-offs when some results went their way the next day. Tigers were on an aeroplane heading for East Midlands airport when they got the Edinburgh-Perpignan result via a satellite phone call to Stockholm – they were still in business and the reaction of everyone present on the flight said it all!

After a week off, the Premiership got under way again at the end of January, with Tigers back in business with a 32-17 win over NEC Harlequins. Six Nations, 'A' team and Under-21 call-ups sucked Tigers' resources dry for their return fixture in the mud against Bath – -resulting in a second successive draw between the teams – before another week off, followed by possibly their most complete showing of 2004-05; an 83-10 triumph over Newcastle, with fly-half Andy Goode kicking 13 from 13 and fellow backs Ollie Smith and Leon Lloyd and flanker Neil Back all scoring two tries.

But Tigers were brought back down to earth with a bang the following week when East Midlands neighbours, Northampton Saints, took advantage of all Leicester's international call-ups, which by then also included Goode and Smith, recording a shock 26-11 win at Franklin's Gardens. March was a better month for Leicester, who played three and won two, losing away to Leeds Tykes, just a week before having to travel to Dublin for their Heineken Cup quarter-final meeting with Leinster. Martin Corry was handed the England captaincy against Italy and Scotland, but the month of March will always be remembered for the unfortunate neck injury suffered by Tigers' young prop Matt Hampson at an England Under-21 training session.

The first weekend of April in Dublin was easily the highlight of

Leicester's season. Nineteen points from Andy Goode's boot and tries from centres Daryl Gibson and Ollie Smith saw Tigers beat Leinster 29-13 at Lansdowne Road, giving the two times champions a very realistic chance of a third European title. A huge victory over Sale the following week added more icing to Tigers' cake, only for Leicester to suffer successive losses to Saracens (compounded by Martin Corry's red card and subsequent two-week suspension and also a facial injury to Louis Deacon), and to Toulouse, in the Heineken Cup semi-final at the Walkers Stadium. Knee injuries to Graham Rowntree and Lewis Moody soured the semi-final loss even more, although the month ended on a high in Tigers' last league game of the season – a 45-10 victory over Wasps, which saw Leicester end the regular season on top of the Premiership standings, although barn-storming back row Henry Tuilagi, who was in fine form, suffered a badly broken leg. The Wasps match was the last time the Welford Road faithful would see Messrs Johnson and Back in action – it was also coach Wells' final home game – and the trio were given an excellent send-off afterwards by supporters, board members and team-mates alike.

Whilst Johnson, Back and Wells managed to end their Welford Road careers on a high, Wasps wrecked their title hopes at Twickenham just two weeks later with a 39-14 victory in the final. Replacement scrum-half Scott Bemand – who came on early for England man Ellis – scored Leicester's only try, with Goode adding three penalty goals.

"It wasn't the real Leicester out there because Wasps didn't allow us to play," said Wells after the final. "If you look at our performances this year, the ones where we haven't been able to perform, teams haven't given us space or time and they did that today. Their defence was rock-solid early on and put pressure on our ball and they got over the gain-line more times in this game than they did in the previous matches."

# Season Preview 2005-06

New Tigers head coach Pat Howard and his squad began preparations for the 2005-06 season with a week-long training camp at the Peebles Hydro in Scotland – as the team did last season. Last year the training camp ended with a match against Edinburgh; this season Tigers signed off with a controlled training session, in match-like conditions, against The Borders in Galashiels.

"It was a nice start and a good crescendo to the week away," said Howard. "There were good things out there and bad things, but as I told the lads before they went out it wasn't about individual performances or the score, I wanted to see how the units performed, which meant everybody had to pull their weight.

"I don't want to change too much from last year, there's no point in tossing the baby out with the bath water. We did well last year; we just didn't know how to win finals, so I don't want to say we had a bad year. At the same time, however, I would like to change a few things and some of the new things we worked on during the week came off, but others didn't. We've got a video of the day, so we can take another good look at what needs working on."

The next week saw a youthful Tigers squad make the trip to Twickenham for the annual Middlesex Sevens. Leicester, under the captaincy of Dan Hipkiss, began with a 40-5 win over Bristol, with speedster Tom Varndell running in a hat-trick of tries. Tigers qualified for the semi-finals courtesy of a 10-0 win over Saracens in Round Two, but their campaign was halted in the last four by Wasps, who inflicted a 22-12 win over Leicester.

Next on Tigers' pre-season agenda was a friendly against Connacht in Galway. Whilst the score went against Tigers – they lost 17-22 – Howard was happy enough with his team's try-scoring abilities; Leicester outscoring their hosts by three tries to one, but the home team took all their kicks at goal in a bid for victory.

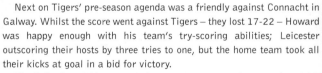

The following Friday saw Leicester come up against another Irish team in the shape of Heineken Cup giants Munster, with Tigers romping to a 50-19 victory at Welford Road.

Tries by Daryl Gibson, Alesana Tuilagi, Sam Vesty, Ephraim Taukafa and Leo Cullen, with Andy Goode adding the necessary with his booming right boot, put Tigers on the road to victory, with head coach Howard saying afterwards: "Look, there were positives and negatives. They did manage to breach our defence at times, but our patience was better than last week (against Connacht), especially when it came to off-loading the ball, and we scored some good tries out there."

# Development Team

Leicester Tigers' development team – under the astute coaching of Andy Key, Dusty Hare and Richard Cockerill – enjoyed a record-breaking season on and off the field as they romped to the 2004-05 Zurich A League title, beating London Wasps in a two-leg final in April.

Tigers, captained by back row Brett Deacon, won the first final, played at the Causeway Stadium in High Wycombe on April 11, by 35-19, before winning the second final – a fortnight later – in atrocious conditions at Welford Road by 29-22. The first final was a particularly memorable encounter, with Tigers having fought back from 18-19 down, before racking up two unanswered tries in the closing stages of the match.

Speedy winger Tom Varndell, who made a massive impact at first-team level this season, scored his customary solo try early on, before fly-half Ross Broadfoot scored his first of two five-pointers on the night. Tigers' other tries were scored by winger Ben Toft and flanker Joe Wheeler.

The second final was also something of a dog-fight, mainly because of the inclement weather; Leicester outscoring the visitors by three tries to two, with Samoan winger Alesana Tuilagi scoring a brace. Tigers' first try was scored by prop Peter Cook, with full back Roger Warren contributing 14 points through his boot.

Tigers finished top of the standings in the Northern Section, having won seven of their 10 league matches, losing just two – to Northampton Wanderers (home) and Newcastle Falcons (away) – and drawing to Sale Jets (away). In the Southern Section, Wasps topped the table with 46 points from their 10 games, losing just once in the regular season.

Tigers' Samoan international, Warren, finished the season as the top points-scorer in the Zurich A League with 94 points (one try, 17 conversions and 17 penalties), and Tuilagi, who scored a record four tries against Leeds Tykes, ended the season with eight tries, which saw him occupy joint third-place in the try-scoring stakes.

Aside from their sparkling play on the field, the other feature of Tigers' development team this season was the huge crowds they managed to attract, setting new standards in Britain for second team fixtures. England flanker Lewis Moody's comeback game against the Wanderers in October 2004, which ended in a 14-20 loss, was watched by 9,209 people, whilst their encounter with Worcester a month later attracted a crowd of 8,257.

The undoubted highlight, however, was the development team clash with Sale Jets on Monday, January 24, 2005, which was watched by an amazing crowd of 12,553. Tigers beat Sale 39-19, virtually securing

their place in the final, before their hard-fought 15-12 win over Northampton in March, which eventually booked their place in the final.

Leicester lost their final league fixture of the regular season, against Newcastle by 26-27, on a Bank Holiday Monday, but they more than made up for it with their wins over Wasps in the two finals. The first final was played in front of just over 1,000 fans, the return leg saw over 11,000 supporters, despite the bad weather.

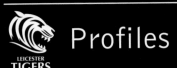

# Profiles

# Coaches

**Head Coach**

# Pat **Howard**

This is Pat Howard's second spell with Tigers, having enjoyed a successful time at the club as a player between 1998 and 2001; playing 94 matches and scoring 10 tries.

Pat, a former Wallaby fly-half or inside centre, then returned to his country of birth where he joined Super 12 outfit, the ACT Brumbies, before enjoying a spell with French club Montferrand ahead of his return to Leicester where he will the role of backline coach.

Pat was born in Sydney on November 14, 1973. He played 20 tests for Australia between 1993 and 1997.

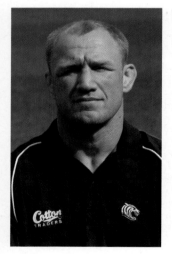

**Technical Director**

# Neil **Back**

Neil Back was one of England's outstanding players during their victorious 2003 Rugby World Cup campaign; starting six of the seven games in the tournament and scoring two tries along the way (the only fixture he missed was the pool game against Uruguay). It was his third successive World Cup campaign, having also been involved in '95 and '99, whilst he also toured with the British & Irish Lions squad three times in a row - to South Africa in 1997, Australia in 2001 and New Zealand in 2005.

He captained his country on four occasions during his 66-test career, including the Cook Cup victory against Australia during 2001-02, the last occasion being the day of his 50th England cap, with him retiring from test rugby during the 2004 Six Nations.

Neil took on coaching responsibilities within the club, whilst still serving as a player during the 2003-04 season, eventually retiring from first-class rugby at the end of 2004-05, after 339 matches for Tigers' first team — which saw him score a staggering 125 tries — and he now finds himself on the academy's coaching staff, as part of his role as the club's technical director, as well as looking after the first team's defence on a full-time basis.

# Chris **Brookes**

Chris Brookes, who was born in Stockton-on-Tees, was educated at the University of Nottingham, graduating with a degree in physiotherapy and as a member of the chartered society of physiotherapy in 1996.

He worked for the NHS for a while, before joining a private practice for two years. He started at Tigers in 2000 on a part-time basis, eventually joining the staff as a full-time employee in 2001.

Chris used to be a member of the Profile Sports injury-risk management team and he also runs a part-time practice in Leicester.

His main duty is looking after the first-team squad – during the week and on matchdays.

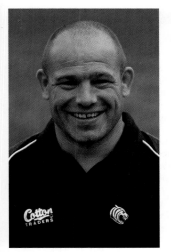

Forwards Coach

# Richard **Cockerill**

This is Richard Cockerill's second spell with Leicester Tigers – he left at the end of Tigers' double-winning session of 2001-02 to join French division club, Montferrand, where he played for two years seeing them through to the final of the Parker Pen Cup in May.

Richard, known as one of the game's most spirited players, hails from Rugby. He was educated at Harris Church of England School and played rugby for Warwickshire Schools.

He went on to represent England at U21 level and then England A, before making his Test debut in 1997. He played in the '98 and '99 Five Nations and the '99 World Cup, missing out on only two possible selections for England's 22 during his test career.

Richard has also been invited to play for the Barbarians, joining them on their Summer 2001 tour of the UK, and then captaining the side that came to Welford Road for the Neil Back Testimonial game in March 2003.

**Athletic Performance Coach**

# John **Dams**

John Dams was born in Lower Hutt, in Wellington, New Zealand, and studied physical education at Otago University in Dunedin. He ran his own business in Dunedin for two years, then moved to Wellington, where again he had his own business, before joining the Wellington Rugby Union, where he spent one-and-a-half years.

In his time with the Wellington Rugby Union, John worked with the Wellington Lions – the National Provincial Championship outfit that boasts the likes of All Blacks Tana Umaga and Jerry Collins – and the Wellington cricket team, before moving to Leicester in 2004.

Recently retired from the game of rugby, John played for the Otago Colts Development side and their Sevens team.

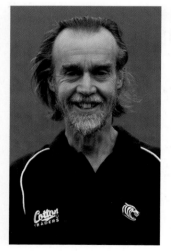

**Team Doctor**

# Dave **Finlay**

Originally from Grimsby, Dr Finlay qualified in medicine at St Andrews University in 1970. He worked in orthopaedics, trauma, casualty and medicine before becoming a radiologist in 1977. He was made a consultant at Queens Medical Centre in Nottingham in 1978 and moved to his current job at Leicester Royal Infirmary in 1981 as Muscular Skeletal Radiologist.

The Doc has been involved with Leicester Tigers since 1982 and has been the first team doctor for over a decade.

**Specialist Scrum-Half Coach & Video Analyst**

# Jamie **Hamilton**

A former pupil of Gleanon School in Sydney, Australia and Stonefield House in Lincoln, Jamie Hamilton played 162 games for Tigers between 1990 and 2001-02, despite taking 12 months out to play for London Scottish for the 1996-97 season.

An experienced Sevens player, his expertise earned him selection in the England Hong Kong Sevens squad and also the squad for the International Rugby Board World Sevens in 2001. Jamie's Sevens experience also resulted in him playing in the Tigers squads which won the Middlesex Sevens in 1995 and the Madrid Sevens in 1997.

The long-serving scrum-half — now the club's specialist Scrum-Half Coach and Video Analyst — is one of only seven Tigers players to gain five league winners medals with the club.

Jamie, who also enjoyed a playing spell in Christchurch (New Zealand), also featured in both of Tigers' Heineken Cup successes — in 2000-01 and 2001-02. His best moment at Tigers was the club's first Heineken Cup triumph in '00-01.

**Rehabilitation Coach**

# Julie **Hayton**

Welsh-born Julie Hayton grew up in Liverpool and studied in Manchester, where she completed a sports rehabilitation degree, before obtaining another degree in physical therapy.

Julie has been with Leicester Tigers since 2001, but she has worked with a lot of the senior players for longer. She used to be in a private practice, which saw her serve as Tigers' masseuse for 18 months before joining the set-up on a full-time basis.

Julie works closely with the physiotherapists and strength and conditioning staff to ensure that players are eased in properly from injuries. She was instrumental in Tigers adapting a "prehab" routine to prevent players from picking up injuries, whilst she also specialises in soft tissue injuries.

### Assistant Backline Coach
# Andy **Key**

Andy Key, who is known to all as Kiwi, was born in Market Harborough, educated at Welland Park High School, Market Harborough Grammar School and Leicester Polytechnic.

He played for Tigers between 1975-81 and again from 1987-92. In between these two periods he played for Bedford and Nottingham. Andy's father, Maurice, played for Tigers in the late '50s, while his two brothers, Richard and Lance, have both been professional footballers.

Andy spent 15 years in total at BSS Group Plc before joining Tigers as the full-time General Operations Manager. He has since been appointed as Head of Rugby Development at the club.

### Performance and Medical Director
# Phil **Mack**

Phil Mack, Tigers' Performance and Medical Director, was born just down the road in Stoke-on-Trent, but he grew up in Aberdeen. He was also schooled in Aberdeen and attended Robert Gordon University, where he studied physiotherapy.

After a two-year stint in America, where he spent time with the Dallas Cowboys, Phil followed his parents to South Africa in the mid-1990s, basing himself in Cape Town.

Phil began working for Western Province at various age-group levels, before graduating to the senior WP and Stormers management under former Northampton Saints coach Alan Solomons.

Phil also enjoyed a stint with the Nick Mallett-coached Springboks in 2000, before following Solomons to Irish Province, Ulster, where he spent nearly three years, before taking a post with Australian Super 12 franchise, the ACT Brumbies.

### Head Physiotherapist
# Paul **Stanton**

Paul Stanton was born in Walsall, West Midlands, and studied at the University Hospital of Wales, qualifying in 1981.

He worked in Walsall for years after completing his studies, before moving to Leicester in 1983. He began working at the Leicester General Hospital, then had a stint at the Leicester Royal Infirmary and also at BUPA.

Paul began working for Leicester Tigers in 1996 and has only recently become a full-time member of staff. His duties include looking after the first team squad along with Chris Brookes.

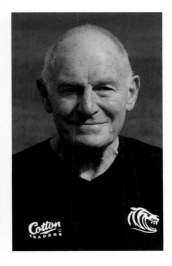

### First Team Kit Man
# Cliff **Shephard**

Cliff Shephard was born in Wigston and educated at Wigston HS. He played as a wing in the Leicester Schools' team and in a final England School's trial. He captained the Leicestershire Alliance Colts and represented the county and RAF.

His Tigers debut was in 1955 against Coventry, and he went on to play for the Tigers First XV 140 times, scoring 36 tries.

Cliff became the LFC first team secretary in 1996 after looking after the Extras in the same capacity for a few years.

Before his retirement, Cliff was a sales representative with Bass Breweries.

### Athletic Performance Coach
# Ollie **Richardson**

Ollie Richardson – who joined Tigers in 2004/05 – is a graduate of the University of Bath's coach education and sports performance programme and he also holds a Sports Science degree. His main duties involve looking after Tigers' first team squad, along with fellow Athletic Performance coach John Dams, whilst he also travels with Tigers' development team.

Ollie has worked as a strength and conditioning coach in athletics, rugby, cricket and swimming. He was based in Christchurch for a while, where he worked as a strength and conditioning coach for New Zealand swimming, whilst he also enjoyed a spell at a rugby club in NZ.

# Luke **ABRAHAM**

Luke Abraham joined the Tigers Academy at the age of 15, only three years after he took up the sport at Bushlow High School and joined his local club, Leicester Vipers.

He has played for Tigers' Youth team, was a member of the U21 squad that claimed the 2002-03 League title and appeared regularly in the Tigers Extras team that won the Zurich A League last season.

Luke was selected for the England U18 Schoolboys squad to face New Zealand Schoolboys at Twickenham at the end of January 2001, and then elevated to the U19 team, playing against Ireland and France in their "shadow" Six Nations. He played in the FIRA U19 Junior World Championship in Italy in March 2002 and more recently has represented England U21A.

A back row forward, Abraham has also been tried out at hooker, a move which led to a brief trip New Zealand playing for Nelson Bays club, Stoke, during the summer.

| Position | Back row |
| --- | --- |
| Date of Birth | 26.9.83 |
| Height | 6'2" |
| Weight | 16st 3lb |
| Tigers Debut | 21.12.02 vs Worcester Warriors |
| Tigers Record | 1+10 apps |
| | 1 try |
| | 5 pts |
| Previous Clubs | N/A |
| Rep Hons | England U21A |

# Scott **BEMAND**

Educated at the Bishop of Hereford's Bluecoat School and Harper Adams University College, Scott Bemand played for Luctonians First XV as an 18-year-old, before moving to Moseley Colts in 1997-98, the season they won the National Colts Cup in an unbeaten season.

He made his debut in the Allied Dunbar Premiership Two for Moseley in 1998, and was selected for England Students whilst with the club. He went on to captain the Students the following season, having previously represented England and The Midlands at Colts level, and winning the County Colts championship at Twickenham with the North Midlands in December 1997.

Scott signed for NEC Harlequins in the summer of 2001, and went on to make 30 Premiership appearances for the club, scoring two tries – one on his Premiership debut against Bristol at the Stoop. His last game for Quins was the Parker Pen Cup Final in May when he helped the team to a 27-26 win over French club Montferrand.

Since joining Leicester he has competed with Harry Ellis as the regular scrum half for the first XV, and captained the Tigers Extras during their successful Zurich A League campaign.

Scott also scored Tigers' only try in the Zurich Premiership Final against London Wasps at Twickenham in May.

An all-round sportsman, Scott played junior County Cricket from Under-13 to Under-16 level.

| | |
|---|---|
| Position | Scrum-half |
| Date of Birth | 21.9.78 |
| Height | 5'11" |
| Weight | 13st 12lb |
| Tigers Debut | 11.9.04 vs Leeds Tykes |
| Tigers Record | 13+10 apps |
| | 2 tries |
| | 10 pts |
| Previous Clubs | Luctonians, Moseley, NEC Harlequins |
| Rep Hons | England Students |

# Ross **BROADFOOT**

Fly-half Ross Broadfoot joined Leicester from the London Irish Academy for the start of the 2003-04 season.

In his first year at Leicester he played for both the Tigers U21/Development team and Tigers Extras in the Zurich A League, scoring 178 points in just 14 appearances.

After making his debut at the start of last season the left footed place kicker made a total of eight appearances in the first team, and was also a member of Tigers' successful A League squad.

Ross had represented England at 16 Group Schools in 1999-2000 and 2000-01, and 18 Group Schools (1 September) in 2001-02, before being selected for England at the FIRA U19s World Championship in France in April 2003. He also appeared in the U19 "shadow" Six Nations, and the IRB U19 World Championship in Durban where he kicked a personal tally of 23 points in England's 33-23 win over Australia in the pool stages. During 2004-05 he progressed to the England U21 team for which he made three appearances during the "shadow" Six Nations campaign.

A former pupil of Whitgift School, Croydon, Ross was a member of their squad that won the Daily Mail Under 15 Cup in 1999. He plays cricket as a hobby.

| | |
|---|---|
| Position | Fly-half |
| Date of Birth | 8.3.85 |
| Height | 5'11" |
| Weight | 14st 2lb |
| Tigers Debut | 11.9.04 vs Leeds Tykes |
| Tigers Record | 5+6 apps |
| | 0 tries |
| | 42 pts (9 C, 8 PG) |
| Previous Clubs | Saracens, London Irish |
| Rep Hons | England U21 |

# James **BUCKLAND**

James Buckland joined the Tigers in the summer of 2002 from Northampton Saints after returning from South Africa where he had travelled with England for the U21 IRB World Championship.

He made his first appearance in Tigers stripes in the Middlesex Sevens tournament at Twickenham in August 2002, then joined the first team at their training camp in France, playing in the friendly match against Agen.

A regular member of Tigers' league winning U21 team in 2002-03, James' 12 tries made him the U21s top try-scorer that season.

The opportunity to progress in the first team was hampered when he broke his leg during a training session at the start of the 2003-04 season. He returned to the fray in February playing six games for Tigers Extras in the Zurich A League, before heading south in the off-season to hone his skills in New Zealand's North Island, playing for the Tawa club near Wellington. He returned in time to make his Leicester first-team debut at the start of last season and has since started in five senior games and come off the bench on 17 further occasions. He was also a member of the Tigers Extras squad that won the Zurich A League championship 2004-05.

| | |
|---|---|
| Position | Hooker |
| Date of Birth | 21.9.81 |
| Height | 5'11" |
| Weight | 17st 2lb |
| Tigers Debut | 11.9.04 vs Leeds Tykes |
| Tigers Record | 5+17 apps |
| | 0 tries |
| | 0 pts |
| Previous Clubs | Aylesbury, Northampton |
| Rep Hons | England U21 |

# George **CHUTER**

After playing for London Division at both U18 and U21 level, George Chuter was invited to trial for Saracens. He joined their first team squad at the age of 19 and had five years with them, including winning the Pilkington Cup in 1998, before taking a break from rugby to travel visiting Australia and the USA.

George joined Tigers in December 2000, vying first with Richard Cockerill then Dorian West as first-choice at hooker, a position he has now made his own.

He made his England A debut in 1998 scoring a try in the game against France at Tours, and went on to be included in the summer '98 tour to Australia and New Zealand featuring in the match at Invercargill against New Zealand Academies.

More recently, impressive club performances in the latter stages of the 2003-04 season earned him selection for the England A side to compete for the Churchill Cup in Canada where England lost in the final to the New Zealand Maoris after extra-time. George returned to Canada the following year with the successful England XV playing in both matches including the final against Argentina.

An old boy of Trinity School in Croydon, George played club rugby for Old Mid-Whitgiftians before studying at the West London Institute for a year.

| | |
|---|---|
| Position | Hooker |
| Date of Birth | 9.7.76 |
| Height | 5'10" |
| Weight | 15st 10lb |
| Tigers Debut | 31.3.01 vs Gloucester |
| Tigers Record | 56+31 apps |
| | 9 tries |
| | 45 pts |
| Previous Clubs | Old Mid-Whitgiftians, Saracens |
| Rep Hons | England XV |

# Matt **CORNWELL**

Matt Cornwell started playing rugby as a seven-year-old with Syston RFC before being invited into Tigers' Under-16 squad.

He attended Oakham school on a rugby scholarship, and played in both of the school's Daily Mail Cup victories at Twickenham.

He has represented Leicestershire at U16 and U18 levels, and England U18 schools.

An ever present in England's 2005 U21 Six Nations campaign, scoring a try in the game against France, Matt was named as captain of the England U21 side that competed in the IRB U21 World Cup in Argentina during the summer.

He was named the NIG Academy Player of the Month for October 2004, and since his senior debut has made 11 appearances for the first team as well as being a member of Tigers' successful Zurich A League squad.

| | |
|---|---|
| Position | Centre / Full back |
| Date of Birth | 16.01.85 |
| Height | 6'0" |
| Weight | 14st 11lb |
| Tigers Debut | 2.10.04 at Newcastle Falcons |
| Tigers Record | 3+10 apps |
| | 1 try |
| | 5 pts |
| Previous Club | Syston |
| Rep Hons | England U21 |

# Martin **CORRY**

Named as Leicester captain for the 2005-06 season, Martin Corry is now in his ninth season with the club, a spell that has seen success with back-to-back Heineken Cup wins and four Premiership titles.

A versatile player who can cover at lock as well as in the back row, Martin has been selected for two British Lions tours – to New Zealand this summer, where he took over as captain in the first test when Brian O'Driscoll was injured, and as late replacement to Australia in 2001 when he put in one of the best performances for the Lions, eventually playing in all three tests.

Martin was also a member of England's 2003 Rugby World Cup-winning squad; again a late selection after putting in some memorable performance during the warm-up games that summer. The trip to Australia was his second World Cup campaign having also played in the 1999 tournament.

Martin has played in four consecutive Five/Six Nations campaigns, 1999 to 2002 and, following his return form World Cup duty, played in all three of the 2004 Autumn Internationals and the last four of the 2005 Six Nations games, captaining his country for the first time in the match against Italy at Twickenham.

Having started playing rugby in the mini section at Tunbridge Wells RFC, Martin first represented England at U18 level in 1992 in the team that won the junior grand slam and triple crown. He had a highly-successful tenure at Northumbria University, which led to his inclusion in the England Students side in 1995 and later that year, England A; Martin made his England test debut in 1997 in Argentina.

He was named as the Members' Player of the Season in 1999-2000, and more recently after outstanding performances for both club and country was named as both the Zurich Premiership and PRA Player of the Season in 2004-05.

He was awarded an MBE in the 2004 New Year's Honours.

| | |
|---|---|
| Position | Back row |
| Date of Birth | 12.10.73 |
| Height | 6'5" |
| Weight | 18st 1lb |
| Tigers Debut | 30.8.97 vs Gloucester |
| Tigers Record | 190+11 apps |
| | 20 tries |
| | 100 pts |
| Previous Clubs | Newcastle-Gosforth, Bristol |
| Rep Hons | England (37), British Lions (6) |

# Tom **CROFT**

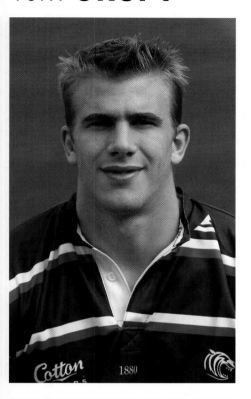

Former Oakham School pupil, second rower Tom Croft, started playing rugby as an 11-year-old, after joining Newbury RFC.

After representing his county at age-group level he was selected to captain the South of England U16 side against France. Tom has also represented England U18 schools.

A member of Tigers' successful Zurich A League squad, Tom was named as the NIG Academy Player of the season for 2004-05.

He recently played at Twickenham for Leicester in the Middlesex Sevens.

| | |
|---|---|
| Position | Lock |
| Date of Birth | 7.11.85 |
| Height | 6'5" |
| Weight | 16st 3lb |
| Tigers Debut | Yet to make Tigers debut |
| Tigers Record | N/A |
| Previous Clubs | Newbury |
| Rep Hons | N/A |

# Leo **CULLEN**

Lock Leo Cullen joined Tigers during the summer from Irish province Leinster. He has played for the Dublin based side since 1998, making his senior debut for the province in September that year against Edinburgh Reivers at Kelso. He has gone on to win the Celtic League title with Leinster in 2001 and played Heineken Cup rugby for the province including four games against Leicester Tigers; the latest occasion being the quarter-final at Lansdowne Road in April 2005.

Leo has gained 17 Ireland caps since his debut in Auckland in June 2002, and toured with Ireland to Japan in June playing in both tests. He has also represented Ireland at Schools, U19 U21 and A level.

| | |
|---|---|
| Position | Lock |
| Date of Birth | 9.1.78 |
| Height | 6'6" |
| Weight | 17st 6lb |
| Tigers Debut | 3.9.05 |
| Tigers Record | 2+1 apps |
| | 0 tries |
| | 0 pts |
| Previous Clubs | Blackrock College, Leinster |
| Rep Hons | Ireland (17) |

# Brett **DEACON**

Brett Deacon started playing rugby at the age of seven for Wigston RFC. He then moved to Syston when he was 11 and went on to represent Leicestershire, the Midlands and England at U16 and U18 levels.

He was selected for the England U19 squad for the "shadow" Six Nations 2001-02, and in fact captained them in their game against Wales U19 in January that year.

The younger brother of Tigers lock, Louis, Brett joined Tigers' Youth Team at the age of 15, and has since played for both the Youth and U21 team, and for Tigers' Extras during last season's successful Zurich A League campaign.

Brett made his first-team debut at the start of the 2003-04 campaign, during the Rugby World Cup, when he partnered his brother Louis in the second row for the game against London Irish, only the second pair of brothers to do so after Mark and Paul Grant against Nottingham in March 1994. He has since made over 20 appearances for the first team, gaining his players' tie.

| | |
|---|---|
| **Position** | Flanker |
| **Date of Birth** | 7.3.82 |
| **Height** | 6'4" |
| **Weight** | 17st |
| **Tigers Debut** | 13.9.03 vs London Irish |
| **Tigers Record** | 19+8 apps |
| | 1 try |
| | 5 pts |
| **Previous Clubs** | Wigston, Syston |
| **Rep Hons** | England U19 |

# Louis **DEACON**

Since making his Tigers first team debut, Louis Deacon has established himself as a highly dependable player – at the front or the middle of the line-out.

The mainstay of Tigers' line-out during the World Cup campaign at the start of the 2003-04 season, Louis gave such impressive performances that it earned him the accolade of the Player's Player of the Season.

A former pupil of Ratcliffe College Leicester, Louis started playing rugby as an eight-year-old with Wigston. He later joined Syston and progressed to play for the County, the Midlands and England at U16 level.

Since joining Tigers' Academy in 1997-98, he has appeared in the Tigers' Youth, U21 and Extras teams.

He has also represented England at U18 and U21 level. He was selected for the England A team for the Churchill Cup in Canada last summer, where he was one of three Tigers players who appeared in the Cup Final team.

After a try-scoring performance for England A in their victory over France at Bath in February, Louis was selected for his second Churchill Cup campaign this summer playing in both games in Edmonton, Canada.

He has also recently been named in the senior England Elite Playing Squad.

| | |
|---|---|
| Position | Lock |
| Date of Birth | 7.10.80 |
| Height | 6'6" |
| Weight | 18st 1lb |
| Tigers Debut | 12.8.00 vs Cardiff |
| Tigers Record | 98+14 apps |
| | 3 tries |
| | 15 pts |
| Previous Clubs | Wigston, Syston |
| Rep Hons | England XV |

# Alex **DODGE**

Alex Dodge made his deserved first-team debut last season, after being a bench replacement twice, following consistently impressive performances for Tigers Extras during their successful Zurich A League campaign.

The son of former Tigers' centre Paul, he joined Tigers in 2000 and attended Queen Elizabeth College, Leicester.

He was named in the England U19 training squad for 2002-03.

| | |
|---|---|
| Position | Centre |
| Date of Birth | 17.11.84 |
| Height | 6'2" |
| Weight | 15st 8lb |
| Tigers Debut | 18.3.05 vs Barbarians |
| Tigers Record | 0+1 apps |
| | 0 tries |
| | 0 pts |
| Previous Clubs | N/A |
| Rep Hons | N/A |

# Harry **ELLIS**

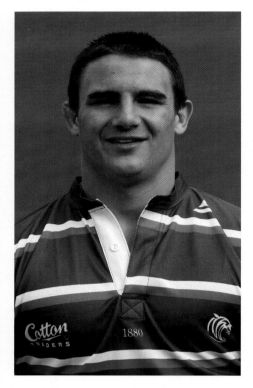

Harry Ellis started playing rugby as a six-year-old with South Leicester, and then moved to Wigston for a year before joining Tigers' Youth Team in 1997 after attending a trial.

The youngest of three rugby-playing brothers, whose father also played for Tigers, Harry studied at Leicester Grammar School and appeared for the County and Midlands at age group level before going on to represent England 'A' U16, U18, U19 and U21 levels, having appeared in the U18 group whilst only 16 years of age. He also featured for England in the World Sevens Series and was named in the England National Academy training squad announced in September 2003.

Harry went on to appear for England A in their game against France in March 2004 and was then selected by Sir Clive Woodward to tour with England to Australia and New Zealand that summer, his first senior tour.

He made his England debut in the game against South Africa at Twickenham in November 2004, and played against Australia the following week. He also appeared in all of last season's Six Nations Championship games, scoring his debut try in the match against Scotland. He is one of nine Tigers players named in the England Elite Player squad for the forthcoming season.

Having made his senior club debut in the Orange Cup game in Toulouse in August 2001, Harry went on to score a superb individual try that helped defeat Llanelli in the Heineken Cup semi-final at Nottingham that season.

He was named as the Tigers' Players Young Player of the Year 2001-02.

| Position | Scrum-half |
| --- | --- |
| Date of Birth | 17.5.82 |
| Height | 5'10" |
| Weight | 14st |
| Tigers Debut | 25.8.01 at Toulouse |
| Tigers Record | 76+25 apps |
| | 22 tries |
| | 110 pts |
| Previous Clubs | South Leicester, Wigston |
| Rep Hons | England (7) |

# Daryl **GIBSON**

Tigers vice-captain, inside centre Daryl Gibson, gained 19 New Zealand caps following his debut against Samoa in Albany in June 1999.

He played throughout the 1999 Rugby World Cup, his only try for the All Blacks coming against Italy at Huddersfield in that competition.

He also appeared in all five games for the New Zealand Maori on their 1998 tour of Scotland and was called into the New Zealand Barbarians side that played England at Twickenham in December 2003 to celebrate the World Champions' homecoming.

Daryl made a team record 78 appearances for the Crusaders in Super 12 rugby from 1996-2002, scoring 14 tries and gaining three winners medals in 1998, 1999 and 2002. He also played 80 matches for Canterbury following his debut in June 1993, claiming 35 tries and winning the New Zealand Provincial Championship with them in 1997 and 2001.

Educated at Christchurch Boys High School and Canterbury University, Gibson played for New Zealand U19 in 1993 and 1994, and New Zealand U21 in 1994, 1995 and 1996. He moved to England joining Bristol Shoguns in September 2002, making his home debut against Leicester Tigers in the Zurich Premiership on September 29.

He has now made over 50 appearances for the club, and has been named as vice-captain for the forthcoming season.

| | |
|---|---|
| Position | Centre |
| Date of Birth | 2.3.75 |
| Height | 5'11" |
| Weight | 15st 8lb |
| Tigers Debut | 13.9.03 vs London Irish |
| Tigers Record | 56+1 apps |
| | 11 tries |
| | 55 pts |
| Previous Clubs | Canterbury (NZ), Crusaders (NZ), Bristol Shoguns |
| Rep Hons | New Zealand (19) |

# Andy **GOODE**

Fly-half Andy Goode rejoined Leicester Tigers in December 2003 after spending almost 18 months with Watford club, Saracens.

He ended the 2003-04 season as the top Premiership points-scorer with 266 in total; his 151 points for Leicester and 115 for Saracens meant he was the top points-scorer in each team!

His personal haul of 28 points in the record 83-10 victory over Newcastle in February 2005 at Welford Road included a Leicester league record of 11 successful conversions, whilst the 12 points he kicked in the defeat at Saracens in April made him only the ninth player to break the 800 career point barrier for Leicester.

In his earlier spell with Leicester, Andy had already picked up two Heineken Cup winners medals – starting as fly-half against Stade Français in Paris in 2001, and being a bench replacement against Munster in Cardiff the following year – an inaugural Zurich Championship medal and despite his youth played a substantial part in Tigers record four successive Premiership titles.

Andy has represented England at U18 and U21 level, and after an impressive performance in the England A game against France at Bath in February 2005, was called into the senior squad and made his England debut as a replacement in the game against Italy during the Six Nations Championship.

Over the summer he was a member of the successful England XV that competed in the Churchill Cup in Canada.

Educated at King Henry VIII School in Coventry, Andy started playing rugby at the age of five. However, his sporting talent stretches beyond the rugby field, having been a bowler and opening batsman at school.

| | |
|---|---|
| Position | Fly-half |
| Date of Birth | 3.4.80 |
| Height | 5'11" |
| Weight | 15st 10lb |
| Tigers Debut | 2.10.98 vs Cardiff |
| Tigers Record | 106+16 apps |
| | 21 tries |
| | 892 pts (152 C, 136 PG, 25 DG) |
| Previous Clubs | Nuneaton Colts, Coventry Colts, Saracens |
| Rep Hons | England (2) |

# James **HAMILTON**

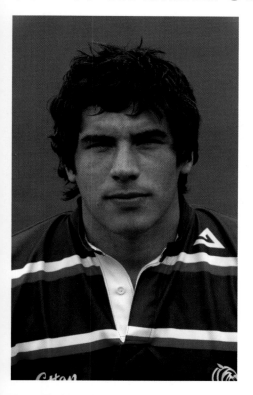

James Hamilton went to Coundon Court School in Coventry and started playing rugby at the age of 15, joining local club Barker's Butts, the club that launched the careers of Neil Back and Leon Lloyd.

He joined the Tigers Academy at the end of 1999 after being spotted by Andy Key and Dusty Hare playing for Warwickshire against Leicestershire.

James was selected for the England Under-19 team that took part in the U19 World Cup in Chile 2000-01. He has also represented England U21 in the "shadow" Six Nations for the last two seasons.

James has played regularly for the Tigers Youth team, as well as being a member of Leicester's Championship-winning U21 side in 2002-03 and successful Zurich A League squad last season.

James is one of three Tigers Academy players who took part in training programme in Durban, South Africa, summer 2001 and this summer journeyed to New Zealand to play for the Marist Albion club in Christchurch.

| | |
|---|---|
| Position | Lock |
| Date of Birth | 17.11.82 |
| Height | 6'8" |
| Weight | 19st 5lb |
| Tigers Debut | 13.9.03 vs London Irish |
| Tigers Record | 10+6 apps |
| | 2 tries |
| | 10 pts |
| Previous Club | Barker's Butts |
| Rep Hons | England U21 |

# Austin **HEALEY**

One of the most experienced players in Tigers' backline, with over 50 international caps and over 200 appearances for Leicester, Austin Healey is hailed as the player who created the break that ended in the winning score in the Heineken Cup Final 2001 in Paris. He then scored the second and decisive try against Munster when Tigers retained the cup the following year.

Now in his 10th season with the club, Austin has played virtually every position behind the scrum, and has tasted success in domestic as well as European competitions, being in the squad that won four consecutive Premiership titles.

Educated at St Anselm's College, Birkenhead and at Leeds Metropolitan University, Austin represented England at U21 and A level, as well as England Sevens whilst playing for Orrell.

After moving to Leicester he made his senior England debut in Ireland in 1997 and was subsequently chosen for the British Lions tour to South Africa later that year where he played in seven matches including the last two tests.

He has now represented England in 5 Five/Six Nations tournaments ('98-'02) and was a key figure in the 1999 World Cup.

He was selected for his second British Lions tours, to Australia in 2001, but unfortunately missed out on further caps due to injury. He was also very unlucky to miss the final cut when the 30-man England squad for the 2003 World Cup was announced. A non-travelling reserve, he made the trip 'Down Under' mid-tournament as cover at scrum-half, but returned to his club when he was not called on to play.

In the 1999-2000 season he was voted both Leicester Tigers' and Allied Dunbar's Player of the Season.

| | |
|---|---|
| Position | Utility back |
| Date of Birth | 26.10.73 |
| Height | 5'10" |
| Weight | 13st 9lb |
| Tigers Debut | 26.8.96 vs Agen |
| Tigers Record | 197+23 apps |
| | 58 tries |
| | 317 pts (3 C, 1 PG, 6 DG) |
| Previous Clubs | Birkenhead Park, Waterloo, Orrell |
| Rep Hons | England (51), British Lions (2) |

# Dan **HIPKISS**

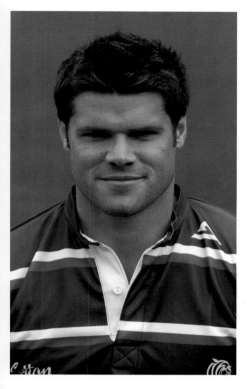

Having learned his "trade" at Hartsmere School and Diss Rugby Club in Norfolk, Leicester offered Dan Hipkiss a scholarship to Uppingham School and the chance to become involved in Tigers' Youth set up.

Following in his father's footsteps (he played for England Schools), Dan has represented England at U16, U17, U18 and U21 levels.

Having overcome a career-threatening injury suffered to his left knee in November 1999, Dan made his first start for the Tigers U21's against Leeds on November 9, 2001, scoring a try on his debut. He was called into the first team squad for summer training in 2002, and scored a stunning solo try to help win the game on his senior debut in the Orange Cup game against Biarritz Olympique in Bayonne.

Dan became a regular member of the successful Tigers 2002-03 U21 team and was one of five Tigers' youngsters called up for the 2003 IRB U21 World Cup. He was included in the England Sevens Squad for the IRB Sevens in 2004 and was again selected for the England Sevens team that played in the tournaments in Wellington, Los Angeles and Singapore Twickenham and Paris.

A member of Tigers' successful Zurich A League squad last season, Dan captained the Leicester side that played in the Middlesex Sevens at Twickenham in August.

| | |
|---|---|
| Position | Centre |
| Date of Birth | 4.6.82 |
| Height | 5'10" |
| Weight | 14st 6lb |
| Tigers Debut | 24.8.02 vs Biarritz Olympique at Bayonne |
| Tigers Record | 8+8 apps |
| | 4 tries |
| | 20 pts |
| Previous Clubs | Diss |
| Rep Hons | England U21 / Sevens |

# Michael **HOLFORD**

Born in Leicester, Michael Holford attended Oakham School, gaining a sport scholarship to study for his A-Levels in Sports Science and Biology.

He started playing rugby at the age of 10 and has since played for the England U18 Schools' team, England U19s, and was one of three young Tigers players to represent England in the IRB U21 World Championship in South Africa in the summer of 2002.

He went on to captain England U21A against their Welsh counterparts in December that year, and play for England U21 in their "shadow" Six Nations Championship 2003 as well as the FIRA World Cup at Henley June later that year.

After playing for Syston, the talented young player joined Tigers' Youth set up in 1998 and has played in the Tigers' U21s, commanding a regular spot in their winning team of 2002-03, and for the Extras, including their successful campaign in the Zurich A league last season.

He was invited to play for the Hong Kong RFU Barbarians in their game against the Penguins marking the 50th Anniversary of the Hong Kong RFU in the summer of 2004.

| | |
|---|---|
| Position | Prop |
| Date of Birth | 11.8.82 |
| Height | 5'11" |
| Weight | 16st 11lb |
| Tigers Debut | 19.10.03 at Leeds Tykes |
| Tigers Record | 12+6 apps |
| | 1 try |
| | 5 pts |
| Previous Club | Syston |
| Rep Hons | England U21 |

# Ian **HUMPHREYS**

Fly-half Ian Humphreys joined Leicester during the summer from the All Ireland League side, Belfast Harlequins.

He has represented Ulster, the province for which his famous brother David also plays, at Under 21 level, captaining them during the 2002-03 season.

He has also represented Ireland at U19 and U21 level, and captained the Irish side at the Rugby World Cup Sevens tournament in Hong Kong in March, the team finally going out to defeat by Samoa in the Plate quarter-finals.

He had previously been named player of the tournament for the European Sevens qualifier in Poland, whilst his first outing in Tigers stripes was at the Middlesex Sevens Tournament at Twickenham in August.

Ian was selected for the Barbarians last November, scoring a try and three conversions in the 36-38 loss to the Combined Services.

| | |
|---|---|
| Position | Fly-half |
| Date of Birth | 24.4.82 |
| Height | 5'11" |
| Weight | 12st 10lb |
| Tigers Debut | Yet to make Tigers debut |
| Tigers Record | N/A |
| Previous Clubs | Ballymena, Belfast Harlequins, Ulster |
| Rep Hons | Ireland U21 / Sevens |

# Shane **JENNINGS**

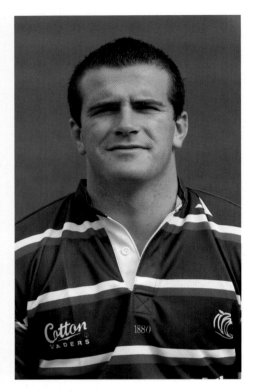

Openside flanker Shane Jennings had an impressive first outing in Tigers' stripes when playing for the club at the Middlesex Sevens at Twickenham scoring a try in just 32 seconds in the first-round game against Bristol, the fastest try of the day.

Shane joined Tigers from Irish province Leinster where he had played in 10 Heineken Cup games since his debut against Biarritz in 2003, his last appearance in the competition appropriately being against Leicester Tigers in the 2005 quarter-finals.

During those games he scored four tries, including two in the pool match against Benetton Treviso in January that earned him not only the Man of the Match accolade, but also the nomination from Leinster supporters as their Player of the Month.

Shane has also made 29 appearances for Leinster in the Celtic League and Cup after making his senior debut for the province against Glasgow at Hughenden in September 2002.

He has represented Ireland at Schools, U19, Under-21 and at A level against France in March.

Still only 23, he has already captained Leinster on several occasions last season in the absence of Reggie Corrigan on World Cup duty.

| | |
|---|---|
| Position | Flanker |
| Date of Birth | 8.7.81 |
| Height | 6' |
| Weight | 16st 3lb |
| Tigers Debut | 3.9.05 |
| Tigers Record | 3+1 apps |
| | 1 try |
| | 5 pts |
| Previous Clubs | St. Mary's College, Leinster |
| Rep Hons | Ireland A |

# Will **JOHNSON**

Educated at Robert Smyth School in Market Harborough then at Birmingham University, before making his Tigers debut in 1994 Will Johnson played Midlands 18, 19 and 21 Group rugby.

His 1999-2000 season was cut short when he fractured his foot in the first week of April. However sparkling form in the 2000-01 season resulted in Will being picked as vice-captain of England A during the 2001 "shadow" Six Nations, after having scored a try on his debut in the 44-3 victory over Italy A at Bedford in February 2001.

Despite this, he unfortunately missed out on the full tour to Canada in the summer that year, but came back into contention for the England A squad, turning out for them against Wales in March 2002.

The following season saw Will consolidate his position in Tigers' back row, despite some stiff opposition. Considered by then head coach John Wells to be "one of the most underrated players in Tigers pack", he was once more called into the England A set up, this time to contest the Churchill Cup in Canada in June, where he was one of three Tigers players to take to the field in the epic final against New Zealand Maori.

Now in his 13th season since his debut, having played almost 200 first-team games, a period that has seen Leicester success in both European and domestic competitions.

Will is celebrating his testimonial season this year.

| | |
|---|---|
| Position | Back row |
| Date of Birth | 18.3.74 |
| Height | 6'4" |
| Weight | 16st 9lb |
| Tigers Debut | 16.4.94 at Sale |
| Tigers Record | 148+46 apps |
| | 9 tries |
| | 45 pts |
| Previous Clubs | Wigston, Kibworth, Linwood (NZ) |
| Rep Hons | England A |

# Ben **KAY**

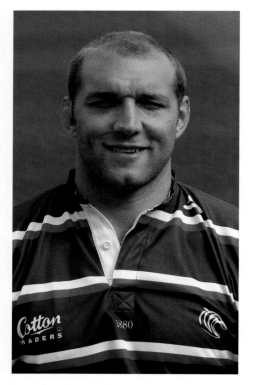

Another of the Tigers' 2005 British Lions contingent, lock Ben Kay gained his Lions cap playing in the first test against New Zealand in Christchurch.

Previously Ben had given an outstanding performance in the second row for England alongside club colleague Martin Johnson during the 2003 Rugby World Cup, never being replaced in the six games he played during the tournament. He also featured in all of England's Six Nations games in the intervening two years.

Ben was educated at Merchant Taylor's School before attending Loughborough University, where he obtained his degree in Sports Science. He has played rugby at Queensland University in Australia, and has represented England U18, U19, Students and U21 and appeared for the Barbarians.

Joining Tigers from Waterloo in 1999, Ben made his England A debut against France in 2000, going on to captain the side in 2001.

He was in tremendous form for Tigers during the 2000-01 season and as a result was chosen for England to tour Canada and the USA, making his senior debut in the test against Canada at Markham.

Ben was in the starting line-up for all the Six Nations games in spring 2002, toured with England to Argentina that summer, went on to compete in both the Autumn internationals and the 2003 Six Nations, before touring to New Zealand and Australia pre-World Cup.

After an impressive season he was named as the Tigers Members' Player of the Year 2001-02, and was also a nominee for the Zurich Premiership Player of the Year.

Ben has been named in the starting line-up on over 100 occasions for the club, gaining his commemorative cap in the Heineken Cup fixture against the Newport Gwent Dragons at Welford Road on 14 December 2003.

He was awarded an MBE in the 2004 New Year's Honours list.

| | |
|---|---|
| Position | Lock |
| Date of Birth | 14.12.75 |
| Height | 6'4" |
| Weight | 19st |
| Tigers Debut | 11.9.99 at Northampton |
| Tigers Record | 124+27 apps |
| | 7 tries |
| | 35 pts |
| Previous Clubs | Waterloo, Queensland University (Aus) |
| Rep Hons | England (40), Lions (1) |

# Leon **LLOYD**

| | |
|---|---|
| Position | Wing / Centre |
| Date of Birth | 22.9.77 |
| Height | 6'4" |
| Weight | 15st 1lb |
| Tigers Debut | 16.10.96 vs Bridgend |
| Tigers Record | 201+17 apps |
| | 72 tries |
| | 360 pts |
| Previous Clubs | Barker's Butts |
| Rep Hons | England (5) |

Prior to making his debut for the Tigers first team, Leon Lloyd was a successful try-scorer for Tigers' Youth XV and Development XV, before a serious car accident sidelined him for six months.

He eventually made his full Tigers debut in 1996 and was part of the squad that won the Madrid Sevens that year. He scored his first memorable try in Tigers' remarkable Heineken Cup victory at Pau.

Leon was selected for England Colts, the Barbarians and England U21 in 1997, two years later he played for England A, and also equalled Rory Underwood's 1985 club record of four tries scored in a single domestic Cup tie.

In 1999 Leon was included in England's World Cup squad, but did not play and, in fact, had to wait until the following summer to win his first cap in South Africa.

He appeared again for England on their tour to Canada and the USA in 2001, unfortunately he suffered a shoulder injury, which required surgery and kept him out of the Tigers squad for the start of the 2001-02 season.

However, Leon recovered well and returned to the form that saw him score the match-winning try in Tigers' first Heineken Cup Final, only to be cruelly struck down by injury again and denied the chance to repeat his performance when Leicester retained the famous trophy in May 2002. That injury also ruled him out of the England Sevens squad for the Commonwealth games in Manchester in which he had been named after his participation in the Brisbane 7s in February 2002.

After a delayed start to the 2002-03 campaign Leon played in 27 of a possible 29 matches following his return against Bath in October, and further consolidated his position at centre the following season.

His appearance at Saracens in September 2004 saw him chalk up his 100th Premiership appearance for the club.

# Daniel **MONTAGU**

Australian Daniel Montagu joined the Tigers Academy at the start of the 2003-04 season, after taking a gap year from his studies at Edith Cowan University in Western Australia.

Dan grew up playing Australian Rules Football, however, he was encouraged to change codes by his school's rugby coach, and made first links with Leicestershire, playing against a touring side that included several future Academy players. His coach, Mike Penhaligon, then arranged for him to make the trip over to England where he started training with the Tigers Academy.

Since then, Dan has appeared for the Under-21/Development team (including playing in the 153-0 victory over India), played for the Tigers Extras, and finally made his first team debut as a replacement during Tigers' 69-21 win over the Barbarians at Welford Road in March 2004.

Last season he turned out regularly for the Tigers Extras during their successful 2004-05 Zurich A league campaign.

| | |
|---|---|
| Position | Lock / Back row |
| Date of Birth | 10.9.83 |
| Height | 6'4" |
| Weight | 17st 2lb |
| Tigers Debut | 3.3.04 vs Barbarians |
| Tigers Record | 1+2 apps |
| | 0 tries |
| | 0 pts |
| Previous Clubs | N/A |
| Rep Hons | N/A |

# Lewis **MOODY**

A British Lion and World Cup winner, at the time of his debut in 1996, Lewis Moody became the youngest first team Tiger to feature in a league game.

He has since made over 100 first team starts for Leicester, gaining his 100 game cap in the Heineken cup game against Wasps in December.

Lewis has played for England Schools, U18, Colts and England U21, and in 1998 was selected for the full England tour to the southern hemisphere where he featured in two games but no tests.

He was finally awarded his full international cap on the England tour to Canada and the USA in 2001 then started in two Six Nations games the following season.

2002-03 saw him play in all three of the Autumn internationals, but unfortunately he was injured in the last game against South Africa. He returned to fitness but a further injury in the first Six Nations match of 2003 against France curtailed the rest of his season for his club. However, he recovered well enough to be included in the 30-man England Rugby World Cup squad and went on to play some part in all seven of the games during the tournament, including coming off the bench in the final itself.

However, on his return to England it was discovered that Lewis had sustained a stress fracture to his foot, and the rest of his season was spent either in plaster or rehabilitation.

He came back into international contention last season, competing in two Autumn international games and the Six Nations championship.

As a result of performances in those, and for his club, he was named in the British & Irish Lions touring party to New Zealand this summer playing the last two tests.

An all-round sportsman Lewis competed in athletics, cricket and swimming at school before deciding to concentrate on rugby.

He was named Zurich Player of the Month for September 2001 and the 2001-02 Zurich Young Player of the Season.

Along with six of his Tigers compatriots he was awarded an MBE in the Queen's New Year's Honours list.

| Position | Flanker |
|---|---|
| Date of Birth | 12.6.78 |
| Height | 6'3" |
| Weight | 16st 3lb |
| Tigers Debut | 25.8.96 vs Boroughmuir |
| Tigers Record | 107+42 apps |
| | 22 tries |
| | 110 pts |
| Previous Clubs | Oakham, Bracknell |
| Rep Hons | England (31), British Lions (2) |

# Alex **MORENO**

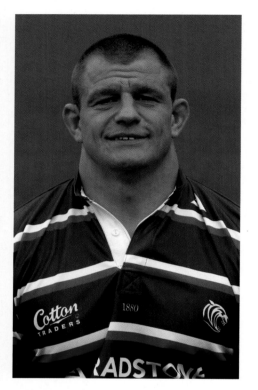

Prop Alex Moreno joined Leicester during the summer from French club Brive, after making 13 appearances for them in France's Top 16 and the European Challenge Cup.

This will not be Alex's first visit to Welford Road; he played there for Italy against Tonga during the 1999 World Cup. That was his debut for Italy having already gained international recognition winning three caps for Argentina during the 1998 South American Championship.

Alex went on to play for Italy against New Zealand also in the 1999 World Cup, and then appeared twice as a replacement during the 2002 Six Nations Championship.

Originally playing his rugby with the San Fernando club in Buenos Aires, Alex switched to play for the French side Agen in 1999. He then joined Worcester in the summer of 2001 playing for a season in English National One. Two seasons in Perpignan followed, during which time he was a bench replacement for the French Championship Final of 2004 in which Perpignan lost to Stade Français.

| | |
|---|---|
| Position | Prop |
| Date of Birth | 26.4.73 |
| Height | 6'1" |
| Weight | 17st 8lb |
| Tigers Debut | 3.9.05 |
| Tigers Record | 3 apps |
| | 0 tries |
| | 0 pts |
| Previous Clubs | San Fernando (AR), Agen (FR), Worcester, Perpignan (FR), Brive (FR) |
| Rep Hons | Argentina (3), Italy (4) |

# Darren **MORRIS**

Educated at Aberdare Boys Comprehensive, Neath College and Glamorgan University, Darren Morris originally came to prominence with Neath before joining Swansea in 1998.

In his time with the 'All-Whites' they lifted the Welsh Cup in 1999 and he was also part of the squad that won the Welsh-Scottish League in 2000-01.

Darren was included in the Swansea team that lost to Leicester in the Heineken Cup quarter-final tie at Welford Road in January 2001.

Darren has won 18 Wales caps since his debut against Zimbabwe in Harare in June 1998, his performances in his first season with Tigers, during which he made most first-team appearances with 28, led to his recall to the national squad and he toured with them to Argentina and South Africa in June, 2004 playing in all three tests. He, in fact, became the first Tigers player to be capped for Wales whilst playing for the club.

Darren toured Australia with the British and Irish Lions in 2001, playing in six matches including coming on as a replacement in the third test in Sydney.

He has also appeared for the Barbarians, making his debut for the invitation side against Australia at Millennium Stadium in November 2001.

| | |
|---|---|
| Position | Prop |
| Date of Birth | 24.9.74 |
| Height | 6'1" |
| Weight | 19st 13lb |
| Tigers Debut | 13.9.03 |
| | vs London Irish |
| Tigers Record | 43+13 apps |
| | 0 tries |
| | 0 pts |
| Previous Clubs | Neath, Swansea |
| Rep Hons | Wales (18), British Lions (1) |

# Geordan **MURPHY**

| | |
|---|---|
| Position | Full back / Wing |
| Date of Birth | 19.4.78 |
| Height | 6'1" |
| Weight | 13st 7lb |
| Tigers Debut | 14.11.97 vs Rotherham |
| Tigers Record | 150+15 apps |
| | 71 tries |
| | 558 pts (49 C, 32 PG, 3 DG) |
| Previous Clubs | Naas, Auckland GS (NZ) |
| Rep Hons | Ireland (31), Lions (1) |

One of eight Tigers players named by Sir Clive Woodward for the British and Irish Lions tour to New Zealand in the summer, Geordan Murphy played in seven games including the third test in Auckland.

Born in Dublin, the youngest of six children who all played rugby union, Geordan was educated at Newbridge College, Naas before attending De Montfort University in Leicester.

Shortly after joining Tigers in 1997, he first represented his country playing at U19 level and in June 2000, after appearing for Ireland A and an Ireland XV, he made his full Ireland debut against the United States, scoring twice.

The 2001-02 season saw Geordan finishing the season as Tigers' top try-scorer in all competitions.

He scored two more tries for Ireland against Wales in Dublin in the 2002 Six Nations tournament, but was then injured in the game against England.

He toured with Ireland in the summer of 2002, adding two more caps to his tally, but missed the start of Tigers 2002-03 campaign after undergoing surgery. He returned to fitness in time to participate in the Autumn internationals, and his form for his country in the 2003 Six Nations, where he was an ever-present, earned him the accolade of being named Irish Player of the Season by the Irish Rugby Writers. He was also voted Tigers' Supporters Player of the season the same year, and his impressive form continued over the summer internationals.

He was tipped to be one of the outstanding players at the Rugby World Cup until fate dealt him a cruel blow. He broke his left leg in a seemingly innocuous tackle in Ireland's last warm-up game against Scotland at Murrayfield in September.

He returned to action earlier than anticipated when he came on as a replacement in Tigers' game at London Irish in February 2004, and was also back in international action, playing for Ireland during the Six Nations and touring with them to South Africa in June 2004.

He appeared in all of Ireland's international tests last season, scoring four tries including two against the USA.

# Ian **NIMMO**

Lock Ian Nimmo joined Tigers from Scottish club Heriots during the summer.

He has played for Scotland at U18, U19, and U21 levels. His U19 honours include the 2004 IRB World Championship in Durban, South Africa. His U21 international debut followed when Scotland only narrowly lost 8-12 to France in Bourgoin in February.

He was an ever-present in the No.4 shirt for Scotland U21 in their own Six Nations Championship this season.

Ian helped Heriot's to second place in the SRU BT Premiership Division 1 last season.

| | |
|---|---|
| Position | Lock |
| Date of Birth | 25.7.85 |
| Height | 6'7" |
| Weight | 17st 6lb |
| Tigers Debut | Yet to make Tigers debut |
| Tigers Record | N/A |
| Previous Club | Heriots |
| Rep Hons | Scotland U21 |

# Seru **RABENI**

A former teacher, Seru Rabeni played for the Fijian first division club side Lautoka whilst at college, before moving on to the capital's club, Suva.

Seru is also an accomplished Sevens player, making his debut in Dubai in 1998, playing in two Hong Kong Sevens tournaments and appearing for Fiji in the 2002 Commonwealth Games in Manchester.

He played at both U21 and U23 level for Fiji, before making his senior test debut in May 2000 against Japan in Tokyo during the Epson Cup tournament.

He has since toured with Fiji to New Zealand in 2002, and the same year played Wales at the Millennium Stadium in Cardiff. The following year he toured with the national side to South America.

Seru started all four of Fiji's pool games in the 2003 World Cup, and more recently played in all three games for the newly-formed unified team, the Pacific Islanders.

In 2001 Seru took up a three-year degree course at Otago University, New Zealand, and the following year played seven games for Otago in the National Provincial Championship before gaining a Super 12 contract with Highlanders, for whom he played a dozen games over the 2003 and 2004 season.

Following his Tigers debut last season, Seru became only the ninth player in the 125-year history of the Tigers to score tries in each of his first three starts, he went on to score eight tries in his first 10 appearances for the club.

| | |
|---|---|
| Position | Centre / wing |
| Date of Birth | 27.12.78 |
| Height | 6'2" |
| Weight | 16st 9lb |
| Tigers Debut | 5.9.04 at Sale Sharks |
| Tigers Record | 12+2 apps |
| | 8 tries |
| | 40 pts |
| Previous Clubs | Lautoka (FJ), Suva (FJ), Otago (NZ), Highlanders (NZ) |
| Rep Hons | Fiji (17), Pacific Islanders (3) |

# John **RAWSON**

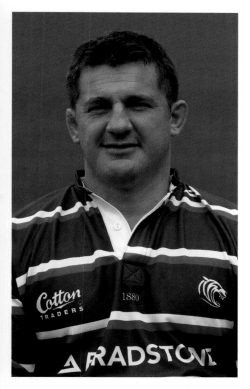

Tighthead prop John Rawson made 25 appearances for First Division Rotherham after joining them in 2003, appearing for the club in both the Powergen Cup and the European Parker Pen Cup, as well as playing 10 games in the Zurich Premiership.

Rawson joined the Yorkshire outfit from Auckland, New Zealand, where he was part of the squad that won the NPC Development Competition in 2002, whilst playing his club rugby for Ponsonby.

He made five appearances for the first team in his first season at Welford Road and was a member of the successful Zurich A League squad.

| | |
|---|---|
| Position | Prop |
| Date of Birth | 6.4.75 |
| Height | 5'7" |
| Weight | 17st 4lb |
| Tigers Debut | 5.2.05 at Bath |
| Tigers Record | 1+4 apps |
| | 0 tries |
| | 0 pts |
| Previous Clubs | Ponsonby (NZ), Auckland (NZ), Rotherham |
| Rep Hons | N/A |

# Graham **ROWNTREE**

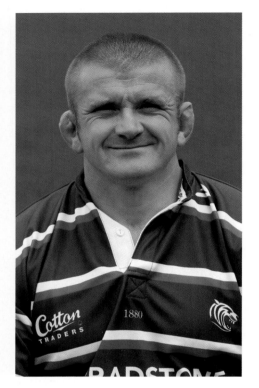

Since joining Tigers Youth set up in 1988, and making his full debut against Oxford University in 1990, Graham Rowntree has gone on to make over 375 first team appearances for the club, placing him ninth on Tigers' all-time list.

Graham also became only the second player from any club to make 200 appearances in the English top division and was the first Leicester player to receive the ERC Elite award for appearing in 50 Heineken Cup games.

In the 1999-2000 season, the former John Cleveland College pupil won the Members' Award for Outstanding Service to the Club.

In 1993 he made his England A, Barbarians and Midlands debuts, and in 1995 he gained his first full England cap against Scotland in the Five Nations tournament.

He was a prominent figure in the next two Five Nations tournaments, the 1995 and 1999 World Cups, and also in the Lions Tour to South Africa in 1997, playing six games, but no tests.

After the World Cup Graham was not capped for almost two years until a series of imperious performances for his club forced him back into international contention.

He was selected for the England squad to tour Canada and the USA in 2001, participated in that season's Autumn internationals and was capped in each of the following Six Nations games.

An ever-present in the 2003 Six Nations Championship he toured with England to New Zealand and Australia that summer, putting in a memorable performance against the All Blacks.

He was very unlucky to miss out on selection for the final World Cup squad, however, he was selected for England in all three of the Autumn international test series and the first four Six Nations games in 2005.

He was one of eight Tigers players named by Sir Clive Woodward for the British & Irish Lions tour to New Zealand in the summer, and finally gained his first Lions cap in the second test, eight years after his original Lions selection.

| Position | Prop |
|---|---|
| Date of Birth | 18.4.71 |
| Height | 6' |
| Weight | 17st 4lb |
| Tigers Debut | 23.10.90 vs Oxford University |
| Tigers Record | 343+35 apps |
| | 18 tries |
| | 87 pts |
| Previous Clubs | Nuneaton Colts |
| Rep Hons | England (52), Lions (2) |

# Will **SKINNER**

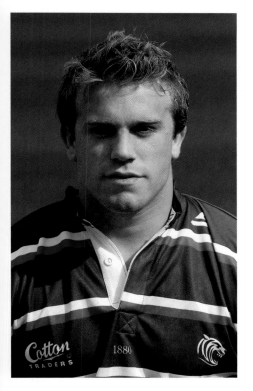

Will Skinner began playing rugby when, at the age of six, he followed in the footsteps of his two older brothers and joined Olney Rugby Club.

He attended Bedford School and moved to Bedford RUFC at U13 level. After earning three caps for England Schoolboys at U16 level, he was invited to join the Tigers Academy and was picked for the England U18 squad that played at Welford Road in February 2001.

Whilst still waiting to make his impressive Tigers first-team debut – scoring a try in the game against Leeds Tykes – the openside flanker played in the England Sevens team that won the Brisbane 7s in February 2003 and for England U19s during the "shadow" Six Nations.

During the 2003-04 season Will took the opportunity afforded by players being absent on England duty to make 16 appearances for the first team, his efforts rewarded by being voted as Young player of the Season. He was also called into the England U21 squad that completed a "Grand Slam", but was unfortunately injured in the game against Wales.

A member of the Tigers Extras squad that won the Zurich A League in 2004-05, Will was a late call-up for the England U21 side that competed in the IRB U21 World Cup in Argentina in June.

| | |
|---|---|
| Position | Flanker |
| Date of Birth | 8.2.84 |
| Height | 5'11" |
| Weight | 14st 13lb |
| Tigers Debut | 26.4.03 vs Leeds Tykes |
| Tigers Record | 8+17 apps |
| | 3 tries |
| | 15 pts |
| Previous Clubs | Olney, Bedford |
| Rep Hons | England U21 / Sevens |

# Ollie **SMITH**

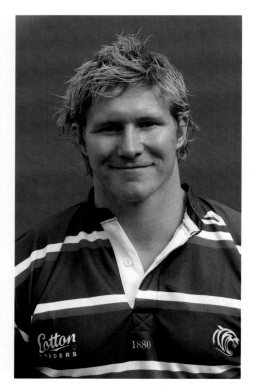

Centre Ollie Smith started playing junior rugby with Old Bosworthians and then switched to Market Bosworth at U14 level.

He joined Tigers in 1999 after attending a trial and went on to surpass Lewis Moody's record for being the youngest Tigers player to play in a league game.

Success in the Heineken Cup Final at Cardiff in 2002 also made him the only teenager to hold a Heineken Cup winners medal.

Ollie had played for England at U18, U19 and U21 levels before finally making his senior debut, coming on as a replacement in the Six Nations game against Italy at Twickenham in March 2003.

Named in Clive Woodward's extended World Cup squad during the summer of 2003, Smith made his first start for England in the game against France in Marseilles.

His performance during a season curtailed by injury earned him a nomination for Young Player of the Season 2002-03 by the Professional Rugby Players Association. He had previously been voted the 2000-01 and 2001-02 Tigers' Members' Young Player of the Season, as well as the Players' Young Player of the Season in 2000-01.

Last season Ollie forced his way back into international contention with an outstanding performance for England A against France A, scoring a try in the game at Bath in February, then played in the final two Six Nations games.

He was selected to tour with the British & Irish Lions party to New Zealand in the summer playing in five games scoring two tries.

He has been included in this season's England Elite Playing squad.

| | |
|---|---|
| Position | Centre / wing |
| Date of Birth | 14.8.82 |
| Height | 6'1" |
| Weight | 15st 6lb |
| Tigers Debut | 16.9.00 vs London Irish |
| Tigers Record | 97+17 apps |
| | 29 tries |
| | 145 pts |
| Previous Clubs | Old Bosworthians, Market Bosworth |
| Rep Hons | England (5) |

# Ephraim **TAUKAFA**

Ephraim Taukafa was the Tongan hooker at the 2003 Rugby World Cup. He played in all four of their pool games making two starts, against Italy and Canada, and coming on twice as a replacement, against Wales and New Zealand.

He had already gained six test caps prior to the competition, his debut being against Papua New Guinea at Port Moresby in a World Cup qualifying match in November 2002.

He also played in the repechage game against Korea in Seoul the following March, where he scored a try in a 75-0 win. The return leg in Nuku'Alofa a week later saw the Tongans improve to win 119-0, with Taukafa grabbing two of their 17 tries scored.

Ephraim also scored two tries in Soa Otuvaka's memorial match at Kingston Park in April a game which pitted him against his future captain, Martin Johnson.

Ephraim played for Tigers Extras in their successful Zurich A League campaign as well as making his first team debut. He also played in the IRB Tsunami appeal match at Twickenham in March and gained two more international caps playing in World Cup qualifying games during the summer, making him the first Tongan to be capped whilst playing for the club.

Auckland-born Ephraim originally played in North Harbour, New Zealand before making his way across the Tasman to play for Northern Suburbs in Sydney in 2003.

| | |
|---|---|
| Position | Hooker |
| Date of Birth | 26.6.76 |
| Height | 5'11" |
| Weight | 16st 7lb |
| Tigers Debut | 21.11.04 at London Wasps |
| Tigers Record | 2+4 apps |
| | 0 tries |
| | 0 pts |
| Previous Club | Northern Suburbs (AU) |
| Rep Hons | Tonga (13) |

# Alesana **TUILAGI**

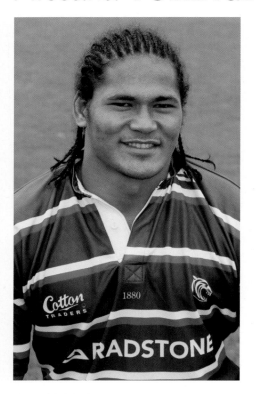

Alesana Tuilagi joined Leicester from Italian club Parma, for whom he had played the previous two seasons, after joining his brother Henry in Europe.

Alesana was equal second top try-scorer in Italy in the 2003-04 season, his 12 tries helping his club to the semi-finals of both the Italian Super 10 Championship and the Parker Pen Shield.

He has gained eight international caps since his debut for Samoa in their World Cup qualifier against Fiji in June 2002, including 5 appearances this summer scoring five tries, four in a single game against Tonga in Apia.

This is Alesana's second spell at Tigers. He made 11 appearances for the Under-21 team during the 2000-01 season, playing alongside future first-teamers Sam Vesty and Harry Ellis.

A member of last season's successful Zurich A League squad, Alesana set a Zurich A League record by scoring five tries in the game against Leeds in September 2004.

| | |
|---|---|
| Position | Wing |
| Date of Birth | 24.2.81 |
| Height | 6'1" |
| Weight | 17st 11lb |
| Tigers Debut | 11.9.04 vs Leeds Tykes |
| Tigers Record | 9+14 apps |
| | 11 tries |
| | 55 pts |
| Previous Club | Parma (IT) |
| Rep Hons | Samoa (8) |

# Henry **TUILAGI**

Henry Tuilagi has made a real impact in the back row since joining his elder brother Fereti when at Leicester.

He made 24 first team appearances in his first season, scoring a try on his debut in the opening game against London Irish, and has since consolidated his position both in the team and as a favourite of the fans.

His 2004-05 season was cruelly cut short, however, when he suffered a broken leg in the final home Premiership match against London Wasps in April.

Henry previously played for Italian club Parma, where his younger brother Alesana had joined him for a season.

He appeared for Parma against London Wasps at High Wycombe in the first round of the European Challenge Cup, and then at Caerphilly in the quarter final of the same competition in January 2003.

The No.8 was first included in the Samoa squad for the 2000 Pacific Rim Championship, but had to wait another two years for his test debut against Fiji in Apia, Samoa in June 2002.

Both Fereti and Alesana joined him in the international team later in the month when all three brothers played together in the World Cup qualifier against Fiji at Nadi.

Henry now has four international caps, but due to injury missed out on further honours last summer. He was also capped for Samoa at Rugby League in 1999.

| Position | Back row / Number 8 |
| --- | --- |
| Date of Birth | 12.8.76 |
| Height | 6'1" |
| Weight | 19st 11lb |
| Tigers Debut | 13.9.03 vs London Irish |
| Tigers Record | 23+21 apps |
| | 7 tries |
| | 35 pts |
| Previous Clubs | Marist St Joseph's (SM), Parma (IT) |
| Rep Hons | Samoa (4) |

# Tom **VARNDELL**

Winger Tom Varndell returned to Leicester Tigers in the summer of 2004 for his second spell at the club, having previously spent two years at the Tigers Academy under the guidance of Dusty Hare.

The speedy youngster made an impressive start in the Zurich Premiership, scoring a hat-trick in his second outing at Worcester in November.

An ever-present in England's U21 squad during last season's "shadow" Six Nations, he also toured with them to Argentina in the summer competing in the IRB U21 World Cup.

Named as the NIG Academy Player of the Month for November 2004, Tom put in an impressive performance for Leicester at the 2005 Middlesex Sevens scoring a hat-trick in the first-round win over Bristol.

| | |
|---|---|
| Position | Wing |
| Date of Birth | 16.9.85 |
| Height | 6'3" |
| Weight | 15st 6lb |
| Tigers Debut | 6.11.04 vs Gloucester |
| Tigers Record | 10+3 apps |
| | 12 tries |
| | 60 pts |
| Previous Clubs | N/A |
| Rep Hons | England U21 |

# Sam **VESTY**

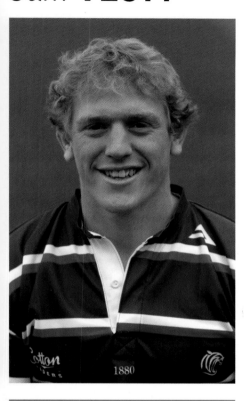

A former pupil of John Cleveland College, Sam Vesty started playing rugby at age 10, having been inspired by his father Phil (who used to play prop for Leicester).

After graduating through Tigers' U21 team, and Tigers Extras, Sam was rewarded with a first team debut, coming on as a second-half replacement in the Orange Cup game against Biarritz Olympique, making him the fourth generation of his family to play for Leicester.

Having already represented his country at U18 level, Sam was one of three Tigers youngsters in the England squad that competed in the IRB U21 World Championship in South Africa during the summer of 2002.

Propelled into the first team for the 2002-03 season due to injuries, Sam acquitted himself well in the pivotal role of fly-half, picking up both the Supporters' and Players' Awards for Young Player of the Season.

Last season Sam consolidated his selection within the team switching to full back, to accommodate the return of Andy Goode, from where he made 14 of his 21 starts including the Heineken Cup quarter-final victory over Leinster in Dublin in April.

His form was such that he was selected for the England XV for the Churchill Cup in Canada during the summer, playing in the first game against the host nation.

Sam's sporting talent stretches beyond the rugby field onto the cricket pitches, where he has played for the Leicestershire second XI and Leicestershire U19, as well as playing tennis at county level.

| | |
|---|---|
| Position | Utility back |
| Date of Birth | 26.11.81 |
| Height | 6'3" |
| Weight | 14st 6lb |
| Tigers Debut | 24.8.02 vs Biarritz Olympique at Bayonne |
| Tigers Record | 46+18 apps |
| | 5 tries |
| | 84 pts (10 C, 13 PG) |
| Previous Clubs | N/A |
| Rep Hons | England XV |

# Julian **WHITE**

After signing for Tigers in the summer of 2003, prop Julian White's Leicester debut was held over as he was in Australia on duty with England at the Rugby World Cup.

After making his international debut at Loftus Versfeld in Pretoria in June 2000, Julian toured with England to North America in 2001, playing in all three tests against Canada and the USA.

A knee injury sustained after a solitary appearance in the 2002-03 Six Nations meant Julian was unavailable for the England tour to Australia and New Zealand that summer, but did regain his fitness in time to be included in the final warm-up games against France and Wales. His performance ensured his place on the plane to Australia, where he made two appearances in the World Cup pool games.

Since then, Julian has played in the 2004 Six Nations championship, toured with England to New Zealand and Australia in the summer of 2004, was an ever-present for that season's Autumn international series and played the first game of this year's Six Nations campaign before succumbing to injury. His form was such that he was named among the Leicester contingent for this summer's tour to New Zealand by the British & Irish Lions playing in all three tests at tighthead.

Julian is one of a select band of England capped players who have appeared in the southern hemisphere's Super 12 tournament, appearing for the Crusaders against Natal at Christchurch in 1997, whilst in New Zealand playing for Hawke's Bay, with whom he appeared in the NZ Provincial Championship (NPC).

Returning to the UK, White played for Bridgend in 1998-99 before switching over to Saracens for two seasons. He joined Bristol at the start of the 2002-03.

Along with his England team-mates, Julian was awarded an MBE in the 2004 New Year's Honours.

| Position | Prop |
|---|---|
| Date of Birth | 14.5.73 |
| Height | 6'1" |
| Weight | 18st 12lb |
| Tigers Debut | 29.11.03 vs Bath |
| Tigers Record | 31+6 apps |
| | 2 tries |
| | 10 pts |
| Previous Clubs | Dannevirke RSC (NZ), Hawke's Bay (NZ), Crusaders (NZ), Bridgend, Saracens, Bristol |
| Rep Hons | England (28) Lions (3) |

# David **YOUNG**

Prop David Young joined Leicester Tigers' Academy in 2004 and has been elevated to the first team squad this season following solid performances for Tigers Extras during their successful Zurich A League campaign.

David played for Scotland U19 at the IRB U19 World Cup in Durban, South Africa in 2004 and for Scotland U21 during last season's "shadow" Six Nations.

Named as the NIG Tigers Academy Player of the Month for December 2004, Young has also attended Murray Mexted's International Rugby Academy in New Zealand.

| | |
|---|---|
| Position | Prop |
| Date of Birth | 18.2.85 |
| Height | 6'1" |
| Weight | 17st 11lb |
| Tigers Debut | Yet to make Tigers debut |
| Tigers Record | N/A |
| Previous Clubs | N/A |
| Rep Hons | Scotland U21 |

# Academy

### Rugby Development Co-ordinator

# Dusty **Hare**

Dusty Hare was a professional cricketer from 1971 to 1976, before seeing the light and moving to rugby union. He joined Tigers in '76 as a full back and was the world's highest points-scorer; achieving 7,137 points in total, with 4,507 being for Tigers alone. He was capped 25 times for England and was a British & Irish Lions tourist in 1983.

He served on the Barbarians Committee between 1989 and 1992, and was awarded an MBE in 1989.

In 1993 Dusty took on the role of Director of Rugby at Nottingham, before coming back to Tigers in 1994 as Development Co-ordinator.

Before becoming a full-time coach, Dusty was a farmer. He also has an honorary Bachelor of Arts degree from Leicester University (1990).

### Academy Physiotherapist

# Jackie **Limna**

Jackie Limna obtained her degree in physiotherapy in Bristol, before going on to get a Masters degree in Sports Medicine from Trinity College in Dublin.

She worked for the NHS for six years, before moving into rugby, which saw her work for National League club Western-Super-Mare, as well as Somerset County Rugby Union. Jackie has also helped out with the RFUW, in their Elite Regional Programme.

Jackie joined Leicester Tigers in 2004/05 and her main role is in Tigers' Academy, whilst she also helps out with the first team and Tigers' development team.

**Academy Conditioning Coach**

# Patrick **Mortimer**

Paddy Mortimer boasts extensive experience in the rugby world, having played and coached for many years. Forced out of rugby at the tender age of 23, he obtained a degree in Physical Education from the Manchester Metropolitan University, whilst he is also a sports psychologist under accreditation.

Paddy, who was born in the Lake District in 1967, played college rugby as well as representing Sale's second team. His coaching experiences saw him coach Fylde for three years, whilst he was also an assistant coach for Sale at first-team level, a head coach at Liverpool St Helens and an assistant coach at Herriots Rugby Club.

Paddy also taught physical education at school, lectured at Manchester Metropolitan University and Edinburgh University, managed Gloucester's Rugby Academy, as well as serving the RFU as its Sports Science Co-ordinator for referees.

Paddy is currently a representative on UK Athletics' Senior Sports Science Performance Group.

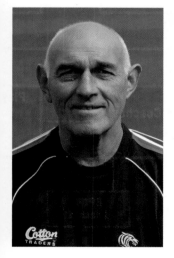

**Academy Kit Man**

# Ray **Needham**

Ray Needham joined Tigers in 1973 after achieving a degree at Exeter University. He made 129 first team appearances until 1982 when he coached Leicester Tigers Extras for a year.

From 1984 he was a full RFU coach and coached Leicester Youth until 1989.

Ray continued to teach throughout his early coaching career at Allderman Newtons from 1973-2000.

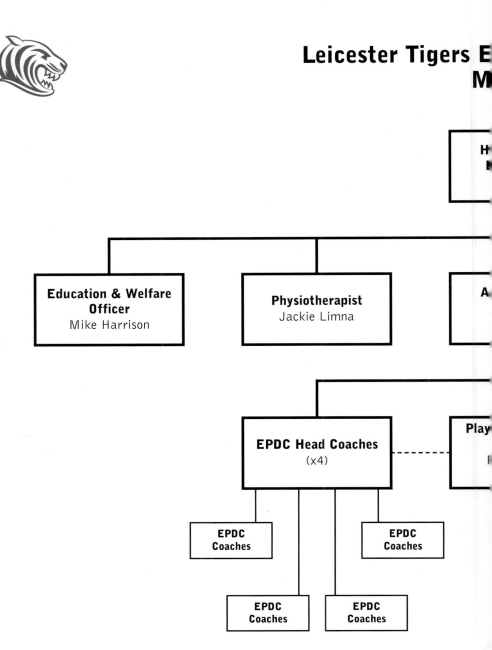

# Leicester Tigers E

## M

**Education & Welfare Officer**
Mike Harrison

**Physiotherapist**
Jackie Limna

**EPDC Head Coaches**
(x4)

**EPDC Coaches**

**EPDC Coaches**

**EPDC Coaches**

**EPDC Coaches**

# d Rugby Academy
## 05

ENGLAND
RUGBY

| | |
|---|---|
| by | |
| it | |

**Strength & Conditioning Coach**
Patrick Mortimer

**Academy Administrator**
Teresa Chester

ment
&

**Academy Head Coach**
Neil Back

**Player Development Coach**
Mike Penistone

**Paul Bailey-Green**

| | |
|---|---|
| Position | Centre |
| Date of Birth | 8.10.87 |
| Height | 6'1" |
| Weight | 14st 2lb |

**Phil Boulton**

| | |
|---|---|
| Position | Prop |
| Date of Birth | 14.12.86 |
| Height | 6'3" |
| Weight | 18st 13lb |

**Alistair Burgess**

| | |
|---|---|
| Position | No 8 |
| Date of Birth | 6.9.85 |
| Height | 6'3" |
| Weight | 15st 6lb |

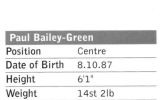

**Jack Cobden**

| | |
|---|---|
| Position | Centre |
| Date of Birth | 26.3.89 |
| Height | 6'1" |
| Weight | 13st 10lb |

**Dan Cole**

| | |
|---|---|
| Position | Prop |
| Date of Birth | 9.5.87 |
| Height | 6'3" |
| Weight | 18t 4lb |

**Tom Collett**

| | |
|---|---|
| Position | Hooker |
| Date of Birth | 5.1.89 |
| Height | 5'10" |
| Weight | 12st 13lb |

| Mitchell Culpin | |
|---|---|
| Position | Wing/Centre |
| Date of Birth | 14.3.89 |
| Height | 5'8" |
| Weight | 12st 4lb |

| Kevin Davis | |
|---|---|
| Position | Prop |
| Date of Birth | 26.1.86 |
| Height | 6' |
| Weight | 18st 4lb |

| Oliver Dodge | |
|---|---|
| Position | Centre/Wing |
| Date of Birth | 27.8.87 |
| Height | 6'1" |
| Weight | 15st 11lb |

| Spencer Eke | |
|---|---|
| Position | Scrum half |
| Date of Birth | 3.3.88 |
| Height | 5'9" |
| Weight | 11st 5lb |

| Chris Fletcher | |
|---|---|
| Position | Centre |
| Date of Birth | 28.10.87 |
| Height | 6' |
| Weight | 15st 11lb |

| Gregor Gillanders | |
|---|---|
| Position | Lock |
| Date of Birth | 12.4.88 |
| Height | 6'4" |
| Weight | 16st 7lb |

| Sam Herrington | |
|---|---|
| Position | Lock |
| Date of Birth | 2.10.86 |
| Height | 6'5" |
| Weight | 18st 2lb |

| Marc Howgate | |
|---|---|
| Position | Openside Flanker |
| Date of Birth | 16.2.86 |
| Height | 5'9" |
| Weight | 13st 10lb |

| Anthony Kane | |
|---|---|
| Position | Prop |
| Date of Birth | 7.11.85 |
| Height | 6' |
| Weight | 17st 2lb |

| Aiden McNulty | |
|---|---|
| Position | Fly half |
| Date of Birth | 21.10.87 |
| Height | 6' |
| Weight | 13st 5lb |

| Chris Mundy | |
|---|---|
| Position | Flanker |
| Date of Birth | 7.9.87 |
| Height | 6' |
| Weight | 13st 8lb |

| Michael Pearson | |
|---|---|
| Position | Lock |
| Date of Birth | 28.9.85 |
| Height | 6'6" |
| Weight | 15st 8lb |

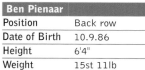

**Ben Pienaar**

| | |
|---|---|
| Position | Back row |
| Date of Birth | 10.9.86 |
| Height | 6'4" |
| Weight | 15st 11lb |

**Greg Sammons**

| | |
|---|---|
| Position | Back row |
| Date of Birth | 31.12.87 |
| Height | 6'10" |
| Weight | 14st 11lb |

**Ian Saxelby**

| | |
|---|---|
| Position | No 8 |
| Date of Birth | 22.5.89 |
| Height | 6'3" |
| Weight | 15st 2lb |

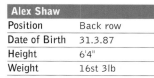

**Alex Shaw**

| | |
|---|---|
| Position | Back row |
| Date of Birth | 31.3.87 |
| Height | 6'4" |
| Weight | 16st 3lb |

**Matt Smith**

| | |
|---|---|
| Position | Utility back |
| Date of Birth | 15.11.85 |
| Height | 6'4" |
| Weight | 14st 13lb |

**Rob Springall**

| | |
|---|---|
| Position | Scrum half |
| Date of Birth | 23.1.87 |
| Height | 5'10" |
| Weight | 12st 13lb |

### Tom Strickland

| | |
|---|---|
| Position | Fly half/Centre |
| Date of Birth | 11.10.88 |
| Height | 6' |
| Weight | 13st 3lb |

### Ben Toft

| | |
|---|---|
| Position | Wing/Full back |
| Date of Birth | 18.3.86 |
| Height | 5'10" |
| Weight | 12st |

### Greig Tonks

| | |
|---|---|
| Position | Centre/ Full back |
| Date of Birth | 20.5.89 |
| Height | 6'1" |
| Weight | 13st 8lb |

### Adam Varley

| | |
|---|---|
| Position | Back row |
| Date of Birth | 3.10.87 |
| Height | 6'2" |
| Weight | 14st 2lb |

### Chris Whitehead

| | |
|---|---|
| Position | Hooker |
| Date of Birth | 9.5.86 |
| Height | 5'10" |
| Weight | 14st 11lb |

### Alex Wright

| | |
|---|---|
| Position | Scrum half |
| Date of Birth | 23.6.86 |
| Height | 5'10" |
| Weight | 12st 8lb |

| Tom Youngs | |
|---|---|
| Position | Inside centre |
| Date of Birth | 28.1.87 |
| Height | 5'10" |
| Weight | 14st 7lb |

# GUINNESS PREMIERSHIP
# KICK OFF
# 2005-06

**STATS & FACTS
ON EVERY TEAM**

# Premiership Roll of Honour

| Season | Champions | Relegated | Promoted |
| --- | --- | --- | --- |
| 2004-05 Premiership | **London Wasps** | NEC Harlequins | Bristol Rugby |
| 2003-04 Premiership | **London Wasps** | Rotherham Titans | Worcester Warriors |
| 2002-03 Premiership | **London Wasps** | Bristol Rugby | Rotherham Titans |
| 2001-02 Premiership | **Leicester Tigers** | N/A | N/A |
| 2000-01 Premiership | **Leicester Tigers** | Rotherham Titans | Leeds Tykes |
| 1999-00 Premiership | **Leicester Tigers** | Bedford Blues | Rotherham |
| 1998-99 Premiership | **Leicester Tigers** | West Hartlepool | Bristol Rugby |
| 1997-98 Premiership | **Newcastle Falcons** | Bristol  Rugby | Bedford<br>West Hartlepool<br>London Scottish |

GUINNESS PREMIERSHIP

# KICK OFF

## 2005-06

# Season Statistics 2004-05

## Final Premiership Table 2004-05

| | Team | RECORD | | | POINTS | | | ATTACK | | | | | DEFENCE | | | | | |
|---|---|---|---|---|---|---|---|---|---|---|---|---|---|---|---|---|---|---|
| | | W | D | L | TB | LB | Tot | T | C | PG | DG | For | T | C | PG | DG | Agst | PD |
| 1 | Leicester | 15 | 3 | 4 | 9 | 3 | 78 | 75 | 58 | 51 | 7 | 665 | 27 | 16 | 49 | 3 | 323 | +342 |
| 2 | London Wasps (C) | 15 | 1 | 6 | 6 | 5 | 73 | 59 | 43 | 55 | 5 | 561 | 40 | 34 | 52 | 6 | 442 | +119 |
| 3 | Sale | 13 | 0 | 9 | 4 | 4 | 60 | 51 | 39 | 53 | 7 | 513 | 43 | 31 | 49 | 6 | 442 | +71 |
| 4 | Bath | 12 | 2 | 8 | 1 | 5 | 58 | 33 | 25 | 53 | 11 | 407 | 35 | 22 | 41 | 8 | 366 | +41 |
| 5 | Saracens | 12 | 2 | 8 | 3 | 2 | 57 | 39 | 24 | 44 | 3 | 384 | 43 | 30 | 47 | 4 | 428 | -44 |
| 6 | Gloucester | 10 | 1 | 11 | 3 | 2 | 47 | 43 | 24 | 41 | 7 | 407 | 43 | 34 | 67 | 1 | 487 | -80 |
| 7 | Newcastle | 9 | 2 | 11 | 3 | 4 | 47 | 43 | 31 | 58 | 8 | 475 | 64 | 45 | 56 | 6 | 596 | -121 |
| 8 | Leeds | 9 | 0 | 13 | 1 | 6 | 43 | 34 | 24 | 53 | 1 | 380 | 40 | 27 | 49 | 10 | 431 | -51 |
| 9 | Worcester | 9 | 0 | 13 | 1 | 5 | 42 | 36 | 25 | 39 | 6 | 365 | 53 | 39 | 46 | 4 | 493 | -128 |
| 10 | London Irish | 8 | 0 | 14 | 1 | 7 | 40 | 28 | 17 | 63 | 5 | 378 | 35 | 21 | 62 | 6 | 421 | -43 |
| 11 | Northampton | 8 | 0 | 14 | 2 | 6 | 40 | 31 | 21 | 67 | 4 | 410 | 44 | 29 | 54 | 11 | 473 | -63 |
| 12 | Harlequins (R) | 6 | 1 | 15 | 3 | 9 | 38 | 41 | 29 | 49 | 2 | 416 | 46 | 32 | 54 | 1 | 459 | -43 |

### Championship Play-Off Semi-Final

Saturday, 7 May 2005 **London Wasps** **43-2** **Sale Sharks**
**Wasps:** Tries: Rees, Lewsey, Erinlee, Shaw; Con: Van Gisbergen (4); Pen: Van Gisbergen (4); DG: King
**Sale:** Tries: Chabel, White, Cueto; Cons: Hodgson(2); Pen: Hodgson          Causeway Stadium, 5,824

### Championship Play-Off Final

Saturday, 14 May 2005 **London Wasps** **34-14** **Leicester Tigers**
**Wasps:** Tries: Voyce, Van Gisbergen, Hoadley; Con: Van Gisbergen (3); Pen: Van Gisbergen (5); DG: King
**Leicester:** Try: Bemand; Pen: Goode (3)          Twickenham, 66,000

## Tries and Points

[includes play-off data]

### Top Try Scorer

| Pos | Player | Team | Tries |
|---|---|---|---|
| W | T.Voyce | London Wasps | 12 |
| C | A.Erinle | London Wasps | 11 |
| W | M.Cueto | Sale Sharks | 11 |
| W | S.Hanley | Sale Sharks | 9 |
| FL | N.Back | Leicester Tigers | 7 |
| W/FB | S.Staniforth | London Irish | 7 |
| W | M.Stephenson | Newcastle Falcons | 7 |
| C | T.Fanolua | Gloucester | 6 |
| W | M.Garvey | Gloucester | 6 |
| C | A.Snyman | Leeds Tykes | 6 |
| UB | A.Healey | Leicester Tigers | 6 |
| W/C | L.Lloyd | Leicester Tigers | 6 |
| C/W | S.Rabeni | Leicester Tigers | 6 |
| W | T.Varndell | Leicester Tigers | 6 |
| FB | M.Van Gisbergen | London Wasps | 6 |
| C | C.Bell | Leeds Tykes | 5 |
| SH | H.Ellis | Leicester Tigers | 5 |
| C | D.Gibson | Leicester Tigers | 5 |
| FB/W | G.Murphy | Leicester Tigers | 5 |
| SH | M.Dawson | London Wasps | 5 |
| SH/W | S.Keogh | NEC Harlequins | 5 |
| FB | M.Burke | Newcastle Falcons | 5 |
| W | T.May | Newcastle Falcons | 5 |
| C | B.Hinshelwood | Worcester Warriors | 5 |

### Top Points Scorer

| Pos | Player | Team | Points |
|---|---|---|---|
| FH | A.Goode | Leicester Tigers | 268 |
| FB | M.Van Gisbergen | London Wasps | 225 |
| FH | C.Hodgson | Sale Sharks | 200 |
| FH | J.Staunton | NEC Harlequins | 186 |
| FH | S.Drahm | Northampton Saints | 180 |
| FH | G.Ross | Leeds Tykes | 161 |
| FH | J.Wilkinson | Newcastle Falcons | 150 |
| FH | B.Everitt | London Irish | 145 |
| C | H.Paul | Gloucester | 136 |
| FH | C.Malone | Bath Rugby | 133 |
| FH/C | O.Barkley | Bath Rugby | 129 |
| FH | J.Brown | Worcester Warriors | 113 |
| FH | M.Mapletoft | London Irish | 99 |
| FH | G.Jackson | Saracens | 77 |
| FH | T.Hayes | Worcester Warriors | 75 |
| FH | P.Grayson | Northampton Saints | 74 |
| FH | A.King | London Wasps | 65 |
| FB | M.Burke | Newcastle Falcons | 64 |
| W | T.Voyce | London Wasps | 60 |
| FH | D.Walder | Newcastle Falcons | 58 |
| C | A.Erinle | London Wasps | 55 |
| W | M.Cueto | Sale Sharks | 55 |
| FH | M.Hercus | Sale Sharks | 53 |
| FH | N.Little | Saracens | 53 |

## Records

[does not include play-off data]

### Average Tries per Game
4

### Average Points per Game
41

### Longest Unbeaten Run
15 matches, Leicester Tigers,
11.9.04 to 19.2.05

### Longest Run Without Winning
9 matches, Northampton Saints,
18.9.04 to 28.11.04

### Best Home Record
Leicester Tigers, W10, D1, L0, Pts: 48

### Best Away Record
London Wasps, W7, D0, L4, Pts: 32
Bath, W7, D1, L3, Pts: 32

### Most Tries Scored in a Game
12, Leicester Tigers (11) vs Newcastle Falcons (1), 83-10,
19.2.05

### Most Points Scored in a Game
93, Leicester Tigers vs Newcastle Falcons, 83-10,
19.2.05

### Most Tries Scored by Backs
53, Leicester Tigers

### Most Tries Scored by Forwards
20, Sale Sharks

### Most Tries Scored (0-10mins)
10, London Wasps

### Most Tries Scored (11-20mins)
8, Gloucester Rugby

### Most Tries Scored (21-30mins)
8, Sale Sharks

### Most Tries Scored (31-40mins)
20, Leicester Tigers

### Most Tries Scored (41-50mins)
8, London Wasps

### Most Tries Scored (51-60mins)
13, Leicester Tigers

### Most Tries Scored (61-70mins)
8, Leicester Tigers

### Most Tries Scored (71-80mins)
10, Gloucester Rugby

### Most Tries Scored injury time
5, London Irish

### Percentage of Half-Time Deficits Turned into Wins
44.45%, Bath, Half-time deficits 9, Wins 4
42.86%, Wasps, Half-time deficits 7, Wins 3
36.36%, Saracens, Half-time deficits 11, Wins 4
30.77%, Gloucester, Half-time deficits 13, Wins 4
28.57%, Northampton, Half-time deficits 11, Wins 1
28.57%, Newcastle, Half-time deficits 11, Wins 4
18.18%, Sale, Half-time deficits 11, Wins 2
18.18%, Irish, Half-time deficits 11, Wins 2
9.09%, Harlequins, Half-time deficits 11, Wins 1
8.34%, Leeds, Half-time deficits 12, Wins 1
0%, Leicester, Half-time deficits 5, Wins 0
0%, Worcester, Half-time deficits 10, Wins 0

### Time Period in which Most Tries Scored
31-40, 82 / 514, 16%

### Time Period in which Least Tries Scored
61-70, 37 / 514, 7.2%

### Highest % Points Scored From Tries
56.39%, 375 / 665, Leicester Tigers

### Highest % Points Conceded From Tries
53.75%, 265 / 493, Worcester Warriors

### Highest % Points Scored From Conversions
17.44%, 116 / 665, Leicester Tigers

### Highest % Points Conceded From Conversions
15.82%, 78 / 493, Worcester Warriors

### Highest % Points Scored From Penalty Goals
50.00%, 189 / 378, London Irish

### Highest % Points Conceded From Penalty Goals
45.51%, 147 / 323, Leicester Tigers

### Highest % Points Scored From Drop Goals
8.11%, 33 / 407, Bath Rugby

### Highest % Points Conceded From Drop Goals
6.98%, 33 / 473, Northampton Saints

### Highest % of Team Points Scored by One Player
44.71%, J.Staunton, NEC Harlequins, 186 / 416

### Tallest Players
O.Hodge, Bristol Shoguns, 6'9"
L.Gross, Newcastle Falcons, 6'9"

### Heaviest Players
T.Collier, Worcester Warriors, 21st 3lb
D. Browne, Northampton Saints, 20st 6lb

### Lightest Players
D.Blair, Sale Sharks, 11st 7lb
J.Brown, Worcester Warriors, 11st 2lb

### Most Time Spent On Pitch
99%, T.Voyce, London Wasps
99%, P.Sanderson, Worcester Warriors

# Bath Rugby

## Season Summary

| Position | Won | Drawn | Lost | For | Against | Bonus Points | Total Points |
|---|---|---|---|---|---|---|---|
| 4 | 12 | 2 | 8 | 407 | 366 | 6 | 58 |

**Despite their injury problems – for two matches they were only able to field 21 players – Bath finished creditably in the league, although they lost the Powergen Cup Final, their first losing appearance in 11 domestic cup finals.**

But failing to make the Championship or Wildcard play-offs was no bad thing after their playing resources had been so stretched. In 2005-06, Lee Mears can be expected to shine again as one of the country's leading hookers, while Chris Malone needs to get the backs going.

**Head Coach:** John Connolly

**Club Honours**
Courage League / Zurich Premiership: 1988-89, 1990-91, 1991-92, 1992-93, 1993-94, 1995-96, 2003-04 (lost play-offs)

John Player Cup / Pilkington Cup: 1984, 1985, 1986, 1987 1989, 1990, 1992, 1994, 1995, 1996
Heineken Cup: 1997-1998

## Season Squad

### Stats 2004-05

| Position | Player | Height | Weight | Apps | Rep | Tries | Points |
|---|---|---|---|---|---|---|---|
| FH/C | O.Barkley | 5'10" | 14st 6lb | 15 | - | 3 | 129 |
| P | D.Barnes | 6'0" | 17st 10lb | 15 | 4 | - | - |
| SH | M.Baxter | 5'10" | 13st 10lb | - | 2 | - | - |
| BR | A.Beattie | 6'5" | 18st 8lb | 13 | - | 1 | 5 |
| P | D.Bell | 6'2" | 19st 8lb | 18 | 2 | 1 | 5 |
| FB/W | L.Best | 6'3" | 15st 2lb | 4 | - | - | - |
| W/FB | S.Booth | 5'8" | 12st 8lb | 3 | - | - | - |
| L | S.Borthwick | 6'6" | 17st 5lb | 13 | - | 1 | 5 |
| C | T.Cheeseman | 6'0" | 14st 2lb | 2 | 2 | - | - |
| C | A.Crockett | 5'11" | 14st 9lb | 11 | - | 2 | 10 |
| W | B.Daniel | 6'1" | 14st 12lb | 13 | 1 | 3 | 15 |
| C | S.Davey | 6'1" | 15st 2lb | 2 | 6 | - | - |
| FB/FH/C | R.Davis | 5'6" | 13st 12lb | 4 | 3 | 1 | 5 |
| BR | G.Delve | 6'3" | 18st 0lb | 2 | 10 | - | - |
| 8 | Z.Fea'unati | 6'2" | 18st 8lb | 21 | - | 2 | 10 |
| L | R.Fidler | 6'5" | 18st 4lb | 7 | 6 | 2 | 10 |
| P | D.Flatman | 6'1" | 18st 12lb | 1 | 1 | - | - |
| C | R.Fleck | 6'0" | 15st 0lb | 6 | 1 | - | - |
| L | D.Grewcock | 6'6" | 18st 10lb | 16 | - | - | - |
| H | R.Hawkins | 6'0" | 16st 4lb | - | 1 | - | - |
| C | A.Higgins | 5'11" | 13st 6lb | 12 | - | 3 | 15 |
| L | J.Hudson | 6'7" | 17st 10lb | 8 | - | - | - |
| H | J.Humphreys | 6'0" | 16st 4lb | 14 | 1 | - | - |
| P | H.Kok | 6'1" | 19st 4lb | 1 | 1 | - | - |
| BR | G.Lewis | 6'3" | 15st 8lb | 6 | 3 | - | - |
| FB/W | K.Lewitt | 6'1" | 13st 9lb | - | 2 | 1 | 5 |
| BR | M.Lipman | 6'1" | 15st 7lb | 14 | 1 | 1 | 5 |
| P | C.Loader | 5'10" | 18st 6lb | 2 | 2 | - | - |
| FB/W | J.Maddock | 5'8" | 13st 5lb | 6 | 5 | 1 | 5 |
| FH | C.Malone | 6'0" | 14st 9lb | 18 | 2 | 1 | 133 |
| H | L.Mears | 5'9" | 15st 8lb | 8 | 12 | 1 | 5 |
| FL | H.Perrett | 6'2" | 15st 0lb | - | 1 | - | - |
| FB | M.Perry | 6'1" | 13st 12lb | 13 | - | - | - |
| FH | R.Pez | 5'9" | 13st 4lb | - | 1 | - | - |
| BR | J.Scaysbrook | 6'3" | 15st 6lb | 10 | 9 | 2 | 10 |
| BR/L | D.Smith | 6'5" | 17st 10lb | - | 1 | - | - |
| P | M.Stevens | 6'0" | 19st 0lb | 7 | 8 | - | - |
| C | M.Tindall | 6'2" | 16st 8lb | 6 | - | 4 | 20 |
| SH | N.Walshe | 5'10" | 13st 6lb | 11 | 7 | - | - |
| H | D.Ward | 5'9" | 15st 8lb | - | 1 | - | - |
| W/C | F.Welsh | 6'1" | 15st 6lb | 8 | 1 | 3 | 15 |
| SH | A.Williams | 5'11" | 13st 12lb | 9 | 1 | - | - |
| SH | M.Wood | 5'10" | 14st 11lb | 11 | 6 | - | - |

# Bath Rugby <sup>185</sup>

## Last Season Form

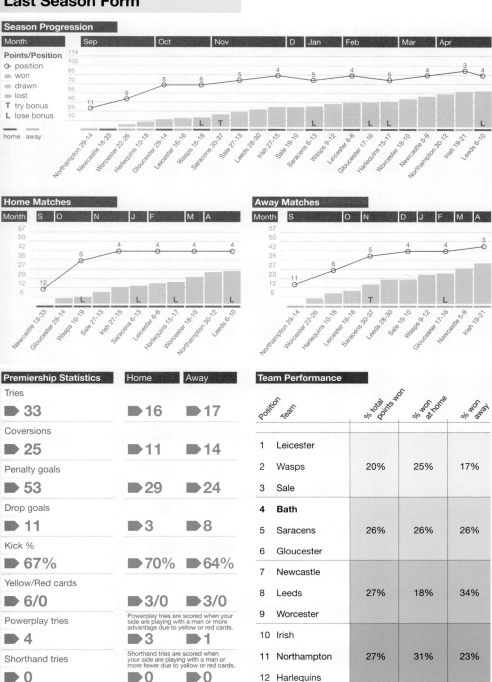

### Season Progression

| Month | Sep | Oct | Nov | D | Jan | Feb | Mar | Apr |

Points/Position
- G— position
- won
- drawn
- lost
- T try bonus
- L lose bonus

home  away

### Home Matches

| Month | S | O | N | J | F | M | A |

### Away Matches

| Month | S | | O | N | | D | J | F | M | A |

### Premiership Statistics

| | Home | Away |
|---|---|---|
| Tries | | |
| ▶ 33 | ▶ 16 | ▶ 17 |
| Coversions | | |
| ▶ 25 | ▶ 11 | ▶ 14 |
| Penalty goals | | |
| ▶ 53 | ▶ 29 | ▶ 24 |
| Drop goals | | |
| ▶ 11 | ▶ 3 | ▶ 8 |
| Kick % | | |
| ▶ 67% | ▶ 70% | ▶ 64% |
| Yellow/Red cards | | |
| ▶ 6/0 | ▶ 3/0 | ▶ 3/0 |
| Powerplay tries | | |
| ▶ 4 | ▶ 3 | ▶ 1 |
| Shorthand tries | | |
| ▶ 0 | ▶ 0 | ▶ 0 |

Powerplay tries are scored when your side are playing with a man or more advantage due to yellow or red cards.

Shorthand tries are scored when your side are playing with a man or more fewer due to yellow or red cards.

### Team Performance

| Position | Team | % total points won | % won at home | % won away |
|---|---|---|---|---|
| 1 | Leicester | | | |
| 2 | Wasps | 20% | 25% | 17% |
| 3 | Sale | | | |
| 4 | **Bath** | | | |
| 5 | Saracens | 26% | 26% | 26% |
| 6 | Gloucester | | | |
| 7 | Newcastle | | | |
| 8 | Leeds | 27% | 18% | 34% |
| 9 | Worcester | | | |
| 10 | Irish | | | |
| 11 | Northampton | 27% | 31% | 23% |
| 12 | Harlequins | | | |

# Bath Rugby

## Top Scorer

**Chris Malone**

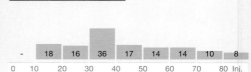

**Points Facts**

| Total points | % team points | Home | Away |
|---|---|---|---|
| 133 | 33 | 55 | 81 |

**Points by Time Period**

| - | 18 | 16 | 36 | 17 | 14 | 14 | 10 | 8 |
|---|----|----|----|----|----|----|----|---|

| 0 | 10 | 20 | 30 | 40 | 50 | 60 | 70 | 80 | Inj. |

## Team Tries and Points

### Tries by Time Period

| 6 | 1 | 6 | 7 | 2 | 4 | 2 | 3 | 2 |
|---|---|---|---|---|---|---|---|---|

| 0 | 10min | 20min | 30min | 40min | 50min | 60min | 70min | 80 Injury time |

| 3 | 5 | 4 | 7 | 2 | 5 | 4 | 2 *League Best* | 3 |
|---|---|---|---|---|---|---|---|---|

scored
conceded

### Tries by Halves

scored

| 33 | 20 | 13 | 61% | 39% |
|---|---|---|---|---|
| Total | 1st half | 2nd half | 1st half % | 2nd half % |

conceded

| 35 | 19 | 16 | 54% | 46% |
|---|---|---|---|---|

### How Points were Scored

- tries: 33
- conversions: 25
- penalty goals: 53 *League Best*
- drop goals: **11** *League Best*

### How Points were Conceded

- tries: 35
- conversions: 22
- penalty goals: **41** *League Best*
- drop goals: 8

### Tries Scored by Player

- backs: 22
- forwards: 11

### Tries Conceded by Player

- backs: 27
- forwards: 7

### Tries Scored/Conceded Across the Pitch

| 3 | 4 | 1 | - | - | 1 | - | 1 | - | - | 2 | 2 | 1 | 3 | 4 | - | 1 | 1 | 1 | - | 2 | - | 3 | 3 | |
|---|---|---|---|---|---|---|---|---|---|---|---|---|---|---|---|---|---|---|---|---|---|---|---|---|

scored
conceded

| 7 | - | - | 2 | - | - | 2 | 1 | - | 3 | 3 | 1 | 2 | 1 | - | 2 | 1 | 2 | - | - | 1 | 4 | 2 | 1 |
|---|---|---|---|---|---|---|---|---|---|---|---|---|---|---|---|---|---|---|---|---|---|---|---|

## Eight-Season Form 1997-2005

### Season Progression

| Season | 97-98 | 98-99 | 99-00 | 00-01 | 01-02 | 02-03 | 03-04 | 04-05 |
|---|---|---|---|---|---|---|---|---|

Points/Position
- G position
- Premiership
- Division 1
- Division 2

| | 3 | 6 | 2 | 3 | 11 | 11 | 1 | 4 |
|---|---|---|---|---|---|---|---|---|
| | 26 | 30 | 43 | 70 | 33 | 36 | 79 | 58 |

### Games

| Season | 97-98 | 98-99 | 99-00 | 00-01 | 01-02 | 02-03 | 03-04 | 04-05 |
|---|---|---|---|---|---|---|---|---|
| won | 13 | 15 | 15 | 14 | 7 | 7 | 18 | 12 |
| drawn | | | 2 | | | 2 | | 2 |
| lost | 9 | 11 | 5 | 8 | 15 | 13 | 4 | 8 |

### Points

| Season | 97-98 | 98-99 | 99-00 | 00-01 | 01-02 | 02-03 | 03-04 | 04-05 |
|---|---|---|---|---|---|---|---|---|
| scored | 575 | 698 | 690 | 680 | 311 | 385 | 508 | 407 |
| conceded | 455 | 574 | 425 | 430 | 524 | 490 | 311 | 366 |

### Points Difference

| Season | 97-98 | 98-99 | 99-00 | 00-01 | 01-02 | 02-03 | 03-04 | 04-05 |
|---|---|---|---|---|---|---|---|---|
| points | +120 | +124 | +265 | +250 | -213 | -105 | +197 | +41 |

### Total Premiership Record

**Largest win**

➡ **76-13**
vs London Scottish (H)
15.05.99

**Largest defeat**

➡ **12-68**
vs Gloucester (A)
04.05.02

**Most tries scored in a game**

➡ **12**
vs London Scottish (H)
15.05.99

**Most tries conceded in a game**

➡ **9**
vs Gloucester (A)
04.05.02

**Top points scorer**

➡ O.Barkley    632

**Top try scorer**

➡ I.Balshaw    36

**Top drop goal scorer**

➡ C.Malone    18

**Most appearances**

➡ S.Borthwick    126

**Longest winning sequence**

➡ **10 wins** from 22.01.00 to 06.05.00

**Longest losing sequence**

➡ **6 defeats** from 31.10.98 to 02.01.99

# Bath Rugby EFL

## ENHANCED FIXTURE LIST
[does not include play-off data]

### GUINNESS PREMIERSHIP 2005-06 — Premiership History

| Date | Team | H/A | 04-05 | Played | 97-98 | 98-99 | 99-00 | 00-01 | 01-02 | 02-03 | 03-04 | 04-05 | Total Points F | A | Outcome after a half-time lead No. | W | D | L | Close games No. | W |
|---|---|---|---|---|---|---|---|---|---|---|---|---|---|---|---|---|---|---|---|---|
| 04.09.05 | Bristol | A | N/A | 5 | | | | | | | | | 99 | 124 | 2 ▶1 | 1 | - | | 2 | 1 |
| 10.09.05 | Northampton | H | 30-12 | 8 | | | | | | | | | 179 | 118 | 4 ▶4 | - | - | | 1 | - |
| 17.09.05 | Leicester | A | 16-16 | 8 | | | | | | | | | 137 | 237 | 5 ▶1 | 1 | 3 | | 2 | 1 |
| 25.09.05 | Newcastle | A | 5-9 | 8 | | | | | | | | | 134 | 159 | 3 ▶2 | - | 1 | | 7 | 3 |
| 15.10.05 | Gloucester | H | 29-14 | 8 | | | | | | | | | 254 | 106 | 7 ▶7 | - | - | | 2 | 2 |
| 05.11.05 | Irish | A | 19-21 | 8 | | | | | | | | | 274 | 203 | 3 ▶3 | - | - | | 3 | 3 |
| 13.11.05 | Saracens | H | 6-13 | 8 | | | | | | | | | 166 | 160 | 5 ▶3 | - | 2 | | 2 | - |
| 20.11.05 | Wasps | A | 9-12 | 8 | | | | | | | | | 147 | 174 | 3 ▶3 | - | - | | 3 | 2 |
| 25.11.05 | Leeds | H | 6-10 | 4 | | | | | | | | | 71 | 57 | 1 ▶- | - | 1 | | 2 | - |
| 26.12.05 | Worcester | A | 22-26 | 1 | | | | | | | | | 26 | 22 | 1 ▶1 | - | - | | 1 | 1 |
| 02.01.06 | Sale | H | 27-13 | 8 | | | | | | | | | 203 | 130 | 7 ▶7 | - | - | | 4 | 4 |
| 08.01.06 | Leeds | A | 28-30 | 4 | | | | | | | | | 87 | 90 | 1 ▶1 | - | - | | 2 | 1 |
| 28.01.06 | Wasps | H | 16-19 | 8 | | | | | | | | | 193 | 163 | 3 ▶3 | - | - | | 4 | 1 |
| 12.02.06 | Saracens | A | 30-37 | 8 | | | | | | | | | 168 | 200 | 4 ▶4 | - | - | | 1 | 1 |
| 18.02.06 | Irish | H | 27-15 | 8 | | | | | | | | | 211 | 130 | 7 ▶6 | 1 | - | | 3 | 3 |
| 25.02.06 | Gloucester | A | 17-16 | 8 | | | | | | | | | 146 | 215 | 5 ▶2 | - | 3 | | 3 | 2 |
| 11.03.06 | Newcastle | H | 18-33 | 8 | | | | | | | | | 179 | 119 | 4 ▶4 | - | - | | 3 | 2 |
| 25.03.06 | Leicester | H | 6-6 | 8 | | | | | | | | | 113 | 116 | 5 ▶3 | - | 2 | | 2 | - |
| 08.04.06 | Northampton | A | 29-14 | 8 | | | | | | | | | 92 | 188 | 2 ▶1 | - | 1 | | 2 | 1 |
| 15.04.06 | Bristol | H | N/A | 5 | | | | | | | | | 136 | 83 | 3 ▶3 | - | - | | 2 | 2 |
| 28.04.06 | Sale | A | 19-10 | 8 | | | | | | | | | 155 | 186 | 3 ▶1 | - | 2 | | 6 | 3 |
| 06.05.06 | Worcester | H | 18-10 | 1 | | | | | | | | | 18 | 10 | 1 ▶1 | - | - | | - | - |

Legend: ■ won ■ drawn ■ lost ☐ not played

# Club Information

## Useful Information

**Founded**
1865
**Address**
The Recreation Ground
Bath
BA2 6PW
**Capacity**
8,182 (5,740 seated)
**Main switchboard**
01225 325200
**Website**
www.bathrugby.com

## Travel Information

**Car**
(Lambridge Park & Ride):
Leave the M4 at Junction 18 and follow the A46 to Bath. Follow the signs for the town centre. The Park & Ride is at Bath Rugby's training ground on your left after the first set of traffic lights.
The Park & Ride is open for all 1st XV weekend fixtures. To go direct to the stadium, carry on past the training ground until you reach the junction on London Road with Bathwick Street. Turn left and then right down Sydney Place. Go straight on at the roundabout then turn left down North Parade. The ground is on your right.

**Train**
Bath has direct links to London, Bristol, Cardiff, Salisbury and Southampton. From Birmingham and the Midlands, there are connecting services at Bristol Temple Meads. National Rail enquiries: 08457 48 49 50.

**Coach**
National Express services operate between most major towns and cities in Britain.
For further information contact Bath Bus Station on 01225 464446 or National Express direct on 08705 80 80 80 or visit www.nationalexpress.com

# Maps

## Area Map

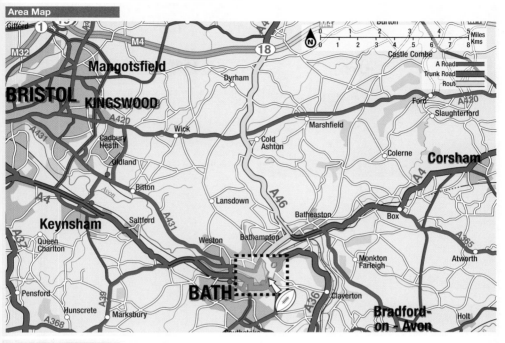

Gifford

M4

M32

M4

**Mangotsfield**

**BRISTOL** **KINGSWOOD**

A420

Wick

Cadbury
Heath

Oldland

Bitton

Avon

Keynsham

Saltford

A4

A431

Queen
Charlton

A37

Pensford

Hunscrete

A368

Marksbury

Dyrham

Cold
Ashton

Lansdown

A46

Weston

Bathampton

BATH

A4

Burton

Castle Combe

Marshfield

Ford

Slaughterford

A420

Colerne

**Corsham**

A4

Batheaston

Box

A365

Monkton
Farleigh

Atworth

Claverton

A36

**Bradford-
on - Avon**

Holt

A Road
Trunk Road
Rout

Miles
Kms

## Local Map

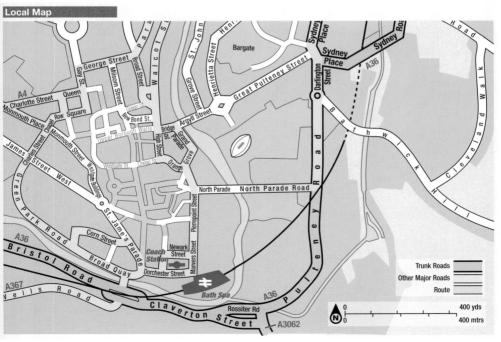

George Street

Gay St

Broad Street

Walcot St

St John

Henrietta Street

Bargate

Sydney
Place

Sydney
Place

Sydney Road

A36

A4

Charlotte Street

Queen

Milsom Street

Grove Street

Great Pulteney Street

Darlington Street

Cleveland Walk

Monmouth Place

Chapel Row Square

Green St

New Bond St.

Argyll Street

Bathwick Hill

James Street West

Charles Street

Monmouth Street

Westgate Buildings

Bridge
St.

High Street

Grand
Parade

Upper Borough Walls

Westgate St.

Cheap St.

Orange Grove

North Parade

North Parade Road

Pulteney Road

Green Park Road

St. James's Parade

Pierrepont Street

A36

Corn Street

Bristol Road

Broad Quay

Coach
Station

Newark
Street

Manvers Street

A367

Wells Road

Dorchester Street

Bath Spa

Claverton Street

Rossiter Rd

A3062

Trunk Roads
Other Major Roads
Route

400 yds
400 mtrs

# Bristol Rugby

## Season Summary

| Position | Won | Drawn | Lost | For | Against | Bonus Points | Total Points |
|---|---|---|---|---|---|---|---|
| **1** | **22** | **0** | **4** | **940** | **355** | **17** | **105** |

A two-year exile from the Premiership has given coaches Richard Hill and Martin Haag the chance to build a squad capable of maintaining their place back in the top flight. Several players with previous Bristol links were key to securing promotion, including Matt Salter, the captain.

Drama in the domestic cup, where they reached the quarter-final, proved they can rise to the big occasion, but in the Premiership Jason Strange and Sean Marsden will need to be as prolific at converting kicks and tries respectively as they were in National One.

**Head Coach:** Richard Hill

**Club Honours**
John Player Cup: 1983

## Season Squad

### Stats 2004-05

| Position | Player | Height | Weight | Apps | Rep | Tries | Points | Position | Player | Height | Weight | Apps | Rep | Tries | Points |
|---|---|---|---|---|---|---|---|---|---|---|---|---|---|---|---|
| FL | R.Bignell | 6'1" | 15st 0lb | - | 1 | - | - | P | M.Irish | 6'0" | 16st 0lb | - | 1 | - | - |
| W/FB | A.Billig | 6'2" | 14st 1lb | 8 | 4 | 2 | 10 | L | O.Kohn | 6'7" | 19st 7lb | 6 | 5 | - | - |
| SH | R.Blake | 5'9" | 12st 7lb | 18 | 2 | 3 | 15 | FB | S.Marsden | 6'0" | 14st 0lb | 24 | - | 21 | 112 |
| BR | J.Brownrigg | 6'6" | 16st 8lb | 23 | 1 | 6 | 30 | SH | H.Martens | 5'10" | 12st 9lb | 8 | 6 | - | - |
| L | D.Bufton | N/A | N/A | - | 1 | - | - | BR | R.Martin-Redman | 6'3" | 17st 0lb | 10 | 5 | 3 | 15 |
| H | N.Clark | 5'11" | 16st 0lb | 5 | 12 | 3 | 15 | FL | C.Morgan | 6'2" | 16st 4lb | 5 | 12 | 1 | 5 |
| P | A.Clarke | 5'11" | 17st 0lb | 19 | 4 | 4 | 20 | W | L.Nabaro | 6'0" | 14st 0lb | 20 | - | 6 | 30 |
| C | M.Contepomi | 6'2" | 14st 2lb | 6 | 1 | 4 | 20 | H | S.Nelson | 5'10" | 14st 9lb | 21 | 2 | 5 | 25 |
| C | S.Cox | 6'0" | 13st 10lb | 15 | 3 | 3 | 15 | SH | G.Nicholls | 5'8" | 12st 0lb | - | 7 | - | - |
| P | D.Crompton | 6'2" | 18st 0lb | 18 | 1 | 4 | 20 | L | E.Pearce | 6'6" | 19st 6lb | 18 | - | 4 | 20 |
| FL | J.El Abd | 6'2" | 16st 0lb | 26 | - | 4 | 20 | C | J.Pritchard | 6'0" | 14st 4lb | 8 | 7 | 2 | 10 |
| W | O.Evans | 5'11" | 13st 5lb | - | 1 | - | - | BR | M.Salter | 6'4" | 16st 4lb | 21 | - | 3 | 15 |
| BR | S.Fox | 5'10" | 14st 0lb | - | 5 | - | - | BR | C.Short | 6'2" | 16st 0lb | 2 | 7 | 1 | 5 |
| FH | D.Gray | 5'10" | 13st 0lb | - | 9 | - | 18 | W | M.Stanojevic | 5'11" | 12st 7lb | 14 | 3 | 11 | 55 |
| C | R.Higgitt | 6'2" | 14st 7lb | 15 | 1 | 7 | 35 | FB | B.Stortoni | 6'1" | 14st 4lb | 18 | - | 13 | 65 |
| P | D.Hilton | 5'11" | 16st 10lb | 12 | 11 | - | - | FH | J.Strange | 5'10" | 13st 3lb | 22 | - | 3 | 287 |
| P | J.Hobson | 5'11" | 17st 0lb | 3 | 5 | 2 | 10 | P | W.Thompson | 6'0" | 16st 3lb | - | 2 | - | - |
| L | O.Hodge | 6'9" | 16st 10lb | 19 | 4 | 1 | 5 | FH | M.Woodrow | 5'7" | 12st 0lb | 4 | 4 | 2 | 53 |
| W | S.Hunt | 6'1" | 15st 0lb | 2 | - | 2 | 10 | | | | | | | | |

## Last Season Form

### Season Progression

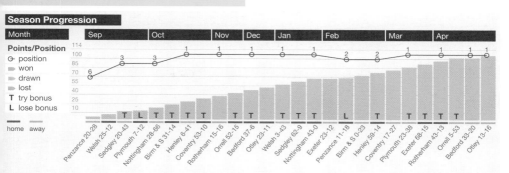

| Month | Sep | Oct | Nov | Dec | Jan | Feb | Mar | Apr |
|---|---|---|---|---|---|---|---|---|

**Points/Position**
- G- position
- won
- drawn
- lost
- T try bonus
- L lose bonus

home  away

### Home Matches

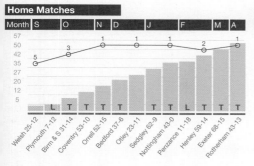

| Month | S | O | N | D | J | F | M | A |
|---|---|---|---|---|---|---|---|---|

### Away Matches

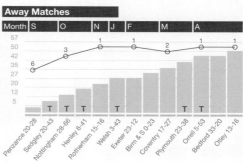

| Month | S | O | N | J | F | M | A |
|---|---|---|---|---|---|---|---|

### Division 1 Statistics

| | Home | Away |
|---|---|---|
| Tries | 66 | 54 |
| Coversions | 53 | 36 |
| Penalty goals | 24 | 28 |
| Drop goals | 2 | 0 |
| Kick % | NA | NA |
| Yellow/Red cards | 5/0 | 9/0 |
| Powerplay tries | 10 | 2 |
| Shorthand tries | 1 | 1 |

Tries: 120
Coversions: 89
Penalty goals: 52
Drop goals: 2
Kick %: NA
Yellow/Red cards: 14/0
Powerplay tries: 12
Shorthand tries: 2

Powerplay tries are scored when your side are playing with a man or more advantage due to yellow or red cards.

Shorthand tries are scored when your side are playing with a man or more fewer due to yellow or red cards.

### Team Performance

| Position | Team | % total points won | % won at home | % won away |
|---|---|---|---|---|
| 1 | **Bristol** | | | |
| 2 | Exeter | | | |
| 3 | Plymouth | | | |
| 4 | Penzance | 40% | 42% | 38% |
| 5 | Otley | | | |
| 6 | Coventry | | | |
| 7 | Bedford | | | |
| 8 | Rotherham | | | |
| 9 | Birm & S | | | |
| 10 | Sedgley | | | |
| 11 | Nottingham | 60% | 58% | 62% |
| 12 | Welsh | | | |
| 13 | Henley | | | |
| 14 | Orrell | | | |

**Bristol Rugby**

## Top Scorer

**Jason Strange**

**Points Facts**

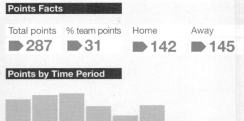

| Total points | % team points | Home | Away |
|---|---|---|---|
| ▶ 287 | ▶ 31 | ▶ 142 | ▶ 145 |

**Points by Time Period**

| 45 | 50 | 52 | 37 | 26 | 38 | 18 | 12 | 9 |
|---|---|---|---|---|---|---|---|---|
| 0 | 10 | 20 | 30 | 40 | 50 | 60 | 70 | 80 Inj. |

## Team Tries and Points

**Tries by Time Period**

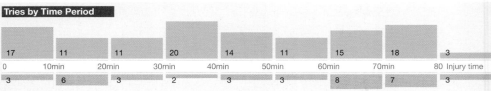

| 17 | 11 | 11 | 20 | 14 | 11 | 15 | 18 | 3 |
|---|---|---|---|---|---|---|---|---|
| 0 | 10min | 20min | 30min | 40min | 50min | 60min | 70min | 80 Injury time |
| 3 | 6 | 3 | 2 | 3 | 3 | 8 | 7 | 3 |

➡ scored
➡ conceded

**Tries by Halves**

➡ scored
➡ conceded

|  | Total | 1st half | 2nd half | 1st half % | 2nd half % |
|---|---|---|---|---|---|
| scored | ▶ 120 | ▶ 59 | ▶ 61 | ▶ 49% | ▶ 51% |
| conceded | ▶ 38 | ▶ 14 | ▶ 24 | ▶ 37% | ▶ 63% |

**How Points were Scored**

➡ tries: 120
➡ conversions: 89
➡ penalty goals: **52**
➡ drop goals: 2

**How Points were Conceded**

➡ tries: 38
➡ conversions: 27
➡ penalty goals: 35
➡ drop goals: 2

**Tries Scored by Player**

➡ backs: 80
➡ forwards: 40

**Tries Conceded by Player**

➡ backs: 28
➡ forwards: 10

**Tries Scored/Conceded Across the Pitch**

N/A

➡ scored
➡ conceded

⊢
⊢

N/A

# Eight-Season Form 1997-2005

## Season Progression

| Season | 97-98 | 98-99 | 99-00 | 00-01 | 01-02 | 02-03 | 03-04 | 04-05 |
|---|---|---|---|---|---|---|---|---|

Points/Position
○ position
■ Premiership
■ Division 1
■ Division 2

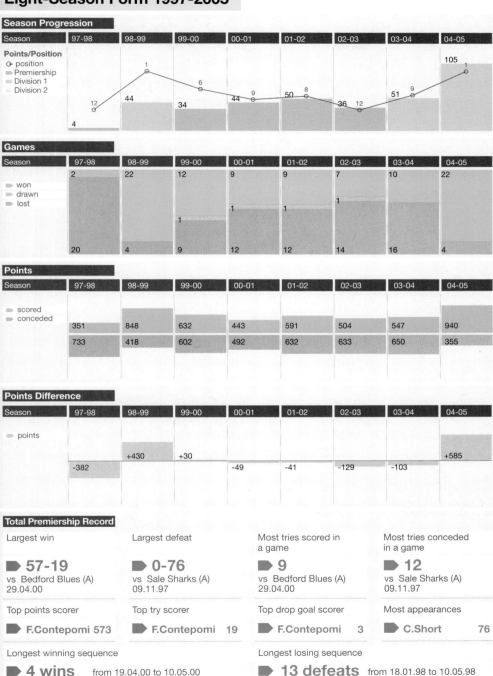

97-98: 4, position 12
98-99: 44, position 1
99-00: 34, position 6
00-01: 44, position 9
01-02: 50, position 8
02-03: 36, position 12
03-04: 51, position 9
04-05: 105, position 1

## Games

| Season | 97-98 | 98-99 | 99-00 | 00-01 | 01-02 | 02-03 | 03-04 | 04-05 |
|---|---|---|---|---|---|---|---|---|

■ won
■ drawn
■ lost

won: 2, 22, 12, 9, 9, 7, 10, 22
drawn: 1 (99-00), 1 (00-01), 1 (01-02), 1 (02-03)
lost: 20, 4, 9, 12, 12, 14, 16, 4

## Points

| Season | 97-98 | 98-99 | 99-00 | 00-01 | 01-02 | 02-03 | 03-04 | 04-05 |
|---|---|---|---|---|---|---|---|---|
| scored | 351 | 848 | 632 | 443 | 591 | 504 | 547 | 940 |
| conceded | 733 | 418 | 602 | 492 | 632 | 633 | 650 | 355 |

## Points Difference

| Season | 97-98 | 98-99 | 99-00 | 00-01 | 01-02 | 02-03 | 03-04 | 04-05 |
|---|---|---|---|---|---|---|---|---|
| points | -382 | +430 | +30 | -49 | -41 | -129 | -103 | +585 |

## Total Premiership Record

**Largest win**
▶ **57-19**
vs Bedford Blues (A)
29.04.00

**Largest defeat**
▶ **0-76**
vs Sale Sharks (A)
09.11.97

**Most tries scored in a game**
▶ **9**
vs Bedford Blues (A)
29.04.00

**Most tries conceded in a game**
▶ **12**
vs Sale Sharks (A)
09.11.97

**Top points scorer**
▶ F.Contepomi 573

**Top try scorer**
▶ F.Contepomi 19

**Top drop goal scorer**
▶ F.Contepomi 3

**Most appearances**
▶ C.Short 76

**Longest winning sequence**
▶ **4 wins** from 19.04.00 to 10.05.00

**Longest losing sequence**
▶ **13 defeats** from 18.01.98 to 10.05.98

# Bristol Rugby EFL

| GUINNESS PREMIERSHIP 2005-06 | | | | Premiership History | | | | | | | | | | Total Points | | Outcome after a half-time lead | | | Close games | |
|---|---|---|---|---|---|---|---|---|---|---|---|---|---|---|---|---|---|---|---|---|
| Date | Team | H/A | 04-05 | Played | 97-98 | 98-99 | 99-00 | 00-01 | 01-02 | 02-03 | 03-04 | 04-05 | | F | A | No. | W | D | L | No. | W |
| | | | | | ■ won | | ▦ drawn | | ■ lost | | ☐ not played | | | | | | | | | | |
| 04.09.05 | Bath | H | N/A | 5 | | | | | | | | | | 124 | 99 | 2 | 2 | - | - | 2 | 1 |
| 11.09.05 | Newcastle | A | N/A | 5 | | | | | | | | | | 110 | 147 | 2 | 2 | - | - | 1 | 1 |
| 18.09.05 | Gloucester | H | N/A | 5 | | | | | | | | | | 117 | 140 | 1 | - | - | 1 | 2 | - |
| 24.09.05 | Irish | A | N/A | 5 | | | | | | | | | | 104 | 164 | - | - | - | - | - | - |
| 16.10.05 | Saracens | H | N/A | 5 | | | | | | | | | | 140 | 163 | 2 | - | - | 2 | 1 | - |
| 04.11.05 | wasps | A | N/A | 5 | | | | | | | | | | 117 | 152 | 2 | 1 | - | 1 | 3 | 1 |
| 13.11.05 | Leeds | H | N/A | 2 | | | | | | | | | | 46 | 46 | 1 | 1 | - | - | 2 | 1 |
| 18.11.05 | Worcester | A | N/A | - | | | | | | | | | | - | - | - | - | - | - | - | - |
| 27.11.05 | Sale | H | N/A | 5 | | | | | | | | | | 106 | 118 | 2 | 2 | - | - | - | - |
| 27.12.05 | Leicester | H | N/A | 5 | | | | | | | | | | 134 | 118 | 3 | 3 | - | - | 4 | 2 |
| 01.01.06 | Northampton | A | N/A | 5 | | | | | | | | | | 77 | 141 | 2 | 1 | - | 1 | 2 | 2 |
| 08.01.06 | Sale | A | N/A | 5 | | | | | | | | | | 127 | 197 | 1 | 1 | - | - | 2 | 1 |
| 28.01.06 | Worcester | H | N/A | - | | | | | | | | | | - | - | - | - | - | - | - | - |
| 10.02.06 | Leeds | A | N/A | 2 | | | | | | | | | | 19 | 49 | - | - | - | - | - | - |
| 19.02.06 | wasps | H | N/A | 5 | | | | | | | | | | 115 | 131 | 3 | 2 | - | 1 | 1 | 1 |
| 26.02.06 | Saracens | A | N/A | 5 | | | | | | | | | | 76 | 135 | - | - | - | - | 2 | 1 |
| 12.03.06 | Irish | H | N/A | 5 | | | | | | | | | | 110 | 124 | 2 | 1 | - | 1 | 2 | 1 |
| 25.03.06 | Gloucester | A | N/A | 5 | | | | | | | | | | 87 | 198 | 3 | - | - | 3 | 1 | - |
| 09.04.06 | Newcastle | H | N/A | 5 | | | | | | | | | | 136 | 102 | 4 | 4 | - | - | - | - |
| 15.04.06 | Bath | A | N/A | 5 | | | | | | | | | | 83 | 136 | 1 | 1 | - | - | 2 | - |
| 30.04.06 | Northampton | H | N/A | 5 | | | | | | | | | | 142 | 133 | 1 | - | - | 1 | 1 | 1 |
| 06.05.06 | Leicester | A | N/A | 5 | | | | | | | | | | 79 | 153 | 1 | - | - | 1 | 2 | - |

# Club Information

## Useful Information

**Founded**
1888
**Address**
The Memorial Stadium
Filton Avenue
Horfield
Bristol
BS7 0AQ
**Stadium capacity**
12,000 (3,000 seated)
**Main switchboard**
0117 952 0500
**Website**
www.bristolrugby.co.uk

## Travel Information

**Car**
From the M4: Exit at junction 19 and follow signs onto the M32. Leave the M32 at junction 2 and at the roundabout turn right towards Horfield and the B4469. Continue for 1.4 miles, then after passing the bus garage (on your right) turn left at the second set of traffic lights into Filton Avenue. Take the first left into the club car park.

From the M5: Exit at junction 16 and join the A38 towards Bristol City Centre. After 5 miles turn left at traffic lights onto B4469. Turn right at the next traffic lights into Filton Avenue and then first left into car park.

**Train**
Nearest mainline rail stations are Bristol Parkway or Bristol Temple Meads.

# Maps

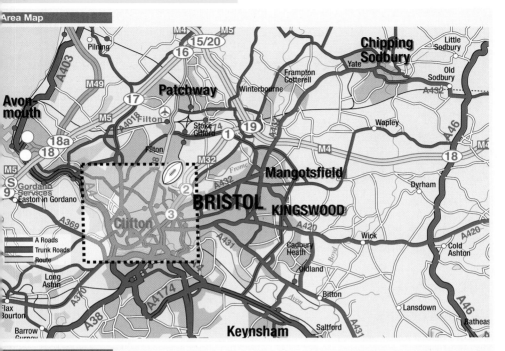

# Gloucester Rugby

## Season Summary

| Position | Won | Drawn | Lost | For | Against | Bonus Points | Total Points |
|---|---|---|---|---|---|---|---|
| **6** | **10** | **1** | **11** | **407** | **487** | **5** | **47** |

Phil Vickery, such a force in the scrum, played his last meaningful league game in February against Bath when he shattered his arm. Cruelly, it was his first game back after recovering from a fractured eye socket. Gloucester needed someone of his ilk to lift them above mid-table mediocrity, and Dean Ryan now in sole charge after Nigel Melville's departure certainly permits no nonsense.

Henry Paul has flourished at club level, if not international, and the incoming Mike Tindall bolsters a back line that, with the likes of James Simpson-Daniel and James Bailey, boasts great speed.

**Head Coach:** Dean Ryan

**Club Honours**
Zurich Premiership: 2002-03 (playoffs won by Wasps)
John Player Cup: 1972, 1978, 1982, 2003

## Season Squad

### Stats 2004-05

| Position | Player | Height | Weight | Apps | Rep | Tries | Points | Position | Player | Height | Weight | Apps | Rep | Tries | Points |
|---|---|---|---|---|---|---|---|---|---|---|---|---|---|---|---|
| FH/SH | S.Amor | 5'7" | 12st 0lb | 3 | 1 | 1 | 25 | W | M.Garvey | 5'8" | 13st 7lb | 18 | - | 6 | 30 |
| H | O.Azam | 6'0" | 18st 0lb | 8 | 4 | 2 | 10 | SH | A.Gomarsall | 5'10" | 14st 4lb | 15 | 1 | 2 | 10 |
| W | J.Bailey | 5'11" | 13st 0lb | 5 | 4 | - | - | FB | J.Goodridge | 6'1" | 13st 8lb | 22 | - | 3 | 15 |
| 8 | A.Balding | 6'2" | 17st 7lb | 18 | 3 | 1 | 5 | FL | A.Hazell | 6'0" | 14st 9lb | 11 | 1 | 1 | 5 |
| P | C.Bezuidenhout | 6'2" | 18st 11lb | 9 | 2 | - | - | W | S.Kiole | 6'6" | 17st 8lb | 11 | 1 | 1 | 5 |
| FL | J.Boer | 6'1" | 16st 8lb | 19 | - | 1 | 5 | C | N.Mauger | 6'0" | 15st 8lb | 6 | 5 | 2 | 10 |
| L | A.Brown | 6'7" | 17st 5lb | 18 | - | 1 | 5 | FH/FB | D.McRae | 5'7" | 12st 10lb | 11 | - | - | 31 |
| BR | P.Buxton | 6'3" | 17st 9lb | 15 | 7 | 1 | 5 | FL | J.Merriman | 6'0" | 14st 7lb | - | 1 | - | - |
| L | M.Cornwell | 6'7" | 18st 2lb | 4 | 4 | - | - | FB | O.Morgan | 6'2" | 14st 0lb | 1 | 1 | 1 | 5 |
| P | N.Currier | 5'11" | 15st 11lb | 2 | 2 | - | - | BR | L.Narraway | 6'3" | 15st 10lb | 2 | 3 | 1 | 5 |
| FH | B.Davies | 5'9" | 14st 1lb | 5 | 2 | - | 20 | SH | A.Page | 5'10" | 13st 3lb | 6 | 3 | - | - |
| H | M.Davies | 5'10" | 15st 0lb | 7 | - | - | - | H | J.Parkes | 5'10" | 15st 6lb | 1 | 1 | 1 | 5 |
| P | S.Emms | 5'11" | 17st 8lb | - | 1 | - | - | C | H.Paul | 5'11" | 14st 10lb | 15 | - | 3 | 136 |
| L | A.Eustace | 6'4" | 17st 0lb | 15 | 4 | 1 | 5 | P | G.Powell | 6'0" | 17st 9lb | 12 | 2 | - | - |
| C | T.Fanolua | 6'0" | 14st 10lb | 20 | - | 6 | 30 | P | T.Sigley | 6'2" | 19st 4lb | 9 | 9 | 1 | 5 |
| 8 | J.Forrester | 6'5" | 15st 9lb | 8 | 9 | 2 | 10 | W/C | J.Simpson-Daniel | 6'0" | 12st 7lb | 14 | - | 3 | 15 |
| H | C.Fortey | 5'11" | 17st 8lb | 5 | 6 | - | - | P | P.Vickery | 6'3" | 18st 4lb | 5 | 2 | - | - |
| W | M.Foster | 6'0" | 14st 4lb | 2 | 1 | - | - | P | N.Wood | 6'1" | 17st 0lb | 8 | 6 | 1 | 5 |

## Last Season Form

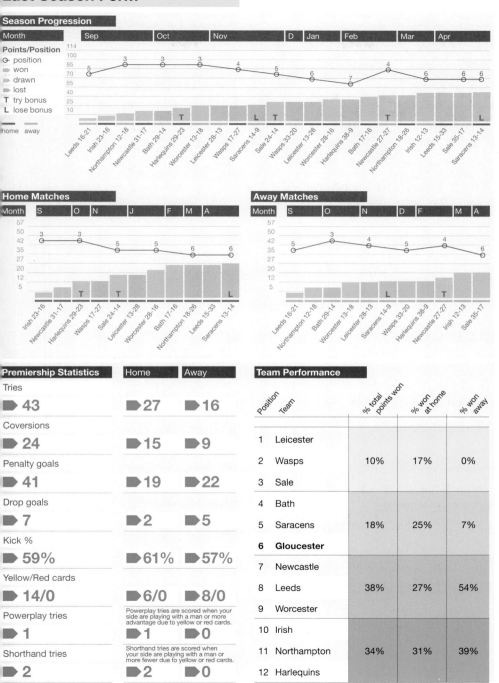

### Season Progression

### Home Matches

### Away Matches

### Premiership Statistics

| | Home | Away |
|---|---|---|
| **Tries** | | |
| 43 | 27 | 16 |
| **Coversions** | | |
| 24 | 15 | 9 |
| **Penalty goals** | | |
| 41 | 19 | 22 |
| **Drop goals** | | |
| 7 | 2 | 5 |
| **Kick %** | | |
| 59% | 61% | 57% |
| **Yellow/Red cards** | | |
| 14/0 | 6/0 | 8/0 |
| **Powerplay tries** | | |
| 1 | 1 | 0 |
| **Shorthand tries** | | |
| 2 | 2 | 0 |

Powerplay tries are scored when your side are playing with a man or more advantage due to yellow or red cards.

Shorthand tries are scored when your side are playing with a man or more fewer due to yellow or red cards.

### Team Performance

| Position | Team | % total points won | % won at home | % won away |
|---|---|---|---|---|
| 1 | Leicester | | | |
| 2 | Wasps | 10% | 17% | 0% |
| 3 | Sale | | | |
| 4 | Bath | | | |
| 5 | Saracens | 18% | 25% | 7% |
| 6 | **Gloucester** | | | |
| 7 | Newcastle | | | |
| 8 | Leeds | 38% | 27% | 54% |
| 9 | Worcester | | | |
| 10 | Irish | | | |
| 11 | Northampton | 34% | 31% | 39% |
| 12 | Harlequins | | | |

# Gloucester Rugby

## Top Scorer

### Henry Paul

### Points Facts

| Total points | % team points | Home | Away |
|---|---|---|---|
| ▶ 136 | ▶ 33 | ▶ 63 | ▶ 73 |

### Points by Time Period

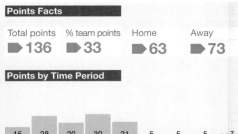

| 15 | 28 | 20 | 30 | 21 | 5 | 5 | 5 | 7 |
|---|---|---|---|---|---|---|---|---|
| 0 | 10 | 20 | 30 | 40 | 50 | 60 | 70 | 80 Inj. |

## Team Tries and Points

### Tries by Time Period

| 1 | 8 | 7 | 4 | 2 | 4 | 4 | 10 | 3 | |
|---|---|---|---|---|---|---|---|---|---|
| 0 | 10min | 20min | 30min | 40min | 50min | 60min | 70min | 80 | Injury time |
| 5 | 7 | 3 | 4 | 5 | 6 | 2 | 9 | 2 | |

➡ scored
➡ conceded

### Tries by Halves

|  | ▶ 43 | ▶ 20 | ▶ 23 | ▶ 47% | ▶ 53% |
|---|---|---|---|---|---|
| ➡ scored | Total | 1st half | 2nd half | 1st half % | 2nd half % |
| ➡ conceded | ▶ 43 | ▶ 19 | ▶ 24 | ▶ 44% | ▶ 56% |

### How Points were Scored

| ➡ tries: | 43 |
|---|---|
| ➡ conversions: | 24 |
| ➡ penalty goals: | 41 |
| drop goals: | 7 |

### How Points were Conceded

| ➡ tries: | 43 |
|---|---|
| ➡ conversions: | 34 |
| ➡ penalty goals: | 67 |
| drop goals: | 1 |

League Best

### Tries Scored by Player

| ➡ backs: | 28 |
|---|---|
| ➡ forwards: | 14 |

### Tries Conceded by Player

| ➡ backs: | 31 |
|---|---|
| ➡ forwards: | 11 |

### Tries Scored/Conceded Across the Pitch

| 3 | 6 | 1 | 3 | - | 1 | 1 | - | 1 | 3 | 5 | 3 | 1 | 1 | 1 | - | 1 | 1 | - | - | 1 | 5 | 3 | 1 |
|---|---|---|---|---|---|---|---|---|---|---|---|---|---|---|---|---|---|---|---|---|---|---|---|

➡ scored
➡ conceded

| 3 | 3 | - | - | 1 | 3 | 2 | - | 1 | - | 2 | 4 | 5 | 1 | 1 | - | 2 | 4 | - | 2 | 1 | 1 | 6 | - |
|---|---|---|---|---|---|---|---|---|---|---|---|---|---|---|---|---|---|---|---|---|---|---|---|

# Eight-Season Form 1997-2005

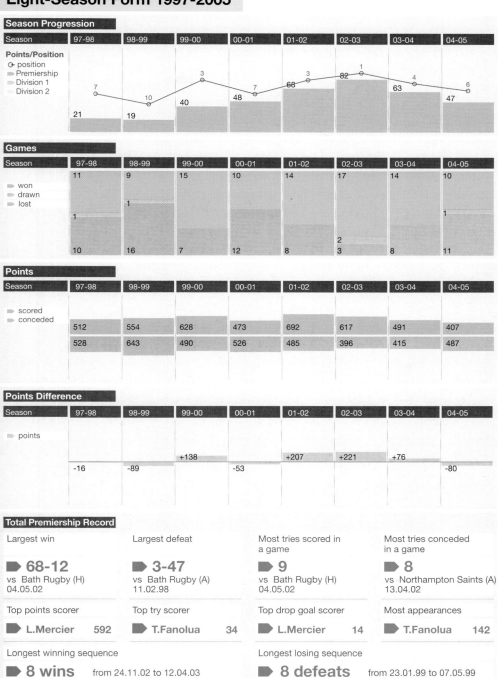

## Season Progression

| Season | 97-98 | 98-99 | 99-00 | 00-01 | 01-02 | 02-03 | 03-04 | 04-05 |
|---|---|---|---|---|---|---|---|---|

**Points/Position**
- position
- Premiership
- Division 1
- Division 2

| | 7 | 10 | 3 | 7 | 3 | 82 | 1 | 4 | 6 |

21 · 19 · 40 · 48 · 68 · 63 · 47

## Games

| Season | 97-98 | 98-99 | 99-00 | 00-01 | 01-02 | 02-03 | 03-04 | 04-05 |
|---|---|---|---|---|---|---|---|---|
| won | 11 | 9 | 15 | 10 | 14 | 17 | 14 | 10 |
| drawn | | 1 | | | | | | |
| lost | 1 | | | | | 2 | | 1 |
| | 10 | 16 | 7 | 12 | 8 | 3 | 8 | 11 |

## Points

| Season | 97-98 | 98-99 | 99-00 | 00-01 | 01-02 | 02-03 | 03-04 | 04-05 |
|---|---|---|---|---|---|---|---|---|
| scored | 512 | 554 | 628 | 473 | 692 | 617 | 491 | 407 |
| conceded | 528 | 643 | 490 | 526 | 485 | 396 | 415 | 487 |

## Points Difference

| Season | 97-98 | 98-99 | 99-00 | 00-01 | 01-02 | 02-03 | 03-04 | 04-05 |
|---|---|---|---|---|---|---|---|---|
| points | -16 | -89 | +138 | -53 | +207 | +221 | +76 | -80 |

## Total Premiership Record

**Largest win**
▶ **68-12**
vs Bath Rugby (H)
04.05.02

**Largest defeat**
▶ **3-47**
vs Bath Rugby (A)
11.02.98

**Most tries scored in a game**
▶ **9**
vs Bath Rugby (H)
04.05.02

**Most tries conceded in a game**
▶ **8**
vs Northampton Saints (A)
13.04.02

**Top points scorer**
▶ L.Mercier 592

**Top try scorer**
▶ T.Fanolua 34

**Top drop goal scorer**
▶ L.Mercier 14

**Most appearances**
▶ T.Fanolua 142

**Longest winning sequence**
▶ **8 wins** from 24.11.02 to 12.04.03

**Longest losing sequence**
▶ **8 defeats** from 23.01.99 to 07.05.99

# Gloucester Rugby `EFL`

## ENHANCED FIXTURE LIST
[does not include play-off data]

**GUINNESS PREMIERSHIP 2005-06** | **Premiership History**

Premiership History bar chart legend: ■ won  ■ drawn  ■ lost  □ not played (years 97-98, 98-99, 99-00, 00-01, 01-02, 02-03, 03-04, 04-05)

| Date | Team | H/A | 04-05 | Played | Total Points F | A | Outcome after a half-time lead No. | W | D | L | Close games No. | W |
|------|------|-----|-------|--------|----|----|-----|---|---|---|-----|---|
| 04.09.05 | Worcester | A | 13-18 | 1 | 18 | 13 | - | - | - | - | 1 | 1 |
| 10.09.05 | Sale | H | 24-14 | 8 | 256 | 134 | 7 | 6 | - | 1 | 1 | - |
| 18.09.05 | Bristol | A | N/A | 5 | 140 | 117 | 4 | 3 | - | 1 | 2 | 2 |
| 24.09.05 | Northampton | H | 18-26 | 8 | 172 | 160 | 3 | 3 | - | - | 2 | 1 |
| 15.10.05 | Bath | A | 29-14 | 8 | 106 | 254 | 1 | - | 1 | - | 2 | - |
| 05.11.05 | Newcastle | H | 31-17 | 8 | 248 | 167 | 5 | 5 | - | - | 3 | 2 |
| 12.11.05 | Leicester | A | 28-13 | 8 | 139 | 204 | 3 | 1 | - | 2 | 3 | - |
| 20.11.05 | Irish | A | 12-13 | 8 | 169 | 206 | 1 | - | - | 1 | 5 | 2 |
| 26.11.05 | Saracens | H | 13-14 | 8 | 227 | 124 | 5 | 5 | - | - | 4 | 3 |
| 26.12.05 | Wasps | A | 33-20 | 8 | 135 | 242 | 1 | - | - | 1 | 3 | - |
| 31.12.05 | Leeds | H | 15-33 | 4 | 125 | 79 | 3 | 3 | - | - | 1 | 1 |
| 08.01.06 | Saracens | A | 14-9 | 8 | 159 | 231 | 2 | 2 | - | - | 3 | 1 |
| 28.01.06 | Irish | H | 23-16 | 8 | 229 | 121 | 5 | 5 | - | - | 4 | 4 |
| 11.02.06 | Leicester | H | 13-28 | 8 | 192 | 151 | 5 | 4 | - | 1 | 2 | 1 |
| 19.02.06 | Newcastle | A | 27-27 | 8 | 176 | 236 | 3 | 1 | 1 | 1 | 3 | 1 |
| 25.02.06 | Bath | H | 17-16 | 8 | 215 | 146 | 3 | 2 | - | 1 | 3 | 1 |
| 11.03.06 | Northampton | A | 12-18 | 8 | 144 | 200 | 4 | 4 | - | - | 3 | 3 |
| 25.03.06 | Bristol | H | N/A | 5 | 198 | 87 | 2 | 2 | - | - | 1 | 1 |
| 07.04.06 | Sale | A | 35-17 | 8 | 200 | 203 | 2 | 2 | - | - | - | - |
| 15.04.06 | Worcester | H | 28-16 | 1 | 28 | 16 | 1 | 1 | - | - | - | - |
| 30.04.06 | Leeds | A | 16-21 | 4 | 112 | 85 | 2 | 2 | - | - | 3 | 1 |
| 06.05.06 | Wasps | H | 17-27 | 8 | 175 | 150 | 6 | 5 | - | 1 | 4 | 3 |

# Club Information

## Useful Information

**Founded**
1873
**Address**
Kingsholm
Kingsholm Road
Gloucester
GL1 3AX
**Capacity**
10,800 (1,498 seated)
**Main switchboard**
01452 381087
**Website**
www.gloucesterrugbyclub.com

## Travel Information

**Car**
From Midlands: From the M5 southbound, exit at junction 11 (Cheltenham south and Gloucester north). Follow A40 to Gloucester/ Ross and Northern Bypass. Turn left at Longford roundabout (where A40 crosses A38) towards the City Centre. Go straight over the Tewkesbury Road roundabout and the ground is on your right after a quarter of a mile.
From South: From the M4 westbound, exit at junction 15 (Swindon) and follow the A419/417 to Gloucester. At Zoons Court roundabout follow the signs A40 to Ross and continue along Northern Bypass until you reach Longford roundabout. The as route for Midlands.
From West Country: Exit the M5 northbound at junction 11A (Gloucester) until you reach Zoons Court roundabout. Then as above. Parking is available approx 5 minutes from the ground. Turn right at the Tewkesbury Road roundabout and follow the signs for the Park and Ride Car Park.
**Train**
Gloucester station is a 5 minute walk from the ground, and is well sign-posted. Virgin Trains, Great Western and Central Trains all serve Gloucester from the Midlands, and there are direct services from all regions.

# Maps

## Area Map

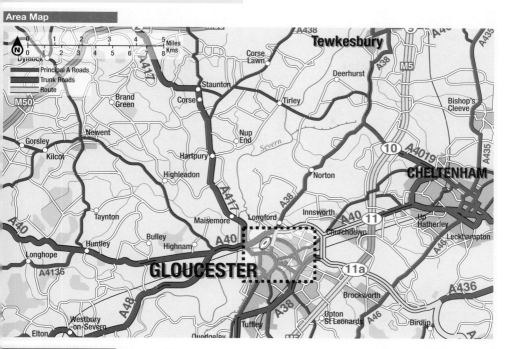

## Local Map

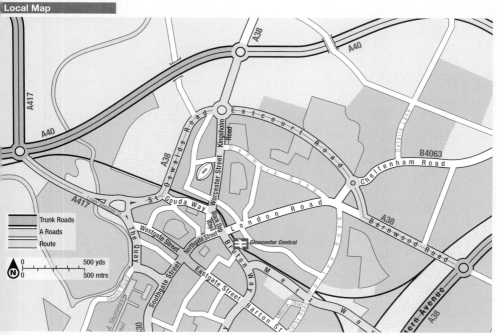

# Leeds Tykes

## Season Summary

| Position | Won | Drawn | Lost | For | Against | Bonus Points | Total Points |
|---|---|---|---|---|---|---|---|
| 8 | 9 | 0 | 13 | 380 | 431 | 7 | 43 |

**Eight points adrift in March, Leeds could have been down and out. But they won their last four matches, beginning with a one-point victory over Leicester, to finish top of the five clubs involved in the relegation dogfight.**

Their triumphant end to the season was capped with winning the domestic cup. Phil Davies, one of the most meticulous coaches in the league, has created an exciting blend of youth – Tom Biggs, Stuart Hooper (captain for 2005-06) et al – and experience – Tim Stimpson, Gordon Ross, inter alia – while former All Black scrum half Justin Marshall will add star quality.

**Director of Rugby:** Phil Davies

**Club Honours**
Powergen Cup: 2005

## Season Squad

### Stats 2004-05

| Position | Player | Height | Weight | Apps | Rep | Tries | Points |
|---|---|---|---|---|---|---|---|
| W | D.Albanese | 5'8" | 12st 4lb | 7 | 3 | 1 | 5 |
| FB | I.Balshaw | 6'0" | 13st 11lb | 8 | 1 | - | 2 |
| C | C.Bell | 6'2" | 14st 9lb | 19 | - | 5 | 25 |
| W | T.Biggs | 5'11" | 12st 4lb | 10 | 6 | 4 | 20 |
| FB | M.Cardey | 6'1" | 13st 10lb | 5 | - | - | - |
| W | P.Christophers | 5'11" | 13st 12lb | 13 | 3 | 2 | 10 |
| P | M.Cusack | 6'0" | 15st 6lb | 1 | 1 | - | - |
| SH | A.Dickens | 5'10" | 12st 9lb | 17 | 2 | - | - |
| W | D.Doherty | 5'11" | 12st 4lb | 2 | - | - | 5 |
| FL | J.Dunbar | 6'5" | 19st 0lb | 11 | 6 | 3 | 15 |
| P | K.Fullman | 5'11" | 17st 0lb | - | 1 | - | - |
| P | R.Gerber | 6'2" | 19st 3lb | 9 | 1 | - | - |
| FH | D.Hodge | 6'0" | 14st 0lb | 1 | - | - | 6 |
| H | M.Holt | 5'11" | 15st 6lb | 2 | 5 | 2 | 10 |
| L | S.Hooper | 6'5" | 16st 7lb | 9 | 2 | - | - |
| 8 | D.Hyde | 6'1" | 15st 0lb | 8 | 4 | 1 | 5 |
| P | G.Kerr | 5'11" | 16st 3lb | 13 | 2 | 2 | 10 |
| P | A.Kershaw | 6'1" | 18st 2lb | - | 1 | - | - |
| P | T.McGee | 6'1" | 16st 7lb | 1 | - | - | - |
| SH | M.McMillan | 5'11" | 13st 11lb | 5 | 3 | - | - |
| FH/C | C.McMullen | 5'11" | 12st 11lb | 2 | 1 | - | - |
| L | S.Morgan | 6'6" | 17st 0lb | 13 | 4 | - | - |
| L | C.Murphy | 6'7" | 17st 3lb | 10 | 8 | - | - |
| L | T.Palmer | 6'6" | 16st 8lb | 17 | - | - | - |
| FL | R.Parks | 6'3" | 16st 5lb | 14 | 2 | 1 | 5 |
| FL | A.Popham | 6'2" | 17st 4lb | 11 | 3 | - | - |
| H | R.Rawlinson | 5'11" | 15st 5lb | 4 | 11 | - | - |
| C | D.Rees | 5'9" | 13st 2lb | 15 | 5 | 2 | 10 |
| H | M.Regan | 5'10" | 15st 2lb | 18 | 3 | 2 | 10 |
| FL | C.Rigney | 6'4" | 17st 10lb | 14 | 3 | - | - |
| FH | G.Ross | 5'8" | 13st 4lb | 15 | 1 | - | 161 |
| P | M.Shelley | 6'2" | 18st 7lb | 18 | - | 2 | 10 |
| C | A.Snyman | 6'2" | 15st 8lb | 21 | - | 6 | 30 |
| FB | T.Stimpson | 6'3" | 16st 8lb | 10 | 3 | 1 | 41 |
| FL | P.Uys | 6'4" | 15st 6lb | 3 | 3 | - | - |
| FH | G.Wright | 5'9" | 14st 7lb | 4 | - | - | - |

## Last Season Form

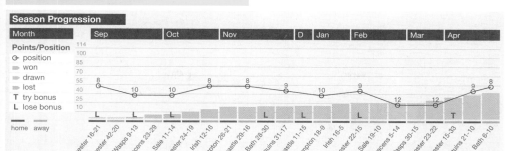

### Season Progression

| Month | Sep | Oct | Nov | D | Jan | Feb | Mar | Apr |
|-------|-----|-----|-----|---|-----|-----|-----|-----|

Points/Position
- G position
- won
- drawn
- lost
- T try bonus
- L lose bonus

home  away

Gloucester 16-21, Leicester 42-20, Wasps 9-13, Saracens 23-29, Sale 11-14, Worcester 24-19, Irish 12-16, Northampton 26-21, Newcastle 29-16, Bath 28-30, Harlequins 31-15, Newcastle 11-15, Northampton 18-9, Irish 16-5, Worcester 22-15, Sale 19-10, Saracens 5-14, Wasps 30-15, Leicester 23-22, Gloucester 15-33, Harlequins 21-10, Bath 6-10

### Home Matches

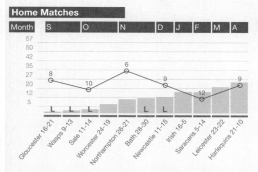

| Month | S | O | N | D | J | F | M | A |
|-------|---|---|---|---|---|---|---|---|

Gloucester 16-21, Wasps 9-13, Sale 11-14, Worcester 24-19, Northampton 26-21, Bath 28-30, Newcastle 11-15, Irish 16-5, Saracens 5-14, Leicester 23-22, Harlequins 21-10

### Away Matches

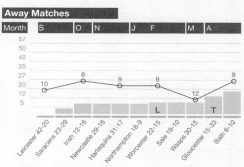

| Month | S | O | N | J | F | M | A |
|-------|---|---|---|---|---|---|---|

Leicester 42-20, Saracens 23-29, Irish 12-16, Newcastle 29-16, Harlequins 31-15, Northampton 18-9, Worcester 22-15, Sale 19-10, Wasps 30-15, Gloucester 15-33, Bath 6-10

### Premiership Statistics

| | Home | Away |
|---|------|------|
| Tries | | |
| 34 | 16 | 18 |
| Coversions | | |
| 24 | 10 | 14 |
| Penalty goals | | |
| 53 | 30 | 23 |
| Drop goals | | |
| 1 | 0 | 1 |
| Kick % | | |
| 69% | 68% | 71% |
| Yellow/Red cards | | |
| 10/0 | 4/0 | 6/0 |
| Powerplay tries | | |
| 4 | 4 | 0 |

Powerplay tries are scored when your side are playing with a man or more advantage due to yellow or red cards.

| Shorthand tries | | |
|---|---|---|
| 1 | 0 | 1 |

Shorthand tries are scored when your side are playing with a man or more fewer due to yellow or red cards.

### Team Performance

| Position | Team | % total points won | % won at home | % won away |
|----------|------|--------------------|---------------|------------|
| 1 | Leicester | | | |
| 2 | Wasps | 13% | 22% | 0% |
| 3 | Sale | | | |
| 4 | Bath | | | |
| 5 | Saracens | 33% | 7% | 70% |
| 6 | Gloucester | | | |
| 7 | Newcastle | | | |
| 8 | **Leeds** | 20% | 27% | 8% |
| 9 | Worcester | | | |
| 10 | Irish | | | |
| 11 | Northampton | 34% | 44% | 22% |
| 12 | Harlequins | | | |

# Leeds Tykes

## Top Scorer

### Points Facts

| Total points | % team points | Home | Away |
|---|---|---|---|
| 161 | 42 | 91 | 70 |

### Points by Time Period

| 24 | 27 | 15 | 31 | 13 | 16 | 14 | 15 | 6 |
|---|---|---|---|---|---|---|---|---|
| 0 | 10 | 20 | 30 | 40 | 50 | 60 | 70 | 80 Inj. |

## Team Tries and Points

### Tries by Time Period

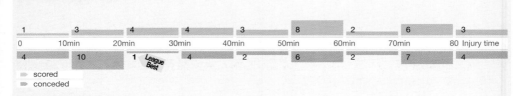

| 1 | 3 | 4 | 4 | 3 | 8 | 2 | 6 | 3 |
|---|---|---|---|---|---|---|---|---|
| 0 | 10min | 20min | 30min | 40min | 50min | 60min | 70min | 80 Injury time |
| 4 | 10 | 1 League Best | 4 | 2 | 6 | 2 | 7 | 4 |

- scored
- conceded

### Tries by Halves

| | scored |
|---|---|

| 34 | 12 | 22 | 35% | 65% |
|---|---|---|---|---|
| Total | 1st half | 2nd half | 1st half % | 2nd half % |
| 40 | 19 | 21 | 48% | 53% |

- scored
- conceded

### How Points were Scored

- tries: 34
- conversions: 24
- penalty goals: 53
- drop goals: 1

### How Points were Conceded

- tries: 40
- conversions: 27
- penalty goals: 49
- drop goals: 10

### Tries Scored by Player

- backs: 21
- forwards: 13

### Tries Conceded by Player

- backs: 22
- forwards: 17

### Tries Scored/Conceded Across the Pitch

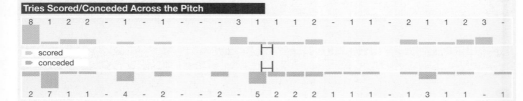

| 8 | 1 | 2 | 2 | - | 1 | - | 1 | - | - | - | 3 | 1 | 1 | 2 | - | 1 | 1 | - | 2 | 1 | 2 | 3 | - |
|---|---|---|---|---|---|---|---|---|---|---|---|---|---|---|---|---|---|---|---|---|---|---|---|

- scored
- conceded

| 2 | 7 | 1 | 1 | - | 4 | - | 2 | - | - | 2 | - | 5 | 2 | 2 | 2 | 1 | 1 | 1 | - | 1 | 3 | 1 | 1 | - | 1 |
|---|---|---|---|---|---|---|---|---|---|---|---|---|---|---|---|---|---|---|---|---|---|---|---|---|---|

## Eight-Season Form 1997-2005

### Season Progression

| Season | 97-98 | 98-99 | 99-00 | 00-01 | 01-02 | 02-03 | 03-04 | 04-05 |
|--------|-------|-------|-------|-------|-------|-------|-------|-------|

**Points/Position**
- ○ position
- ▬ Premiership
- ▬ Division 1
- ▬ Division 2

116

2 — 2 — 1

6

5

12 — 58 — 11 — 8

43 — 28 — 44 — 28 — 37 — 43

### Games

| Season | 97-98 | 98-99 | 99-00 | 00-01 | 01-02 | 02-03 | 03-04 | 04-05 |
|--------|-------|-------|-------|-------|-------|-------|-------|-------|
| won | 21 | 16 | 22 | 24 | 6 | 12 | 7 | 9 |
| drawn | | | | | | | 1 | |
| lost | 1 / 4 | 10 | 4 | 2 | 16 | 2 / 8 | 14 | 13 |

### Points

| Season | 97-98 | 98-99 | 99-00 | 00-01 | 01-02 | 02-03 | 03-04 | 04-05 |
|--------|-------|-------|-------|-------|-------|-------|-------|-------|
| scored | 858 | 713 | 792 | 1032 | 406 | 478 | 449 | 380 |
| conceded | 407 | 367 | 269 | 407 | 654 | 435 | 588 | 431 |

### Points Difference

| Season | 97-98 | 98-99 | 99-00 | 00-01 | 01-02 | 02-03 | 03-04 | 04-05 |
|--------|-------|-------|-------|-------|-------|-------|-------|-------|
| points | +451 | +346 | +523 | +625 | -248 | +43 | -139 | -51 |

### Total Premiership Record

**Largest win**

▶ **41-16**
vs London Irish (H)
08.09.02

**Largest defeat**

▶ **14-64**
vs London Wasps (A)
18.11.01

**Most tries scored in a game**

▶ **6**
vs Saracens (H)
12.10.03

**Most tries conceded in a game**

▶ **8**
vs Gloucester (A)
01.12.01

**Top points scorer**

▶ B.van Straaten 384

**Top try scorer**

▶ D.Scarbrough 27

**Top drop goal scorer**

▶ G.Ross 8

**Most appearances**

▶ M.Shelley 73

**Longest winning sequence**

▶ **4 wins** from 27.03.05 to date

**Longest losing sequence**

▶ **7 defeats** from 16.03.02 to 12.05.02

# Leeds Tykes  EFL

## ENHANCED FIXTURE LIST
[does not include play-off data]

| GUINNESS PREMIERSHIP 2005-06 | | | | Premiership History | | | | | | | | | | | | | | | | |

| Date | Team | H/A | 04-05 | Played | 97-98 | 98-99 | 99-00 | 00-01 | 01-02 | 02-03 | 03-04 | 04-05 | F | A | No. | W | D | L | No. | W |
|---|---|---|---|---|---|---|---|---|---|---|---|---|---|---|---|---|---|---|---|---|
| 03.09.05 | Irish | H | 16-5 | 4 | | | | | | | | | 90 | 66 | 3 | 2 | - | 1 | 2 | - |
| 11.09.05 | Saracens | A | 23-29 | 4 | | | | | | | | | 75 | 76 | 2 | 2 | - | - | 2 | 1 |
| 18.09.05 | Wasps | H | 9-13 | 4 | | | | | | | | | 49 | 70 | 1 | - | - | 1 | 3 | - |
| 25.09.05 | Leicester | H | 23-22 | 4 | | | | | | | | | 125 | 69 | 3 | 3 | - | - | 1 | 1 |
| 14.10.05 | Worcester | A | 22-15 | 1 | | | | | | | | | 15 | 22 | - | - | - | - | 1 | - |
| 05.11.05 | Sale | H | 11-14 | 4 | | | | | | | | | 80 | 121 | 1 | - | 1 | - | 1 | - |
| 13.11.05 | Bristol | A | N/A | 2 | | | | | | | | | 46 | 46 | 1 | 1 | - | - | 2 | 1 |
| 20.11.05 | Northampton | H | 26-21 | 4 | | | | | | | | | 73 | 97 | 3 | 2 | - | 1 | 2 | 2 |
| 25.11.05 | Bath | A | 6-10 | 4 | | | | | | | | | 57 | 71 | 2 | 1 | - | 1 | 2 | 2 |
| 27.12.05 | Newcastle | H | 11-15 | 4 | | | | | | | | | 62 | 81 | 2 | - | 1 | 1 | 2 | - |
| 31.12.05 | Gloucester | A | 15-33 | 4 | | | | | | | | | 79 | 125 | 1 | 1 | - | - | 1 | - |
| 08.01.06 | Bath | H | 28-30 | 4 | | | | | | | | | 90 | 87 | 2 | 1 | - | 1 | 2 | 1 |
| 28.01.06 | Northampton | A | 18-9 | 4 | | | | | | | | | 53 | 128 | - | - | - | - | - | - |
| 10.02.06 | Bristol | H | N/A | 2 | | | | | | | | | 49 | 19 | 2 | 2 | - | - | - | - |
| 17.02.06 | Sale | A | 19-10 | 4 | | | | | | | | | 71 | 123 | - | - | - | - | - | - |
| 24.02.06 | Worcester | H | 24-19 | 1 | | | | | | | | | 24 | 19 | 1 | 1 | - | - | 1 | 1 |
| 11.03.06 | Leicester | A | 42-20 | 4 | | | | | | | | | 58 | 130 | - | - | - | - | - | - |
| 26.03.06 | Wasps | A | 30-15 | 4 | | | | | | | | | 66 | 154 | - | - | - | - | - | - |
| 09.04.06 | Saracens | H | 5-14 | 4 | | | | | | | | | 100 | 77 | 2 | 2 | - | - | - | - |
| 15.04.06 | Irish | A | 12-16 | 4 | | | | | | | | | 72 | 99 | 3 | 2 | - | 1 | 1 | 1 |
| 30.04.06 | Gloucester | H | 16-21 | 4 | | | | | | | | | 85 | 112 | 2 | 2 | - | - | 3 | 2 |
| 06.05.06 | Newcastle | A | 29-16 | 4 | | | | | | | | | 72 | 100 | 1 | - | - | 1 | 2 | 1 |

Total Points: F / A. Outcome after a half-time lead: No. W D L. Close games: No. W.

Legend: ■ won   ■ drawn   ■ lost   □ not played

# Club Information

## Useful Information

**Founded**
1997

**Address**
Headingley Stadium
St Michael's Lane
Headingley
Leeds
LS6 3BR

**Capacity**
23,000 (9,000 seated)

**Main switchboard**
0113 278 6181

**Website**
www.leedsrugby.com

## Travel Information

**Car**
From South:
Take the M62 and exit onto the M621 at junction 27. Continue along the M621 before exiting at junction 2 (signposted Headingly Stadium). Take the A643 (A58) Wetherby Road until you come to a roundabout, then follow the exit for the City Centre/Wetherby. Take the first left towards Ilkley then left again at the traffic lights into Kirkstall Road. Continue until you see Yorkshire Television on the right, and turn right at the traffic lights. Carry on straight ahead, passing another set of traffic lights, and turn left into St Michael's Lane. The stadium is on the right.

**Train**
Leeds City station is in the City Centre, and is on the Eastcoast Rail Network. Headingly and Burley stations are approx 5 minutes away from the stadium.

**Air**
Leeds and Bradford International Airport is located in the north of the city, and is served by most major European airports.

# Maps

## Area Map

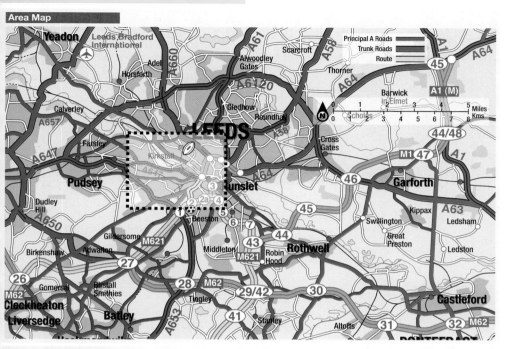

## Local Map

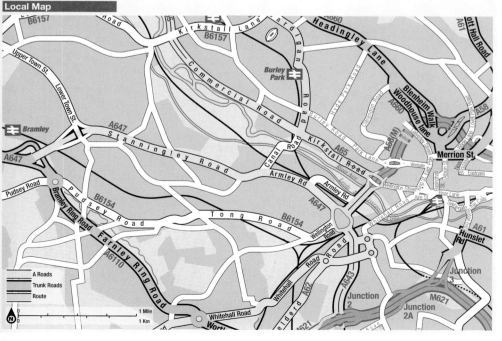

# Leicester Tigers

## Season Summary

| Position | Won | Drawn | Lost | For | Against | Bonus Points | Total Points |
|---|---|---|---|---|---|---|---|
| **1** | **15** | **3** | **4** | **665** | **323** | **12** | **78** |

**Despite helping Leicester to finish top of the league, Martin Johnson and Neil Back bowed out without securing any silverware. But the hard-nosed club have no complaints, after being soundly beaten by Wasps in the Championship Final, and are nevertheless one of the best squads in terms of depth, talent, skill and ambition. International call-ups seem not to harm their league progress.**

Pat Howard takes over from John Wells as Head Coach, while the grit of captain Martin Corry and Back's coaching input will be important.

**Head Coach:** Pat Howard

**Club Honours**
Courage League / Allied Dunbar Premiership / Zurich Premiership: 1987-88, 1994-95, 1998-99 1999-2000, 2000-01, 2001-02, 2004-05 (lost in play-offs)

John Player Cup / Pilkington Cup: 1979, 1980, 1981, 1993, 1997
Heineken Cup: 2000-01 2001-02

## Season Squad

### Stats 2004-05

| Position | Player | Height | Weight | Apps | Rep | Tries | Points | Position | Player | Height | Weight | Apps | Rep | Tries | Points |
|---|---|---|---|---|---|---|---|---|---|---|---|---|---|---|---|
| FL/H | L.Abraham | 6'2" | 16st 5lb | - | 3 | 1 | 5 | BR | W.Johnson | 6'4" | 17st 0lb | 11 | 8 | 1 | 5 |
| FL | N.Back | 5'10" | 14st 8lb | 20 | 1 | 7 | 35 | L | B.Kay | 6'6" | 17st 9lb | 9 | 3 | - | - |
| SH | S.Bemand | 5'11" | 13st 5lb | 11 | 6 | 2 | 10 | W/C | L.Lloyd | 6'4" | 15st 2lb | 9 | 1 | 6 | 30 |
| FH | R.Broadfoot | 5'11" | 13st 2lb | 3 | 4 | - | 24 | L/BR | D.Montagu | 6'4" | 16st 7lb | - | 1 | - | - |
| H | J.Buckland | 5'11" | 16st 11lb | 4 | 13 | - | - | FL | L.Moody | 6'3" | 16st 8lb | 3 | 4 | 1 | 5 |
| H | G.Chuter | 5'10" | 15st 12lb | 18 | 1 | 1 | 5 | P | D.Morris | 6'1" | 19st 10lb | 16 | 4 | - | - |
| H | R.Cockerill | 5'10" | 16st 13lb | 1 | 2 | - | - | FB/W | G.Murphy | 6'1" | 13st 3lb | 15 | 1 | 5 | 35 |
| C/FB | M.Cornwell | 6'1" | 14st 2lb | 2 | 6 | - | - | P | C.Noon | 5'11" | 18st 3lb | - | 1 | - | - |
| FL | M.Corry | 6'5" | 17st 10lb | 14 | - | 2 | 10 | C/W | S.Rabeni | 6'2" | 15st 0lb | 10 | 2 | 6 | 30 |
| FL | B.Deacon | 6'4" | 17st 0lb | 9 | 6 | 1 | 5 | P | J.Rawson | 5'9" | 16st 2lb | - | 4 | - | - |
| L | L.Deacon | 6'5" | 17st 10lb | 16 | 2 | - | - | P | G.Rowntree | 6'0" | 17st 3lb | 11 | 3 | - | - |
| SH | H.Ellis | 5'10" | 13st 4lb | 12 | 4 | 5 | 25 | FL | W.Skinner | 5'11" | 14st 2lb | 1 | 1 | - | - |
| C | D.Gibson | 5'11" | 15st 6lb | 19 | 1 | 5 | 25 | C/W | O.Smith | 6'1" | 14st 7lb | 14 | 3 | 4 | 20 |
| FH | A.Goode | 5'11" | 13st 9lb | 18 | - | 3 | **268** League Best | H | E.Taukafa | 5'11" | 17st 0lb | - | 1 | - | - |
| L | J.Hamilton | 6'8" | 19st 4lb | 1 | 1 | - | - | W/C | A.Tuilagi | 6'1" | 17st 7lb | 3 | 9 | 4 | 20 |
| UB | A.Healey | 5'10" | 13st 9lb | 14 | 1 | 6 | 33 | BR/8 | H.Tuilagi | 6'1" | 18st 10lb | 9 | 7 | 3 | 15 |
| C | D.Hipkiss | 5'10" | 14st 2lb | 3 | 4 | 2 | 10 | W | T.Varndell | 6'3" | 14st 13lb | 6 | 1 | 6 | 30 |
| P | M.Holford | 5'11" | 16st 1lb | 6 | 2 | - | - | FH/FB | S.Vesty | 6'0" | 14st 2lb | 15 | 2 | - | 9 |
| W | J.Holtby | 6'3" | 15st 11lb | 7 | 1 | - | - | FH | R.Warren | 5'11" | 13st 5lb | - | 1 | - | - |
| L | M.Johnson | 6'7" | 18st 9lb | 22 | - | 2 | 10 | P | J.White | 6'1" | 18st 0lb | 13 | 2 | - | - |

# Last Season Form

## Season Progression

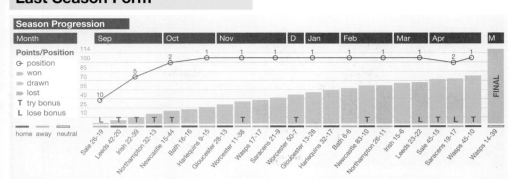

| Month | Sep | Oct | Nov | D | Jan | Feb | Mar | Apr | M |
|---|---|---|---|---|---|---|---|---|---|

Points/Position
- G position
- won
- drawn
- lost
- T try bonus
- L lose bonus

home  away  neutral

Sale 26-19, Leeds 42-20, Irish 22-39, Northampton 32-13, Newcastle 15-44, Bath 16-16, Harlequins 9-15, Gloucester 28-13, Worcester 11-38, Wasps 17-17, Saracens 21-9, Worcester 50-7, Gloucester 13-28, Harlequins 32-17, Bath 6-6, Newcastle 83-10, Northampton 26-11, Irish 15-6, Leeds 23-22, Sale 45-15, Saracens 19-17, Wasps 45-10, Wasps 14-39

FINAL

## Home Matches

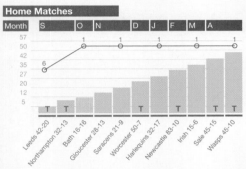

| Month | S | O | N | D | J | F | M | A |
|---|---|---|---|---|---|---|---|---|

Leeds 42-20, Northampton 32-13, Bath 16-16, Gloucester 28-13, Saracens 21-9, Worcester 50-7, Harlequins 32-17, Newcastle 83-10, Irish 15-6, Sale 45-15, Wasps 45-10

## Away Matches

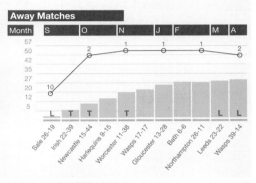

| Month | S | O | N | J | F | M | A |
|---|---|---|---|---|---|---|---|

Sale 26-19, Irish 22-39, Newcastle 15-44, Harlequins 9-15, Worcester 11-38, Wasps 17-17, Gloucester 13-28, Bath 6-6, Northampton 26-11, Leeds 23-22, Wasps 39-14

## Premiership Stats

| | Home | Away | Neutral |
|---|---|---|---|
| Tries | | | |
| 76 | 49 | 26 | 1 |
| Coversions | | | |
| 58 | 40 | 18 | 0 |
| Penalty goals | | | |
| 54 | 26 | 25 | 3 |
| Drop goals | | | |
| 7 | 2 | 5 | 0 |
| Kick % | | | |
| 72% | 79% | 65% | 60% |
| Yellow/Red cards | | | |
| 14/1 | 4/0 | 10/1 | 0/0 |
| Powerplay tries | Powerplay tries are scored when your side are playing with a man or more advantage due to yellow or red cards. | | |
| 0 | 0 | 0 | 0 |
| Shorthand tries | Shorthand tries are scored when your side are playing with a man or more fewer due to yellow or red cards. | | |
| 1 | 0 | 1 | 0 |

## Team Performance

| Position | Team | % total points won | % won at home | % won away |
|---|---|---|---|---|
| 1 | **Leicester** | | | |
| 2 | Wasps | 23% | 28% | 14% |
| 3 | Sale | | | |
| 4 | Bath | | | |
| 5 | Saracens | 20% | 19% | 22% |
| 6 | Gloucester | | | |
| 7 | Newcastle | | | |
| 8 | Leeds | 31% | 28% | 35% |
| 9 | Worcester | | | |
| 10 | Irish | | | |
| 11 | Northampton | 26% | 25% | 29% |
| 12 | Harlequins | | | |

# Leicester Tigers

## Top Scorer

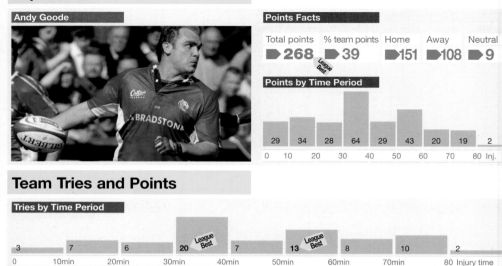

### Points Facts

| | Total points | % team points | Home | Away | Neutral |
|---|---|---|---|---|---|
| | 268 | 39 | 151 | 108 | 9 |

*League Best*

### Points by Time Period

| 29 | 34 | 28 | 64 | 29 | 43 | 20 | 19 | 2 |
|---|---|---|---|---|---|---|---|---|
| 0 | 10 | 20 | 30 | 40 | 50 | 60 | 70 | 80 Inj. |

## Team Tries and Points

### Tries by Time Period

| 3 | 7 | 6 | 20 | 7 | 13 | 8 | 10 | 2 |
|---|---|---|---|---|---|---|---|---|

*League Best (20)*, *League Best (13)*

| 0 | 10min | 20min | 30min | 40min | 50min | 60min | 70min | 80 Injury time |
|---|---|---|---|---|---|---|---|---|

| 7 | 6 | 1 | 2 | 1 | 2 | 4 | 5 | 2 |
|---|---|---|---|---|---|---|---|---|

*League Best (1)*, *League Best (2)*, *League Best (1)*, *League Best (2)*

 scored
conceded

### Tries by Halves

| | Total | 1st half | 2nd half | 1st half % | 2nd half % |
|---|---|---|---|---|---|
| scored | 76 | 36 | 40 | 47% | 53% |
| conceded | 30 | 16 | 14 | 53% | 47% |

*League Best* (76, 36, 40, 30, 16, 14)

### How Points were Scored

| | | |
|---|---|---|
| tries: | 75 | *League Best* |
| conversions: | 58 | *League Best* |
| penalty goals: | 51 | |
| drop goals: | 7 | |

### How Points were Conceded

| | | |
|---|---|---|
| tries: | 27 | *League Best* |
| conversions: | 16 | *League Best* |
| penalty goals: | 49 | |
| drop goals: | 3 | |

### Tries Scored by Player

| | | |
|---|---|---|
| backs: | 54 | *League Best* |
| forwards: | 19 | |

### Tries Conceded by Player

| | | |
|---|---|---|
| backs: | 25 | |
| forwards: | 4 | *League Best* |

### Tries Scored/Conceded Across the Pitch

scored: 8 6 1 2 1 4 3 1 1 - 1 1 10 3 1 1 1 1 3 4 2 3 4 3 6 4

conceded: 1 1 2 2 2 - - - - 1 - 3 2 1 - 1 - 1 - 1 1 1 6 1

## Eight-Season Form 1997-2005

### Season Progression

| Season | 97-98 | 98-99 | 99-00 | 00-01 | 01-02 | 02-03 | 03-04 | 04-05 |
|---|---|---|---|---|---|---|---|---|

Points/Position
- ○ position
- ▬ Premiership
- ▬ Division 1
- ▬ Division 2

| position | 4 | 1 | 1 | 1 | 1 | 6 | 5 | 1 |
| points | 26 | 44 | 51 | 82 | 83 | 55 | 55 | 78 |

### Games

| Season | 97-98 | 98-99 | 99-00 | 00-01 | 01-02 | 02-03 | 03-04 | 04-05 |
|---|---|---|---|---|---|---|---|---|
| won | 12 | 22 | 18 | 18 | 18 | 12 | 11 | 15 |
| drawn | 2 | | 1 | 1 | | | 3 | 3 |
| lost | 8 | 4 | 3 | 3 | 4 | 10 | 8 | 4 |

### Points

| Season | 97-98 | 98-99 | 99-00 | 00-01 | 01-02 | 02-03 | 03-04 | 04-05 |
|---|---|---|---|---|---|---|---|---|
| scored | 569 | 771 | 687 | 571 | 658 | 448 | 537 | 665 |
| conceded | 449 | 423 | 425 | 346 | 349 | 396 | 430 | 323 |

### Points Difference

| Season | 97-98 | 98-99 | 99-00 | 00-01 | 01-02 | 02-03 | 03-04 | 04-05 |
|---|---|---|---|---|---|---|---|---|
| points | +120 | +348 | +262 | +225 | +309 | +52 | +107 | +342 |

### Total Premiership Record

| Largest win | Largest defeat | Most tries scored in a game | Most tries conceded in a game |
|---|---|---|---|
| ▶ **83-10** | ▶ **6-34** | ▶ **12** | ▶ **6** |
| vs Newcastle Falcons (H) 19.02.05 | vs Gloucester (A) 01.10.99 | vs West Hartlepool (H) 16.05.99 | vs Northampton Saints (A) 11.09.99 |

| Top points scorer | Top try scorer | Top drop goal scorer | Most appearances |
|---|---|---|---|
| ▶ T.Stimpson 1180 | ▶ N.Back 59 | ▶ A.Goode 14 | ▶ M.Johnson 139 |

| Longest winning sequence | Longest losing sequence |
|---|---|
| ▶ **17 wins** from 26.12.99 to 06.09.00 | ▶ **5 defeats** from 04.10.03 to 01.11.03 |

# Leicester Tigers EFL

## GUINNESS PREMIERSHIP 2005-06 — Premiership History

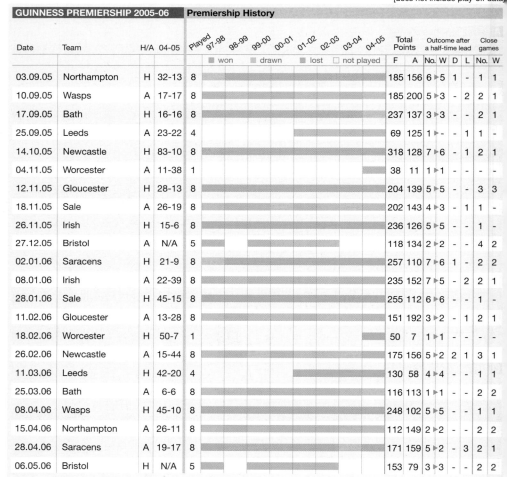

| Date | Team | H/A | 04-05 | Played | F | A | No. | W | D | L | No. | W |
|------|------|-----|-------|--------|---|---|-----|---|---|---|-----|---|
| 03.09.05 | Northampton | H | 32-13 | 8 | 185 | 156 | 6 | ►5 | 1 | - | 1 | 1 |
| 10.09.05 | Wasps | A | 17-17 | 8 | 185 | 200 | 5 | ►3 | - | 2 | 2 | 1 |
| 17.09.05 | Bath | H | 16-16 | 8 | 237 | 137 | 3 | ►3 | - | - | 2 | 1 |
| 25.09.05 | Leeds | A | 23-22 | 4 | 69 | 125 | 1 | ►- | - | 1 | 1 | - |
| 14.10.05 | Newcastle | H | 83-10 | 8 | 318 | 128 | 7 | ►6 | - | 1 | 2 | 1 |
| 04.11.05 | Worcester | A | 11-38 | 1 | 38 | 11 | 1 | ►1 | - | - | - | - |
| 12.11.05 | Gloucester | H | 28-13 | 8 | 204 | 139 | 5 | ►5 | - | - | 3 | 3 |
| 18.11.05 | Sale | A | 26-19 | 8 | 202 | 143 | 4 | ►3 | - | 1 | 1 | - |
| 26.11.05 | Irish | H | 15-6 | 8 | 236 | 126 | 5 | ►5 | - | - | 1 | - |
| 27.12.05 | Bristol | A | N/A | 5 | 118 | 134 | 2 | ►2 | - | - | 4 | 2 |
| 02.01.06 | Saracens | H | 21-9 | 8 | 257 | 110 | 7 | ►6 | 1 | - | 2 | 2 |
| 08.01.06 | Irish | A | 22-39 | 8 | 235 | 152 | 7 | ►5 | - | 2 | 2 | 1 |
| 28.01.06 | Sale | H | 45-15 | 8 | 255 | 112 | 6 | ►6 | - | - | 1 | - |
| 11.02.06 | Gloucester | A | 13-28 | 8 | 151 | 192 | 3 | ►2 | - | 1 | 2 | 1 |
| 18.02.06 | Worcester | H | 50-7 | 1 | 50 | 7 | 1 | ►1 | - | - | - | - |
| 26.02.06 | Newcastle | A | 15-44 | 8 | 175 | 156 | 5 | ►2 | 2 | 1 | 3 | 1 |
| 11.03.06 | Leeds | H | 42-20 | 4 | 130 | 58 | 4 | ►4 | - | - | 1 | 1 |
| 25.03.06 | Bath | A | 6-6 | 8 | 116 | 113 | 1 | ►1 | - | - | 2 | 2 |
| 08.04.06 | Wasps | H | 45-10 | 8 | 248 | 102 | 5 | ►5 | - | - | 1 | 1 |
| 15.04.06 | Northampton | A | 26-11 | 8 | 112 | 149 | 2 | ►2 | - | - | 2 | 2 |
| 28.04.06 | Saracens | A | 19-17 | 8 | 171 | 159 | 5 | ►2 | - | 3 | 2 | 1 |
| 06.05.06 | Bristol | H | N/A | 5 | 153 | 79 | 3 | ►3 | - | - | 2 | 2 |

Premiership History columns: Played | 97-98 | 98-99 | 99-00 | 00-01 | 01-02 | 02-03 | 03-04 | 04-05 | Total Points (F, A) | Outcome after a half-time lead (No. W D L) | Close games (No. W)

Legend: ■ won   ■ drawn   ■ lost   □ not played

# Club Information

## Useful Information

**Founded**
1880
**Address**
Welford Road Stadium
Aylestone Road
Leicester LE2 7TR
**Capacity**
16,000 (12,411 seated)
**Main switchboard**
08701 28 34 30
**Website**
www.leicestertigers.com

## Travel Information

**Car**
From M1 (North and South) and M69 (East): Exit the motorway at Junction 21 (M1). Follow the signs for the city centre via Narborough Road (A5460). After 3 miles, at the crossroad junction with Upperton Road, turn right. The stadium is 1/2 mile ahead (past Leicester City Football ground on the right).
From A6 (South): Follow the signs for the city centre, coming in via London Road. At the main set of lights opposite the entrance to the railway station (on the right), turn left onto the Waterloo Way. The stadium is 1/2 mile further on.
From A47 (East): Follow the signs for the city centre, coming in via Uppingham Road. At the St Georges Retail Park roundabout, take the second exit into St Georges Way (A594). Carry on past the Leicester Mercury offices on the right, and then filter off right into Waterloo Way just before the Railway Station. The stadium is 1/2 mile further on.

**Train**
Leicester Station is a ten minute walk away, along Waterloo Way.

## Maps

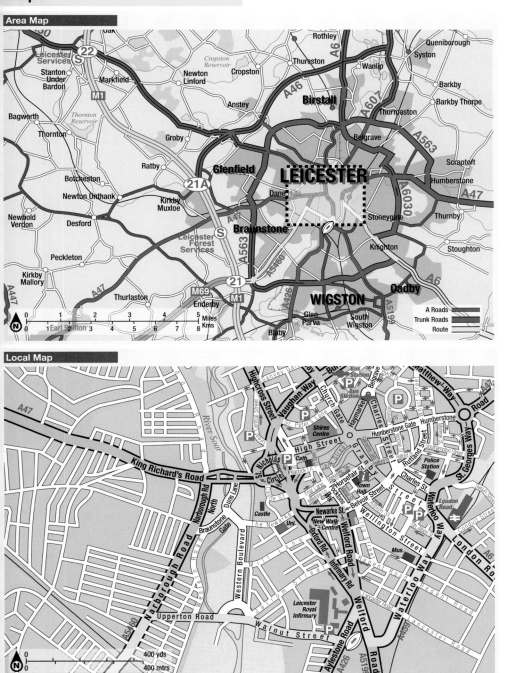

# London Irish

## Season Summary

| Position | Won | Drawn | Lost | For | Against | Bonus Points | Total Points |
|----------|-----|-------|------|-----|---------|--------------|--------------|
| 10 | 8 | 0 | 14 | 378 | 421 | 8 | 40 |

**It is an extraordinary fact that Irish failed to win at home from January onwards. Despite the solid platform created by forwards such as Bob Casey and Nick Kennedy – so handy in the lineout – they repeatedly failed to find the try line, as their total of 28 in the league illustrates.**

Director of Rugby Gary Gold grew frustrated at their inability to produce the goods on match day. His replacement Brian Smith has recruited sensibly to try to give more back-up to the thin squad of 2004-05.

**Director of Rugby:** Brian Smith

**Club Honours**
Powergen Cup: 2002

## Season Squad

### Stats 2004-05

| Position | Player | Height | Weight | Apps | Rep | Tries | Points | Position | Player | Height | Weight | Apps | Rep | Tries | Points |
|----------|--------|--------|--------|------|-----|-------|--------|----------|--------|--------|--------|------|-----|-------|--------|
| C | G.Appleford | 6'3" | 14st 13lb | 13 | 1 | 2 | 10 | FB | M.Horak | 6'3" | 14st 6lb | 15 | 1 | 2 | 10 |
| W/FB | D.Armitage | 6'1" | 12st 8lb | 14 | 1 | 4 | 22 | L | N.Kennedy | 6'8" | 17st 10lb | 14 | 7 | - | - |
| W/C | J.Bishop | 6'1" | 13st 10lb | 15 | - | 2 | 10 | FH | M.Mapletoft | 5'7" | 14st 1lb | 10 | 6 | 2 | 99 |
| L | B.Casey | 6'7" | 19st 3lb | 21 | - | 1 | 5 | C | N.Mordt | 6'1" | 14st 12lb | 7 | 9 | - | - |
| C/FH | M.Catt | 5'10" | 13st 8lb | 16 | - | 1 | 7 | 8 | P.Murphy | 6'5" | 17st 3lb | 12 | 5 | - | - |
| BR | D.Danaher | 6'4" | 16st 3lb | 9 | 8 | - | - | H | D.Paice | 6'1" | 15st 12lb | 3 | 2 | - | - |
| FL | K.Dawson | 6'1" | 15st 3lb | 18 | - | 1 | 5 | C | R.Penney | 6'0" | 14st 7lb | 4 | - | 1 | 5 |
| P | P.Durant | 6'1" | 18st 2lb | 1 | 8 | - | - | BR | R.Reid | 6'4" | 16st 12lb | 6 | 7 | 1 | 5 |
| SH | D.Edwards | 5'8" | 12st 9lb | 9 | 7 | - | - | L/BR | K.Roche | 6'7" | 18st 2lb | 4 | 7 | - | - |
| FH | B.Everitt | 5'9" | 12st 13lb | 12 | 7 | - | 145 | H | R.Russell | 5'10" | 15st 4lb | 10 | 3 | - | - |
| H | A.Flavin | 5'10" | 16st 7lb | 8 | 1 | - | - | W | P.Sackey | 6'2" | 13st 10lb | 6 | - | 1 | 5 |
| BR | P.Gustard | 6'4" | 17st 0lb | 15 | - | - | - | W | D.Shabbo | N/A | N/A | 1 | - | - | - |
| P | A.Halsey | 6'0" | 17st 8lb | - | 2 | - | - | W/FB | S.Staniforth | 6'2" | 15st 11lb | 19 | - | 7 | 35 |
| P | R.Hardwick | 5'11" | 18st 10lb | 21 | - | - | - | L | R.Strudwick | 6'5" | 17st 0lb | 11 | 11 | 2 | 10 |
| P | N.Hatley | 6'1" | 18st 11lb | 19 | - | - | - | H | J.Van der Walt | 6'0" | 16st 2lb | 1 | 3 | - | - |
| SH | P.Hodgson | 5'8" | 12st 9lb | 13 | 8 | 1 | 5 | P | D.Wheatley | 6'2" | 18st 12lb | 3 | 7 | - | - |

## Last Season Form

### Season Progression

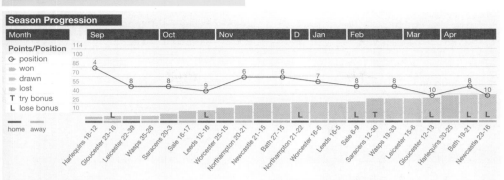

### Home Matches

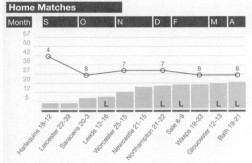

### Away Matches

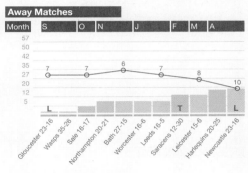

### Premiership Statistics

| | Home | Away |
|---|---|---|
| **Tries** | | |
| 28 | 11 | 17 |
| **Coversions** | | |
| 17 | 7 | 10 |
| **Penalty goals** | | |
| 63 | 37 | 26 |
| **Drop goals** | | |
| 5 | 5 | 0 |
| **Kick %** | | |
| 71% | 70% | 72% |
| **Yellow/Red cards** | | |
| 7/0 | 4/0 | 3/0 |
| **Powerplay tries** | | |
| 2 | 1 | 1 |
| **Shorthand tries** | | |
| 1 | 1 | 0 |

Powerplay tries are scored when your side are playing with a man or more advantage due to yellow or red cards.

Shorthand tries are scored when your side are playing with a man or more fewer due to yellow or red cards.

### Team Performance

| Position | Team | % total points won | % won at home | % won away |
|---|---|---|---|---|
| 1 | Leicester | | | |
| 2 | Wasps | 11% | 4% | 17% |
| 3 | Sale | | | |
| 4 | Bath | | | |
| 5 | Saracens | 26% | 26% | 26% |
| 6 | Gloucester | | | |
| 7 | Newcastle | | | |
| 8 | Leeds | 22% | 38% | 4% |
| 9 | Worcester | | | |
| 10 | **Irish** | | | |
| 11 | Northampton | 41% | 32% | 53% |
| 12 | Harlequins | | | |

# London Irish

## Top Scorer

**Barry Everitt**

**Points Facts**

| Total points | % team points | Home | Away |
|---|---|---|---|
| ▶ 145 | ▶ 38 | ▶ 71 | ▶ 74 |

**Points by Time Period**

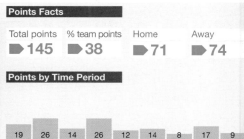

| 19 | 26 | 14 | 26 | 12 | 14 | 8 | 17 | 9 |
|---|---|---|---|---|---|---|---|---|
| 0 | 10 | 20 | 30 | 40 | 50 | 60 | 70 | 80 Inj. |

## Team Tries and Points

**Tries by Time Period**

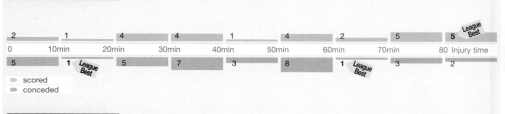

| 2 | | 1 | | 4 | | 4 | | 1 | | 4 | | 2 | | 5 | | 5 League Best |
|---|---|---|---|---|---|---|---|---|---|---|---|---|---|---|---|---|
| 0 | 10min | 20min | 30min | 40min | 50min | 60min | 70min | 80 Injury time |

| 5 | 1 League Best | 5 | 7 | 3 | 8 | 1 League Best | 3 | 2 |
|---|---|---|---|---|---|---|---|---|

▶ scored
▶ conceded

**Tries by Halves**

▶ scored
▶ conceded

| | Total | 1st half | 2nd half | 1st half % | 2nd half % |
|---|---|---|---|---|---|
| ▶ | ▶ 28 | ▶ 11 | ▶ 17 | ▶ 39% | ▶ 61% |
| ▶ | ▶ 35 | ▶ 18 | ▶ 17 | ▶ 51% | ▶ 49% |

**How Points were Scored**

| ▶ tries: | 28 |
|---|---|
| ▶ conversions: | 17 |
| ▶ penalty goals: | 63 |
| drop goals: | 5 |

**How Points were Conceded**

| ▶ tries: | 35 |
|---|---|
| ▶ conversions: | 21 |
| ▶ penalty goals: | 62 |
| drop goals: | 6 |

**Tries Scored by Player**

| ▶ backs: | 23 |
|---|---|
| ▶ forwards: | 5 |

**Tries Conceded by Player**

| ▶ backs: | 20 League Best |
|---|---|
| ▶ forwards: | 14 |

**Tries Scored/Conceded Across the Pitch**

| 2 | 1 | 1 | 1 | - | 4 | 1 | - | - | 1 | - | 2 | 3 | 1 | - | - | - | 3 | - | 1 | - | - | 3 | 3 |
|---|---|---|---|---|---|---|---|---|---|---|---|---|---|---|---|---|---|---|---|---|---|---|---|

▶ scored
▶ conceded

| 6 | 4 | - | 1 | - | 1 | 1 | 1 | - | 1 | 1 | 2 | 3 | 2 | 1 | 2 | - | 2 | 1 | - | 1 | - | 1 | 3 | 1 |
|---|---|---|---|---|---|---|---|---|---|---|---|---|---|---|---|---|---|---|---|---|---|---|---|---|

# Eight-Season Form 1997-2005

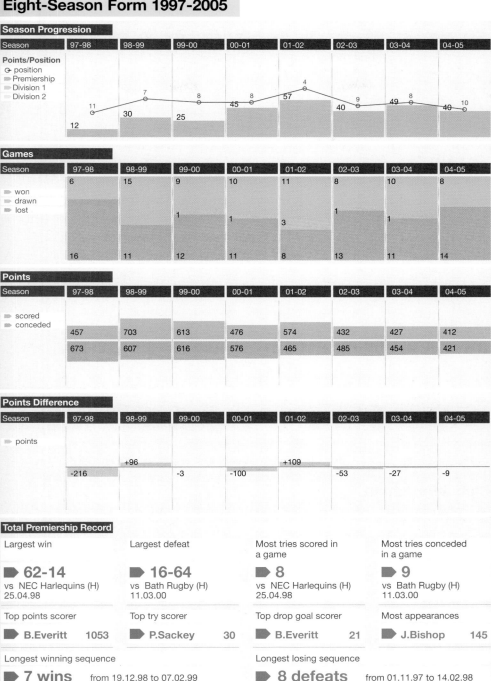

## Season Progression

| Season | 97-98 | 98-99 | 99-00 | 00-01 | 01-02 | 02-03 | 03-04 | 04-05 |
|---|---|---|---|---|---|---|---|---|

Points/Position
- position
- Premiership
- Division 1
- Division 2

11 • 12 | 30 • 7 | 25 • 8 | 45 • | 57 • 8 | 40 • 9 | 49 • 8 | 40 • 10

(positions: 11, 7, 8, 8, 4, 9, 8, 10)

## Games

| Season | 97-98 | 98-99 | 99-00 | 00-01 | 01-02 | 02-03 | 03-04 | 04-05 |
|---|---|---|---|---|---|---|---|---|
| won | 6 | 15 | 9 | 10 | 11 | 8 | 10 | 8 |
| drawn | | | 1 | 1 | 3 | 1 | 1 | |
| lost | 16 | 11 | 12 | 11 | 8 | 13 | 11 | 14 |

## Points

| Season | 97-98 | 98-99 | 99-00 | 00-01 | 01-02 | 02-03 | 03-04 | 04-05 |
|---|---|---|---|---|---|---|---|---|
| scored | 457 | 703 | 613 | 476 | 574 | 432 | 427 | 412 |
| conceded | 673 | 607 | 616 | 576 | 465 | 485 | 454 | 421 |

## Points Difference

| Season | 97-98 | 98-99 | 99-00 | 00-01 | 01-02 | 02-03 | 03-04 | 04-05 |
|---|---|---|---|---|---|---|---|---|
| points | -216 | +96 | -3 | -100 | +109 | -53 | -27 | -9 |

## Total Premiership Record

| Largest win | Largest defeat | Most tries scored in a game | Most tries conceded in a game |
|---|---|---|---|
| **62-14** | **16-64** | **8** | **9** |
| vs NEC Harlequins (H) 25.04.98 | vs Bath Rugby (H) 11.03.00 | vs NEC Harlequins (H) 25.04.98 | vs Bath Rugby (H) 11.03.00 |

| Top points scorer | Top try scorer | Top drop goal scorer | Most appearances |
|---|---|---|---|
| **B.Everitt** 1053 | **P.Sackey** 30 | **B.Everitt** 21 | **J.Bishop** 145 |

| Longest winning sequence | Longest losing sequence |
|---|---|
| **7 wins** from 19.12.98 to 07.02.99 | **8 defeats** from 01.11.97 to 14.02.98 |

# London Irish EFL

## ENHANCED FIXTURE LIST
[does not include play-off data]

### GUINNESS PREMIERSHIP 2005-06 | Premiership History

| Date | Team | H/A | 04-05 | Played | 97-98 | 98-99 | 99-00 | 00-01 | 01-02 | 02-03 | 03-04 | 04-05 | Total Points F | A | No. | W | D | L | No. | W |
|------|------|-----|-------|--------|-------|-------|-------|-------|-------|-------|-------|-------|----------------|---|-----|---|---|---|-----|---|
| | | | | | won | | drawn | | lost | | not played | | | | Outcome after a half-time lead | | | | Close games | |
| 03.09.05 | Leeds | A | 16-5 | 4 | | | | | | | | | 66 | 90 | - | - | - | - | 2 | 2 |
| 11.09.05 | Worcester | H | 25-15 | 1 | | | | | | | | | 25 | 15 | 1 | 1 | - | - | - | - |
| 16.09.05 | Sale | A | 16-17 | 8 | | | | | | | | | 170 | 235 | 6 | 3 | 1 | 2 | 4 | 3 |
| 24.09.05 | Bristol | H | N/A | 5 | | | | | | | | | 164 | 104 | 5 | 4 | 1 | - | - | - |
| 15.10.05 | Northampton | A | 20-21 | 8 | | | | | | | | | 167 | 170 | 7 | 4 | - | 3 | 3 | 2 |
| 05.11.05 | Bath | H | 19-21 | 8 | | | | | | | | | 203 | 274 | 3 | 2 | - | 1 | 3 | - |
| 11.11.05 | Newcastle | A | 23-16 | 8 | | | | | | | | | 178 | 224 | 1 | - | - | 1 | 6 | 2 |
| 20.11.05 | Gloucester | H | 12-13 | 8 | | | | | | | | | 206 | 169 | 5 | 3 | - | 2 | 5 | 3 |
| 26.11.05 | Leicester | A | 15-6 | 8 | | | | | | | | | 126 | 236 | 2 | 1 | - | 1 | 1 | 1 |
| 27.12.05 | Saracens | A | 12-30 | 8 | | | | | | | | | 230 | 195 | 3 | 2 | - | 1 | 3 | 3 |
| 31.12.05 | Wasps | H | 19-33 | 8 | | | | | | | | | 195 | 205 | 3 | 3 | - | - | 2 | 2 |
| 08.01.06 | Leicester | H | 22-39 | 8 | | | | | | | | | 152 | 235 | 1 | - | - | 1 | 2 | 1 |
| 28.01.06 | Gloucester | A | 23-16 | 8 | | | | | | | | | 121 | 229 | 2 | - | - | 2 | 4 | - |
| 12.02.06 | Newcastle | H | 21-15 | 8 | | | | | | | | | 184 | 130 | 5 | 4 | - | 1 | 5 | 3 |
| 18.02.06 | Bath | A | 27-15 | 8 | | | | | | | | | 130 | 211 | 1 | - | - | 1 | 3 | - |
| 26.02.06 | Northampton | H | 21-22 | 8 | | | | | | | | | 149 | 215 | 3 | 2 | - | 1 | 3 | 1 |
| 12.03.06 | Bristol | A | N/A | 5 | | | | | | | | | 124 | 110 | 4 | 1 | 2 | 1 | 2 | 1 |
| 25.03.06 | Sale | H | 6-9 | 8 | | | | | | | | | 157 | 144 | 5 | 3 | - | 2 | 5 | 1 |
| 08.04.06 | Worcester | A | 16-6 | 1 | | | | | | | | | 6 | 16 | - | - | - | - | - | - |
| 15.04.06 | Leeds | H | 12-16 | 4 | | | | | | | | | 99 | 72 | 1 | 1 | - | - | 1 | - |
| 30.04.06 | Wasps | A | 35-26 | 8 | | | | | | | | | 173 | 236 | 4 | 2 | - | 2 | 2 | 1 |
| 06.05.06 | Saracens | H | 20-3 | 8 | | | | | | | | | 181 | 170 | 5 | 3 | - | 2 | 4 | 2 |

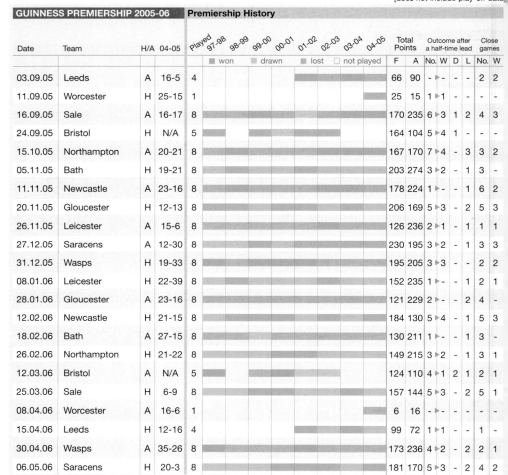

# Club Information

## Useful Information

**Founded**
1898
**Address**
Madejski Stadium
Reading
Berkshire
RG2 0FL
**Capacity**
25,000 (all seated)
**Main switchboard**
0118 987 9730
**Website**
www.london-irish.com

## Travel Information

**Car**
Approaching on the M4, exit at junction 11 onto the A33 towards Reading. When you reach a roundabout, take the 2nd exit onto the Reading Relief Road, the stadium is on your left.
For parking, carry on past the stadium and turn left onto Northern Way and follow the signs for the car parks.

**Train**
Trains run from London Paddington and London Waterloo to Reading station. A shuttle bus runs from Reading station to the ground on matchdays, costing £2 for adults and £1 for children.

**Coach**
National Express coaches run from London Victoria station approx every half hour.
Visit
www.nationalexpress.com
for further information.

# Maps

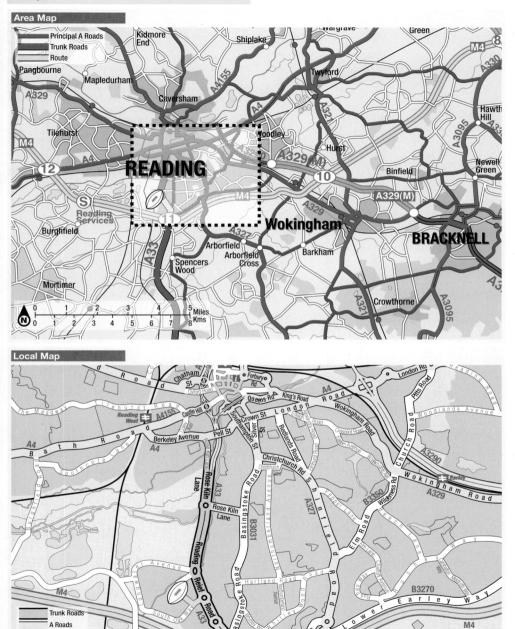

# London Wasps

## Season Summary

| Position | Won | Drawn | Lost | For | Against | Bonus Points | Total Points |
|---|---|---|---|---|---|---|---|
| **2** | **15** | **1** | **6** | **561** | **442** | **11** | **73** |

They did it again: second in the league, but undoubtedly supreme in winning the Championship Final, for the third successive year. Captain Lawrence Dallaglio, freed from international duty, had one of his best seasons, while Mark Van Gisbergen proved dependable and reliable as full back and kicker, though he will now face competition from Jeremy Staunton.

Youth thrived too – Thom Evans is just one player to keep an eye on – and the astute Warren Gatland leaves them in the safe hands of one of rugby's finest and most experienced coaches, Ian McGeechan.

**Director of Rugby:** Ian McGeechan

**Club Honours**
Courage League / Zurich Premiership: 1989-90, 1996-97, 2002-03, 2003-04, 2004-05
Tetley's Bitter Cup: 1998-99, 1999-2000

Heineken Cup: 2003-04
Parker Pen Shield: 2002-03

# Season Squad

### Stats 2004-05

| Position | Player | Height | Weight | Apps | Rep | Tries | Points | Position | Player | Height | Weight | Apps | Rep | Tries | Points |
|---|---|---|---|---|---|---|---|---|---|---|---|---|---|---|---|
| C | S.Abbott | 6'0" | 14st 2lb | 3 | - | 1 | 5 | FL | M.Lock | 6'2" | 16st 7lb | 1 | 8 | - | - |
| H | J.Barrett | 5'11" | 16st 5lb | - | 4 | - | - | W | J.Mbu | 6'1" | 16st 7lb | - | 2 | - | - |
| SH | H.Biljon | 5'11" | 13st 2lb | 2 | 6 | - | - | P | A.McKenzie | 6'3" | 18st 12lb | 3 | 7 | - | - |
| L | R.Birkett | 6'4" | 17st 2lb | 21 | 1 | 2 | 10 | P | H.Nwume | 6'3" | 19st 1lb | 1 | 3 | - | - |
| FH | J.Brooks | 5'10" | 13st 9lb | 6 | 15 | - | 8 | FL | J.O'Connor | 5'11" | 15st 10lb | 12 | 2 | 2 | 10 |
| 8 | L.Dallaglio | 6'4" | 18st 2lb | 22 | 2 | 1 | 8 | P | T.Payne | 6'1" | 18st 4lb | 18 | 3 | 1 | 5 |
| SH | M.Dawson | 5'10" | 14st 2lb | 18 | - | 5 | 25 | W | M.Priscott | 6'1" | 15st 0lb | 4 | 1 | - | - |
| P | C.Dowd | 6'3" | 18st 8lb | 11 | 4 | - | - | L | M.Purdy | 6'7" | 17st 9lb | 3 | 5 | - | - |
| C | A.Erinle | 6'3" | 17st 5lb | 20 | 1 | 11 | 55 | FL | T.Rees | 6'0" | 15st 6lb | 10 | 2 | 2 | 10 |
| W | T.Evans | N/A | N/A | 1 | - | - | - | SH | P.Richards | 5'9" | 14st 10lb | 12 | 4 | 1 | 5 |
| SH | W.Fury | 6'0" | 13st 1lb | 2 | 5 | - | - | W | M.Roberts | 6'3" | 16st 5lb | 3 | - | 2 | 10 |
| H | B.Gotting | 6'1" | 16st 11lb | 6 | 3 | - | - | W | P.Sackey | 6'2" | 13st 10lb | 8 | - | 3 | 15 |
| P | W.Green | 6'0" | 18st 4lb | 15 | 5 | 1 | 5 | L | S.Shaw | 6'8" | 19st 1lb | 16 | 1 | 3 | 15 |
| H | P.Greening | 5'11" | 16st 10lb | 18 | 2 | - | - | L | G.Skivington | 6'7" | 17st 4lb | 4 | 3 | - | - |
| 8 | J.Hart | 6'5" | 17st 10lb | 13 | 6 | - | - | FB | E.Thrower | 6'0" | 14st 11lb | 5 | 3 | 2 | 52 |
| FL | J.Haskell | 6'4" | 17st 7lb | 2 | 2 | - | - | FB | M.Van Gisbergen | 5'11" | 14st 0lb | 24 | *League Best* | 6 | 225 |
| C | R.Hoadley | 6'1" | 14st 0lb | 7 | 6 | 2 | 10 | W | T.Voyce | 6'1" | 14st 13lb | 24 | *League Best* | 12 | 60 |
| FH | A.King | 6'0" | 14st 7lb | 17 | 3 | - | 65 | C | F.Waters | 6'0" | 14st 11lb | 1 | *League Best* | - | - |
| H | T.Leota | 5'9" | 19st 9lb | - | 13 | 1 | 5 | FL | J.Worsley | 6'5" | 17st 7lb | 16 | 2 | 4 | 20 |
| W | J.Lewsey | 5'11" | 13st 7lb | 11 | 2 | 4 | 20 | | | | | | | | |

## Last Season Form

### Season Progression

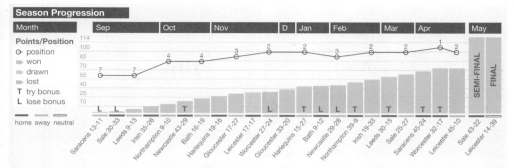

| Month | Sep | Oct | Nov | D | Jan | Feb | Mar | Apr | May |

Points/Position
- ○ position
- won
- drawn
- lost
- T try bonus
- L lose bonus

home away neutral

Saracens 13-11, Sale 30-35, Leeds 9-13, Irish 35-26, Northampton 9-10, Newcastle 43-29, Bath 16-19, Harlequins 19-16, Gloucester 17-27, Leicester 17-17, Worcester 27-24, Gloucester 33-20, Harlequins 15-27, Bath 9-12, Newcastle 29-28, Northampton 39-9, Irish 19-33, Leeds 30-15, Sale 25-27, Saracens 45-24, Worcester 32-17, Leicester 45-10, Sale 43-22, Leicester 14-39

SEMI-FINAL / FINAL

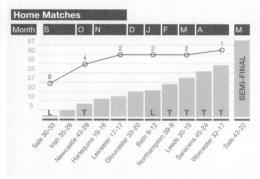

### Home Matches

| Month | S | | O | N | | D | J | F | M | A | | M |

Sale 30-33, Irish 35-26, Newcastle 43-29, Harlequins 19-16, Leicester 17-17, Gloucester 33-20, Bath 9-12, Northampton 39-9, Leeds 30-15, Saracens 45-24, Worcester 32-17, Sale 43-22

SEMI-FINAL

### Away Matches

| Month | S | | O | | N | | J | F | | M | A |

Saracens 13-11, Leeds 9-13, Northampton 9-10, Bath 16-19, Gloucester 17-27, Worcester 27-24, Harlequins 15-27, Newcastle 29-28, Irish 19-33, Sale 25-27, Leicester 14-39

### Premiership Stats

| | Home | Away | Neutral |
|---|---|---|---|
| Tries | | | |
| 66 | 40 | 23 | 3 |
| Coversions | | | |
| 50 | 29 | 18 | 3 |
| Penalty goals | | | |
| 64 | 35 | 24 | 5 |
| Drop goals | | | |
| 7 | 4 | 2 | 1 |
| Kick % | | | |
| 73% | 75% | 68% | 89% |
| Yellow/Red cards | | | |
| 7/0 | 3/0 | 4/0 | 0/0 |
| Powerplay tries | | | |
| 9 | 5 | 4 | 0 |
| Shorthand tries | | | |
| 1 | 1 | 0 | 0 |

Powerplay tries are scored when your side are playing with a man or more advantage due to yellow or red cards.

Shorthand tries are scored when your side are playing with a man or more fewer due to yellow or red cards.

### Team Performance

| Position | Team | % total points won | % won at home | % won away |
|---|---|---|---|---|
| 1 | Leicester | | | |
| 2 | **Wasps** | 14% | 11% | 18% |
| 3 | Sale | | | |
| 4 | Bath | | | |
| 5 | Saracens | 25% | 24% | 26% |
| 6 | Gloucester | | | |
| 7 | Newcastle | | | |
| 8 | Leeds | 27% | 35% | 18% |
| 9 | Worcester | | | |
| 10 | Irish | | | |
| 11 | Northampton | 34% | 30% | 38% |
| 12 | Harlequins | | | |

# London Wasps

## Top Scorer

**Mark Van Gisbergen**

### Points Facts

| | | | | |
|---|---|---|---|---|
| Total points | % team points | Home | Away | Neutral |
| ▶ **225** | ▶ **35** | ▶ **124** | ▶ **75** | ▶ **26** |

### Points by Time Period

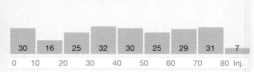

| 30 | 16 | 25 | 32 | 30 | 25 | 29 | 31 | 7 |
|---|---|---|---|---|---|---|---|---|
| 0 | 10 | 20 | 30 | 40 | 50 | 60 | 70 | 80 Inj. |

## Team Tries and Points

### Tries by Time Period

| 11 | 6 | 7 | 8 | 9 | 8 | 4 | 10 | 3 |
|---|---|---|---|---|---|---|---|---|
| 0 | 10min | 20min | 30min | 40min | 50min | 60min | 70min | 80 Injury time |
| 1 *League Best* | 6 | 6 | 5 | 5 | 5 | 2 | 11 | 3 |

- scored
- conceded

### Tries by Halves

| | | | | |
|---|---|---|---|---|
| ▶ **66** | ▶ **32** | ▶ **34** | ▶ **48%** | ▶ **52%** |
| Total | 1st half | 2nd half | 1st half % | 2nd half % |
| ▶ **44** | ▶ **18** | ▶ **26** | ▶ **41%** | ▶ **59%** |

- scored
- conceded

### How Points were Scored

- tries: 59
- conversions: 43
- penalty goals: 55
- drop goals: 5

### How Points were Conceded

- tries: 40
- conversions: 34
- penalty goals: 52
- drop goals: 6

### Tries Scored by Player

- backs: 48
- forwards: 17

### Tries Conceded by Player

- backs: 30
- forwards: 14

### Tries Scored/Conceded Across the Pitch

| 2 | 7 | 2 | 2 | 1 | 3 | 1 | 3 | 1 | 2 | 1 | 4 | 8 | 3 | 3 | 2 | - | 2 | 3 | - | 3 | 1 | - | 3 | 2 | - |
|---|---|---|---|---|---|---|---|---|---|---|---|---|---|---|---|---|---|---|---|---|---|---|---|---|---|

- scored
- conceded

| 3 | 2 | 2 | 1 | 1 | 2 | - | 1 | 1 | 1 | 1 | 9 | 5 | 1 | - | 1 | 1 | 2 | 1 | - | 2 | 1 | 1 | 1 |
|---|---|---|---|---|---|---|---|---|---|---|---|---|---|---|---|---|---|---|---|---|---|---|---|

## Eight-Season Form 1997-2005

### Season Progression

| Season | 97-98 | 98-99 | 99-00 | 00-01 | 01-02 | 02-03 | 03-04 | 04-05 |
|---|---|---|---|---|---|---|---|---|

Points/Position
- position
- Premiership
- Division 1
- Division 2

| | 97-98 | 98-99 | 99-00 | 00-01 | 01-02 | 02-03 | 03-04 | 04-05 |
|---|---|---|---|---|---|---|---|---|
| position | 9 | 5 | 7 | 74 | 2 | 67 | 2 73 | 2 73 |
| points | 17 | 31 | 31 | | 54 7 | 2 | | |

### Games

| Season | 97-98 | 98-99 | 99-00 | 00-01 | 01-02 | 02-03 | 03-04 | 04-05 |
|---|---|---|---|---|---|---|---|---|
| won | 8 | 15 | 11 | 16 | 12 | 13 | 16 | 15 |
| drawn | | 1 | 1 | | | 2 | | 1 |
| lost | 1 13 | 10 | 10 | 6 | 10 | 7 | 6 | 6 |

### Points

| Season | 97-98 | 98-99 | 99-00 | 00-01 | 01-02 | 02-03 | 03-04 | 04-05 |
|---|---|---|---|---|---|---|---|---|
| scored | 490 | 717 | 640 | 663 | 519 | 553 | 575 | 561 |
| conceded | 609 | 506 | 461 | 428 | 507 | 460 | 406 | 442 |

### Points Difference

| Season | 97-98 | 98-99 | 99-00 | 00-01 | 01-02 | 02-03 | 03-04 | 04-05 |
|---|---|---|---|---|---|---|---|---|
| points | -119 | +211 | +179 | +235 | +12 | +93 | +169 | +119 |

### Total Premiership Record

| Largest win | Largest defeat | Most tries scored in a game | Most tries conceded in a game |
|---|---|---|---|
| **71-14** | **21-59** | **10** | **8** |
| vs West Hartlepool (H) 27.09.98 | vs Newcastle Falcons (A) 23.09.00 | vs West Hartlepool (H) 27.09.98 | vs Richmond (A) 02.05.98 |

| Top points scorer | Top try scorer | Top drop goal scorer | Most appearances |
|---|---|---|---|
| A.King 882 | J.Lewsey 38 | A.King 31 | W.Green 164 |

| Longest winning sequence | Longest losing sequence |
|---|---|
| **11 wins** from 21.11.03 to 18.04.04 | **6 defeats** from 08.09.01 to 11.11.01 |

# London Wasps EFL

## ENHANCED FIXTURE LIST
[does not include play-off data]

## GUINNESS PREMIERSHIP 2005-06 — Premiership History

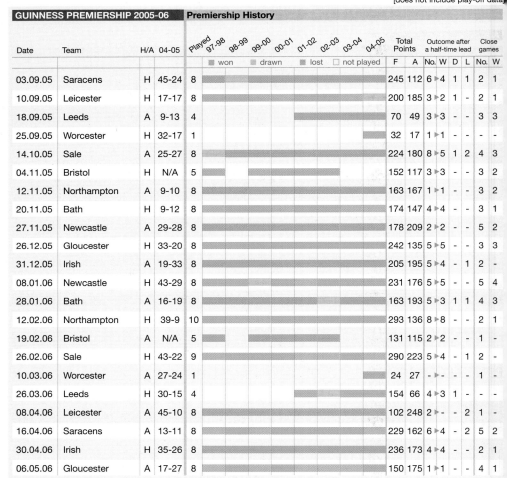

| Date | Team | H/A | 04-05 | Played | Total Points F | A | Outcome after a half-time lead No. | W | D | L | Close games No. | W |
|------|------|-----|-------|--------|---------------|---|------|---|---|---|------|---|
| 03.09.05 | Saracens | H | 45-24 | 8 | 245 | 112 | 6 | 4 | 1 | 1 | 2 | 1 |
| 10.09.05 | Leicester | H | 17-17 | 8 | 200 | 185 | 3 | 2 | 1 | - | 2 | 1 |
| 18.09.05 | Leeds | A | 9-13 | 4 | 70 | 49 | 3 | 3 | - | - | 3 | 3 |
| 25.09.05 | Worcester | H | 32-17 | 1 | 32 | 17 | 1 | 1 | - | - | - | - |
| 14.10.05 | Sale | A | 25-27 | 8 | 224 | 180 | 8 | 5 | 1 | 2 | 4 | 3 |
| 04.11.05 | Bristol | H | N/A | 5 | 152 | 117 | 3 | 3 | - | - | 3 | 2 |
| 12.11.05 | Northampton | A | 9-10 | 8 | 163 | 167 | 1 | 1 | - | - | 3 | 2 |
| 20.11.05 | Bath | H | 9-12 | 8 | 174 | 147 | 4 | 4 | - | - | 3 | 1 |
| 27.11.05 | Newcastle | A | 29-28 | 8 | 178 | 209 | 2 | 2 | - | - | 5 | 2 |
| 26.12.05 | Gloucester | H | 33-20 | 8 | 242 | 135 | 5 | 5 | - | - | 3 | 3 |
| 31.12.05 | Irish | A | 19-33 | 8 | 205 | 195 | 5 | 4 | - | 1 | 2 | - |
| 08.01.06 | Newcastle | H | 43-29 | 8 | 231 | 176 | 5 | 5 | - | - | 5 | 4 |
| 28.01.06 | Bath | A | 16-19 | 8 | 163 | 193 | 5 | 3 | 1 | 1 | 4 | 3 |
| 12.02.06 | Northampton | H | 39-9 | 10 | 293 | 136 | 8 | 8 | - | - | 2 | 1 |
| 19.02.06 | Bristol | A | N/A | 5 | 131 | 115 | 2 | 2 | - | - | 1 | - |
| 26.02.06 | Sale | H | 43-22 | 9 | 290 | 223 | 5 | 4 | - | 1 | 2 | - |
| 10.03.06 | Worcester | A | 27-24 | 1 | 24 | 27 | - | - | - | - | 1 | - |
| 26.03.06 | Leeds | H | 30-15 | 4 | 154 | 66 | 4 | 3 | 1 | - | - | - |
| 08.04.06 | Leicester | A | 45-10 | 8 | 102 | 248 | 2 | - | - | 2 | 1 | - |
| 16.04.06 | Saracens | A | 13-11 | 8 | 229 | 162 | 6 | 4 | - | 2 | 5 | 2 |
| 30.04.06 | Irish | H | 35-26 | 8 | 236 | 173 | 4 | 4 | - | - | 2 | 1 |
| 06.05.06 | Gloucester | A | 17-27 | 8 | 150 | 175 | 1 | 1 | - | - | 4 | 1 |

Legend: ■ won ■ drawn ■ lost ☐ not played
History columns: 97-98, 98-99, 99-00, 00-01, 01-02, 02-03, 03-04, 04-05

# Club Information

## Useful Information

**Founded**
1867

**Address**
Causeway Stadium
Hillbottom Road
Sands
High Wycombe
Buckinghamshire
HP12 4HJ

**Capacity**
10,200 (all seated)

**Main switchboard**
0208 993 8298

**Website**
www.wasps.co.uk

## Travel Information

**Car**
From North
Approaching on the M1, exit onto the M25 at junction 6a (anti-clockwise). Continue on the M25 until junction 16 (M40), then head to junction 4 for the A404 High Wycombe. When you reach the junction take the slip road and turn right, taking the exit for the A4010 John Hall Way. Continue on this road, which becomes New Road, until you reach a mini roundabout with a left turn on to Lane End Road. Take this left turning and continue straight ahead onto Hillbottom Road, which leads to Causeway Stadium.

**Train**
Train services run from London Marylebone to High Wycombe.

## Maps

**Area Map**

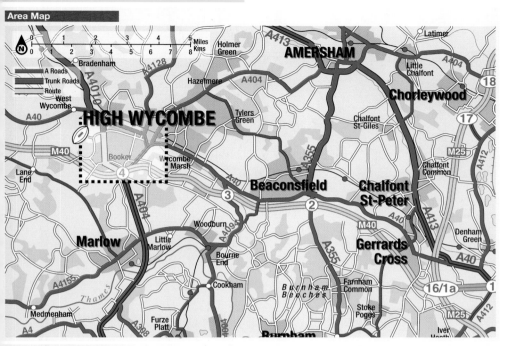

**Local Map**

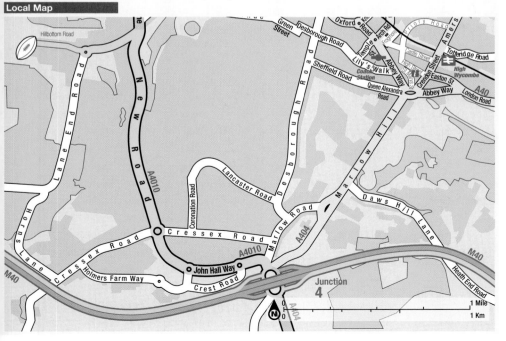

# Newcastle Falcons

## Season Summary

| Position | Won | Drawn | Lost | For | Against | Bonus Points | Total Points |
|---|---|---|---|---|---|---|---|
| **7** | **9** | **2** | **11** | **475** | **596** | **7** | **47** |

**Individual contributions from Jamie Noon, Matt Burke and Colin Charvis, among others, meant Newcastle were not to be disregarded. Charvis, now captain, certainly leads from the front and covers a lot of ground, but Jonny Wilkinson was in and out with injury.**

A small squad struggled to make a big impression, and may do so again, despite the unquestionable talent it contains under the guiding hand of Rob Andrew as Director of Rugby. Mathew Tait should continue to be nurtured after his disappointing England experience in the Six Nations.

**Director of Rugby:** Rob Andrew

**Club Honours**
Allied Dunbar Premiership: 1997-98
John Player Cup / Powergen Cup: 1976, 1977, 2001, 2004

## Season Squad

### Stats 2004-05

| Position | Player | Height | Weight | Apps | Rep | Tries | Points | Position | Player | Height | Weight | Apps | Rep | Tries | Points |
|---|---|---|---|---|---|---|---|---|---|---|---|---|---|---|---|
| P | G.Alvarez Quinones | 6'0" | 18st 6lb | 3 | 2 | - | - | C | M.Mayerhofler | 6'0" | 15st 2lb | 11 | 2 | 4 | 20 |
| L | A.Buist | 6'6" | 17st 0lb | 4 | 2 | - | - | FL | M.McCarthy | 6'4" | 17st 0lb | 14 | 7 | 2 | 10 |
| FB | M.Burke | 6'0" | 14st 10lb | 12 | 2 | 5 | 64 | C | J.Noon | 5'10" | 13st 5lb | 16 | 1 | 4 | 20 |
| SH | H.Charlton | 5'11" | 14st 4lb | 10 | 7 | - | - | L/FL | G.Parling | 6'5" | 16st 5lb | 2 | 7 | - | - |
| BR | C.Charvis | 6'3" | 16st 10lb | 11 | 2 | 1 | 5 | P | I.Peel | 5'11" | 18st 0lb | 15 | 2 | - | - |
| C | A.Dehaty | N/A | N/A | - | 1 | - | - | W | O.Phillips | 5'11" | 14st 7lb | 2 | 2 | 1 | 5 |
| SH | L.Dickson | 5'11" | 12st 6lb | - | 3 | - | - | FB/C | J.Shaw | 6'0" | 15st 2lb | 4 | 5 | - | - |
| 8 | P.Dowson | 6'3" | 16st 10lb | 16 | 2 | 2 | 10 | FL | S.Sititi | 6'3" | 15st 6lb | 9 | 7 | 1 | 5 |
| FH/FB | T.Flood | 6'2" | 15st 0lb | 2 | 1 | - | - | W | M.Stephenson | 6'0" | 13st 0lb | 17 | - | 7 | 35 |
| L | S.Grimes | 6'5" | 17st 3lb | 14 | 1 | 1 | 5 | C/W/BR | E.Taione | 6'4" | 19st 6lb | 9 | 2 | 1 | 5 |
| SH | J.Grindal | 5'9" | 13st 4lb | 12 | 8 | - | - | C/W | M.Tait | 5'11" | 13st 4lb | 10 | 5 | 4 | 20 |
| L | L.Gross | 6'9" | 19st 8lb | 16 | 2 | - | - | H | M.Thompson | 6'2" | 18st 0lb | 6 | 7 | - | - |
| L | C.Hamilton | 6'8" | 17st 9lb | 7 | 7 | - | - | FH | D.Walder | 5'10" | 12st 9lb | 13 | 3 | 1 | 58 |
| FL | C.Harris | 6'0" | 17st 0lb | 15 | - | 1 | 5 | P | M.Ward | 5'11" | 18st 9lb | 15 | 6 | - | - |
| P | M.Hurter | 6'2" | 19st 6lb | 6 | 3 | - | - | FH | J.Wilkinson | 5'10" | 13st 5lb | 10 | 2 | 1 | 150 |
| P/H | J.Isaacson | 5'11" | 17st 4lb | 3 | 13 | - | - | C | M.Wilkinson | 6'3" | 17st 0lb | 5 | - | 1 | 5 |
| H | A.Long | 5'11" | 16st 3lb | 16 | 6 | - | - | FL | E.Williamson | 6'2" | 14st 9lb | 2 | 1 | - | - |
| W | T.May | 5'10" | 14st 5lb | 21 | 1 | 5 | 48 | P | D.Wilson | 6'1" | 18st 7lb | 2 | 2 | - | - |

## Last Season Form

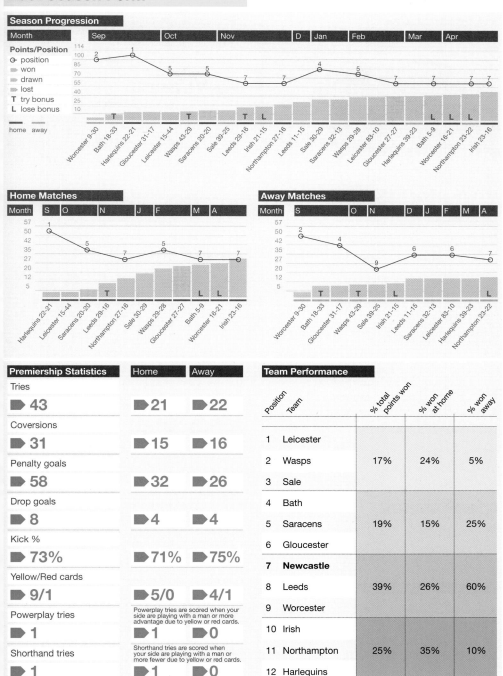

### Season Progression

| Month | Sep | Oct | Nov | D | Jan | Feb | Mar | Apr |

Points/Position
- ○ position
- won
- drawn
- lost
- T try bonus
- L lose bonus

home away

Worcester 9-30, Bath 18-33, Harlequins 22-21, Gloucester 31-17, Leicester 15-44, Wasps 43-29, Saracens 20-20, Sale 39-25, Leeds 29-16, Irish 21-15, Northampton 27-16, Leeds 11-15, Sale 30-29, Saracens 32-13, Wasps 29-28, Leicester 83-10, Gloucester 27-27, Harlequins 39-23, Bath 5-9, Worcester 16-21, Northampton 23-22, Irish 23-16

### Home Matches

| Month | S | O | N | J F | M A |

Harlequins 22-21, Leicester 15-44, Saracens 20-20, Leeds 29-16, Northampton 27-16, Sale 30-29, Wasps 29-28, Gloucester 27-27, Bath 5-9, Worcester 16-21, Irish 23-16

### Away Matches

| Month | S | O | N | D J | F | M | A |

Worcester 9-30, Bath 18-33, Gloucester 31-17, Wasps 43-29, Sale 39-25, Irish 21-15, Leeds 11-15, Saracens 32-13, Leicester 83-10, Harlequins 39-23, Northampton 23-22

### Premiership Statistics

| | Home | Away |
|---|---|---|
| Tries | | |
| 43 | 21 | 22 |
| Coversions | | |
| 31 | 15 | 16 |
| Penalty goals | | |
| 58 | 32 | 26 |
| Drop goals | | |
| 8 | 4 | 4 |
| Kick % | | |
| 73% | 71% | 75% |
| Yellow/Red cards | | |
| 9/1 | 5/0 | 4/1 |
| Powerplay tries | | |
| 1 | 1 | 0 |

Powerplay tries are scored when your side is playing with a man or more advantage due to yellow or red cards.

| Shorthand tries | | |
|---|---|---|
| 1 | 1 | 0 |

Shorthand tries are scored when your side is playing with a man or more fewer due to yellow or red cards.

### Team Performance

| Position | Team | % total points won | % won at home | % won away |
|---|---|---|---|---|
| 1 | Leicester | | | |
| 2 | Wasps | 17% | 24% | 5% |
| 3 | Sale | | | |
| 4 | Bath | | | |
| 5 | Saracens | 19% | 15% | 25% |
| 6 | Gloucester | | | |
| 7 | **Newcastle** | | | |
| 8 | Leeds | 39% | 26% | 60% |
| 9 | Worcester | | | |
| 10 | Irish | | | |
| 11 | Northampton | 25% | 35% | 10% |
| 12 | Harlequins | | | |

# Newcastle Falcons

## Top Scorer

**Jonny Wilkinson**

**Points Facts**

| Total points | % team points | Home | Away |
|---|---|---|---|
| ▶150 | ▶32 | ▶70 | ▶80 |

**Points by Time Period**

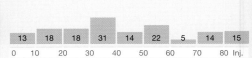

| 13 | 18 | 18 | 31 | 14 | 22 | 5 | 14 | 15 |
|---|---|---|---|---|---|---|---|---|
| 0 | 10 | 20 | 30 | 40 | 50 | 60 | 70 | 80 Inj. |

## Team Tries and Points

**Tries by Time Period**

| 5 | 5 | 5 | 6 | 5 | 4 | 3 | 6 | 4 |
|---|---|---|---|---|---|---|---|---|
| 0 | 10min | 20min | 30min | 40min | 50min | 60min | 70min | 80 Injury time |
| 4 | 5 | 11 | 13 | 5 | 8 | 7 | 8 | 3 |

➥ scored
➥ conceded

**Tries by Halves**

➥ scored
➥ conceded

| | ▶ 43 | ▶ 21 | ▶ 22 | ▶ 49% | ▶ 51% |
|---|---|---|---|---|---|
| scored | Total | 1st half | 2nd half | 1st half % | 2nd half % |
| conceded | ▶ 64 | ▶ 33 | ▶ 31 | ▶ 52% | ▶ 48% |

**How Points were Scored**

➥ tries: 43
➥ conversions: 31
➥ penalty goals: 58
➥ drop goals: 8

**How Points were Conceded**

➥ tries: 64
➥ conversions: 45
➥ penalty goals: 56
➥ drop goals: 6

**Tries Scored by Player**

➥ backs: 34
➥ forwards: 8

**Tries Conceded by Player**

➥ backs: 39
➥ forwards: 24

**Tries Scored/Conceded Across the Pitch**

| 6 | 1 | - | 1 | - | 4 | - | - | 1 | 1 | 1 | 2 | 8 | 1 | 2 | 1 | - | 1 | 2 | - | 1 | 2 | - | 1 | 4 | 3 |
|---|---|---|---|---|---|---|---|---|---|---|---|---|---|---|---|---|---|---|---|---|---|---|---|---|---|

➥ scored
➥ conceded

| 4 | 5 | 2 | 6 | 2 | 3 | 2 | 1 | - | 1 | 3 | 10 | 1 | - | 2 | - | - | 1 | 1 | 2 | 2 | 3 | 2 | 7 | 2 |
|---|---|---|---|---|---|---|---|---|---|---|---|---|---|---|---|---|---|---|---|---|---|---|---|---|

## Eight-Season Form 1997-2005

### Season Progression

| Season | 97-98 | 98-99 | 99-00 | 00-01 | 01-02 | 02-03 | 03-04 | 04-05 |
|---|---|---|---|---|---|---|---|---|
| Points/Position | | | | | | | | |

Position: 1 (97-98), 8 (98-99), 9 (99-00), 6 (00-01), 6 (01-02), 10 (02-03), 9 (03-04), 7 (04-05)

Points: 38, 28, 19, 57, 56, 40, 45, 47

### Games

| Season | 97-98 | 98-99 | 99-00 | 00-01 | 01-02 | 02-03 | 03-04 | 04-05 |
|---|---|---|---|---|---|---|---|---|
| won | 19 | 14 | 6 | 11 | 12 | 8 | 7 | 9 |
| drawn | | | 2 | | 1 | | 2 | 2 |
| lost | 3 | 12 | 14 | 11 | 9 | 14 | 13 | 11 |

### Points

| Season | 97-98 | 98-99 | 99-00 | 00-01 | 01-02 | 02-03 | 03-04 | 04-05 |
|---|---|---|---|---|---|---|---|---|
| scored | 645 | 719 | 377 | 554 | 490 | 388 | 497 | 475 |
| conceded | 387 | 639 | 630 | 568 | 458 | 545 | 525 | 596 |

### Points Difference

| Season | 97-98 | 98-99 | 99-00 | 00-01 | 01-02 | 02-03 | 03-04 | 04-05 |
|---|---|---|---|---|---|---|---|---|
| points | +258 | +80 | -253 | -14 | +32 | -157 | -28 | -121 |

### Total Premiership Record

| Largest win | Largest defeat | Most tries scored in a game | Most tries conceded in a game |
|---|---|---|---|
| ▶ 56-10 | ▶ 10-83 | ▶ 8 | ▶ 11 |
| vs Rotherham Titans (H) 09.11.03 | vs Leicester Tigers (A) 19.02.05 | vs London Irish (H) 11.01.98 | vs Leicester Tigers (A) 19.02.05 |

| Top points scorer | Top try scorer | Top drop goal scorer | Most appearances |
|---|---|---|---|
| ▶ J.Wilkinson 1251 | ▶ G.Armstrong 35 | ▶ J.Wilkinson 17 | ▶ I.Peel 120 |

| Longest winning sequence | Longest losing sequence |
|---|---|
| ▶ 12 wins from 23.08.97 to 10.03.98 | ▶ 7 defeats from 03.11.02 to 03.01.03 |

# Newcastle Falcons EFL

## ENHANCED FIXTURE LIST
[does not include play-off data]

### GUINNESS PREMIERSHIP 2005-06 — Premiership History

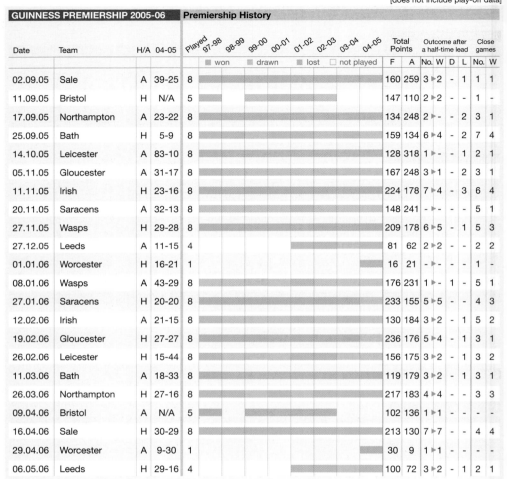

Key: ■ won  ■ drawn  ■ lost  ☐ not played

| Date | Team | H/A | 04-05 | Played | Total Points F | A | Outcome after a half-time lead No. | W | D | L | Close games No. | W |
|---|---|---|---|---|---|---|---|---|---|---|---|---|
| 02.09.05 | Sale | A | 39-25 | 8 | 160 | 259 | 3 ►2 | - | 1 | 1 | 1 | |
| 11.09.05 | Bristol | H | N/A | 5 | 147 | 110 | 2 ►2 | - | - | 1 | - | |
| 17.09.05 | Northampton | A | 23-22 | 8 | 134 | 248 | 2 ►- | - | 2 | 3 | 1 | |
| 25.09.05 | Bath | H | 5-9 | 8 | 159 | 134 | 6 ►4 | - | 2 | 7 | 4 | |
| 14.10.05 | Leicester | A | 83-10 | 8 | 128 | 318 | 1 ►- | - | 1 | 2 | 1 | |
| 05.11.05 | Gloucester | A | 31-17 | 8 | 167 | 248 | 3 ►1 | - | 2 | 3 | 1 | |
| 11.11.05 | Irish | H | 23-16 | 8 | 224 | 178 | 7 ►4 | - | 3 | 6 | 4 | |
| 20.11.05 | Saracens | A | 32-13 | 8 | 148 | 241 | - ►- | - | - | 5 | 1 | |
| 27.11.05 | Wasps | H | 29-28 | 8 | 209 | 178 | 6 ►5 | - | 1 | 5 | 3 | |
| 27.12.05 | Leeds | A | 11-15 | 4 | 81 | 62 | 2 ►2 | - | - | 2 | 2 | |
| 01.01.06 | Worcester | H | 16-21 | 1 | 16 | 21 | - ►- | - | - | 1 | - | |
| 08.01.06 | Wasps | A | 43-29 | 8 | 176 | 231 | 1 ►- | 1 | - | 5 | 1 | |
| 27.01.06 | Saracens | H | 20-20 | 8 | 233 | 155 | 5 ►5 | - | - | 4 | 3 | |
| 12.02.06 | Irish | A | 21-15 | 8 | 130 | 184 | 3 ►2 | - | 1 | 5 | 2 | |
| 19.02.06 | Gloucester | H | 27-27 | 8 | 236 | 176 | 5 ►4 | - | 1 | 3 | 1 | |
| 26.02.06 | Leicester | H | 15-44 | 8 | 156 | 175 | 3 ►2 | - | 1 | 3 | 2 | |
| 11.03.06 | Bath | A | 18-33 | 8 | 119 | 179 | 3 ►2 | - | 1 | 3 | 1 | |
| 26.03.06 | Northampton | H | 27-16 | 8 | 217 | 183 | 4 ►4 | - | - | 3 | 3 | |
| 09.04.06 | Bristol | A | N/A | 5 | 102 | 136 | 1 ►1 | - | - | - | - | |
| 16.04.06 | Sale | H | 30-29 | 8 | 213 | 130 | 7 ►7 | - | - | 4 | 4 | |
| 29.04.06 | Worcester | A | 9-30 | 1 | 30 | 9 | 1 ►1 | - | - | - | - | |
| 06.05.06 | Leeds | H | 29-16 | 4 | 100 | 72 | 3 ►2 | - | 1 | 2 | 1 | |

## Club Information

### Useful Information

**Founded**
1995
(Gosforth formed in 1877)
**Address**
Kingston Park
Brunton Road
Kenton Bank Foot
Newcastle NE13 8AF
**Capacity**
10,000
**Main switchboard**
0191 214 5588
**Website**
www.newcastle-falcons.co.uk

### Travel Information

**Car**
From South:
Take the M1 and turn right onto the M62 at junction 42, towards the A1. Follow the A1 all the way into Newcastle, heading for the junction for Newcastle Airport. When you reach that junction, take the Kingston Park exit then continue straight ahead over two mini roundabouts. After passing under a bridge, turn right into Brunton Road then continue until you see the ground on your left.
From West:
Follow the A69 until it joins the A1, and follow signs for the Newcastle Airport junction. Then as route for South.

**Train**
GNER and Virgin Trains run services to Newcastle Central. From there, catch the Tyne and Wear Metro to Kingston Park station.

**Air**
Newcastle International Airport is a short cab ride from the stadium.

## Maps

**Area Map**

**Local Map**

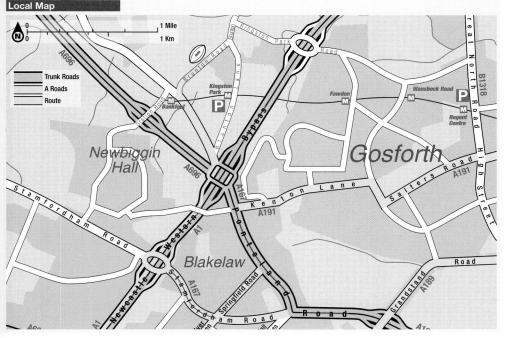

# Northampton Saints

## Season Summary

| Position | Won | Drawn | Lost | For | Against | Bonus Points | Total Points |
|---|---|---|---|---|---|---|---|
| 11 | 8 | 0 | 14 | 410 | 473 | 8 | 40 |

**Eight losses on the trot represented the Saints' worst ever league run and ended Alan Solomons' tenure as coach. The squad rallied behind Corné Krige, the South African captain, but he chose to stand down, leaving the role to Steve Thompson. Budge Pountney and Paul Grayson picked up the pieces as coaches, narrowly avoiding relegation.**

The supporters at the newly expanded Franklin's Gardens – now able to hold 13,500 – will give a hearty welcome to All Black fly-half Carlos Spencer, and hope he settles quickly to steer them to better things.

**Head Coach:** Budge Pountney

**Club Honours**
Heineken Cup: 1999-2000

## Season Squad

### Stats 2004-05

| Position | Player | Height | Weight | Apps | Rep | Tries | Points |
|---|---|---|---|---|---|---|---|
| BR/L | R.Beattie | 6'5" | 17st 8lb | 4 | 3 | - | - |
| FL | A.Blowers | 6'5" | 16st 4lb | 17 | 1 | 1 | 5 |
| L | S.Boome | 6'3" | 17st 0lb | 13 | - | - | - |
| L | D.Browne | 6'6" | 20st 6lb | 12 | 9 | - | - |
| P | C.Budgen | 5'8" | 17st 10lb | 6 | 2 | 1 | 5 |
| FB/W | J.Clarke | 6'3" | 14st 1lb | 3 | 1 | 1 | 5 |
| L | A.Codling | 6'6" | 17st 10lb | - | 2 | - | - |
| W | B.Cohen | 6'2" | 15st 10lb | 13 | 3 | 3 | 15 |
| W | P.Diggin | 5'8" | 13st 2lb | 4 | 1 | 2 | 10 |
| FH | S.Drahm | 5'9" | 12st 10lb | 14 | 7 | 1 | 180 |
| P | S.Emms | 5'11" | 17st 8lb | 9 | 1 | - | - |
| FL | D.Fox | 6'0" | 15st 10lb | 11 | 5 | 1 | 5 |
| SH | B.Fulton | 5'9" | 13st 8lb | 1 | 2 | - | - |
| FH | P.Grayson | 5'11" | 13st 13lb | 8 | 2 | - | 74 |
| SH | J.Howard | 5'9" | 12st 7lb | 10 | 5 | 1 | 5 |
| W | W.Human | 5'11" | 14st 12lb | 13 | 3 | 3 | 15 |
| C | C.Hyndman | 5'9" | 13st 9lb | 6 | - | 1 | 5 |
| SH | B.Jones | 5'5" | 13st 0lb | 1 | 5 | - | - |
| P | R.Kempson | 6'0" | 16st 7lb | 10 | - | - | - |
| FL | C.Krige | 6'3" | 16st 0lb | 19 | - | 3 | 15 |
| L | M.Lord | 6'4" | 17st 2lb | 14 | 5 | - | - |
| P | R.Morris | 6'2" | 18st 11lb | 6 | 5 | - | - |
| FH | L.Myring | 6'0" | 14st 3lb | - | 1 | - | - |
| L | E.O'Donoghue | 6'6" | 17st 4lb | 1 | 3 | - | - |
| FB | B.Patston | 5'10" | 12st 10lb | - | 2 | - | - |
| FB | B.Reihana | 6'0" | 13st 7lb | 21 | - | 1 | 11 |
| H | D.Richmond | 5'11" | 15st 6lb | 7 | 6 | - | - |
| SH | M.Robinson | 5'10" | 13st 8lb | 10 | - | 1 | 5 |
| W | J.Rudd | 6'2" | 17st 0lb | 14 | 4 | 3 | 15 |
| BR/L | G.Seely | 6'4" | 17st 0lb | 12 | 5 | 2 | 10 |
| FL | I.Sipa | 6'2" | 15st 10lb | - | 1 | - | - |
| P | T.Smith | 5'10" | 16st 3lb | 10 | 1 | - | - |
| BR | M.Soden | 6'2" | 16st 4lb | 7 | 6 | - | - |
| C | N.Starling | 6'5" | 14st 4lb | 4 | 1 | 1 | 5 |
| C | M.Stcherbina | 6'0" | 15st 0lb | 20 | - | 1 | 5 |
| P | B.Sturgess | 6'1" | 17st 10lb | 3 | 8 | - | - |
| H | S.Thompson | 6'2" | 18st 2lb | 15 | 1 | 1 | 5 |
| C/W | M.Tucker | 6'0" | 15st 10lb | 8 | 3 | 3 | 15 |
| H | J.Van Wyk | 6'0" | 15st 6lb | - | 1 | - | - |
| C | A.Vilk | 5'11" | 15st 6lb | 4 | 4 | - | - |

## Last Season Form

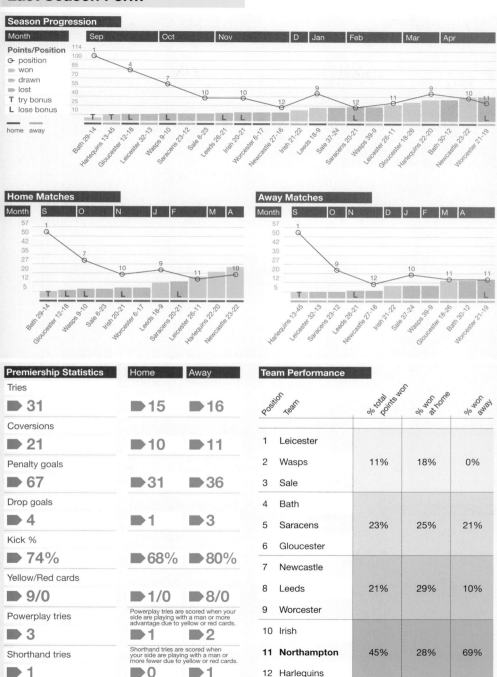

### Season Progression

| Month | Sep | Oct | Nov | D | Jan | Feb | Mar | Apr |

Points/Position
- G position
- won
- drawn
- lost
- T try bonus
- L lose bonus

home  away

Bath 29-14, Harlequins 13-45, Gloucester 12-18, Leicester 32-13, Wasps 9-10, Saracens 23-12, Sale 6-23, Leeds 26-21, Irish 20-21, Worcester 6-17, Newcastle 27-16, Irish 21-22, Leeds 18-9, Sale 37-24, Saracens 20-21, Wasps 39-9, Leicester 26-11, Gloucester 18-26, Harlequins 22-20, Bath 30-12, Newcastle 23-22, Worcester 21-19

### Home Matches

| Month | S | O | N | J F | M A |

Bath 29-14, Gloucester 12-18, Wasps 9-10, Sale 6-23, Irish 20-21, Worcester 6-17, Leeds 18-9, Saracens 20-21, Leicester 26-11, Harlequins 22-20, Newcastle 23-22

### Away Matches

| Month | S | O | N | D J | F M | A |

Harlequins 13-45, Leicester 32-13, Saracens 23-12, Leeds 26-21, Newcastle 27-16, Irish 21-22, Sale 37-24, Wasps 39-9, Gloucester 18-26, Bath 30-12, Worcester 21-19

### Premiership Statistics

| | Home | Away |
|---|---|---|
| Tries | | |
| ▶ 31 | ▶ 15 | ▶ 16 |
| Coversions | | |
| ▶ 21 | ▶ 10 | ▶ 11 |
| Penalty goals | | |
| ▶ 67 | ▶ 31 | ▶ 36 |
| Drop goals | | |
| ▶ 4 | ▶ 1 | ▶ 3 |
| Kick % | | |
| ▶ 74% | ▶ 68% | ▶ 80% |
| Yellow/Red cards | | |
| ▶ 9/0 | ▶ 1/0 | ▶ 8/0 |
| Powerplay tries | | |
| ▶ 3 | ▶ 1 | ▶ 2 |
| Shorthand tries | | |
| ▶ 1 | ▶ 0 | ▶ 1 |

Powerplay tries are scored when your side are playing with a man or more advantage due to yellow or red cards.

Shorthand tries are scored when your side are playing with a man or more fewer due to yellow or red cards.

### Team Performance

| Position | Team | % total points won | % won at home | % won away |
|---|---|---|---|---|
| 1 | Leicester | | | |
| 2 | Wasps | 11% | 18% | 0% |
| 3 | Sale | | | |
| 4 | Bath | | | |
| 5 | Saracens | 23% | 25% | 21% |
| 6 | Gloucester | | | |
| 7 | Newcastle | | | |
| 8 | Leeds | 21% | 29% | 10% |
| 9 | Worcester | | | |
| 10 | Irish | | | |
| 11 | **Northampton** | 45% | 28% | 69% |
| 12 | Harlequins | | | |

# Northampton Saints

## Top Scorer

### Points Facts

| Total points | % team points | Home | Away |
|---|---|---|---|
| ▶ 180 | ▶ 44 | ▶ 95 | ▶ 85 |

### Points by Time Period

| 34 | 33 | 21 | 16 | 3 | 16 | 26 | 23 | 8 |
|---|---|---|---|---|---|---|---|---|
| 0 | 10 | 20 | 30 | 40 | 50 | 60 | 70 | 80 Inj. |

## Team Tries and Points

### Tries by Time Period

| 2 | 5 | 5 | 7 | 1 | 2 | 2 | 4 | 3 |
|---|---|---|---|---|---|---|---|---|
| 0 | 10min | 20min | 30min | 40min | 50min | 60min | 70min | 80 Injury time |
| 2 | 4 | 6 | 8 | 6 | 3 | 2 | 9 | 4 |

▬ scored
▬ conceded

### Tries by Halves

▬ scored
▬ conceded

| | Total | 1st half | 2nd half | 1st half % | 2nd half % |
|---|---|---|---|---|---|
| scored | ▶ 31 | ▶ 19 | ▶ 12 | ▶ 61% | ▶ 39% |
| conceded | ▶ 44 | ▶ 20 | ▶ 24 | ▶ 45% | ▶ 55% |

### How Points were Scored

▬ tries: 31
▬ conversions: 21
▬ penalty goals: **67** *League Best*
▬ drop goals: 4

### How Points were Conceded

▬ tries: 44
▬ conversions: 29
▬ penalty goals: 54
▬ drop goals: 11

### Tries Scored by Player

▬ backs: 22
▬ forwards: 9

### Tries Conceded by Player

▬ backs: 33
▬ forwards: 10

### Tries Scored/Conceded Across the Pitch

| 3 | 1 | 2 | - | 3 | - | - | 1 | - | 1 | 1 | 1 | 2 | 3 | - | 2 | - | - | 1 | 1 | - | 2 | 2 | 2 | 2 | 1 |
|---|---|---|---|---|---|---|---|---|---|---|---|---|---|---|---|---|---|---|---|---|---|---|---|---|---|

▬ scored
▬ conceded

| 1 | 6 | 1 | - | - | 4 | - | - | 3 | - | 5 | 3 | 1 | 2 | 1 | - | 2 | 3 | 1 | 2 | 1 | 2 | 4 | 1 |
|---|---|---|---|---|---|---|---|---|---|---|---|---|---|---|---|---|---|---|---|---|---|---|---|

# Eight-Season Form 1997-2005

## Season Progression

| Season | 97-98 | 98-99 | 99-00 | 00-01 | 01-02 | 02-03 | 03-04 | 04-05 |
|--------|-------|-------|-------|-------|-------|-------|-------|-------|

**Points/Position**
- ⟲ position
- ➡ Premiership
- ➡ Division 1
- ➡ Division 2

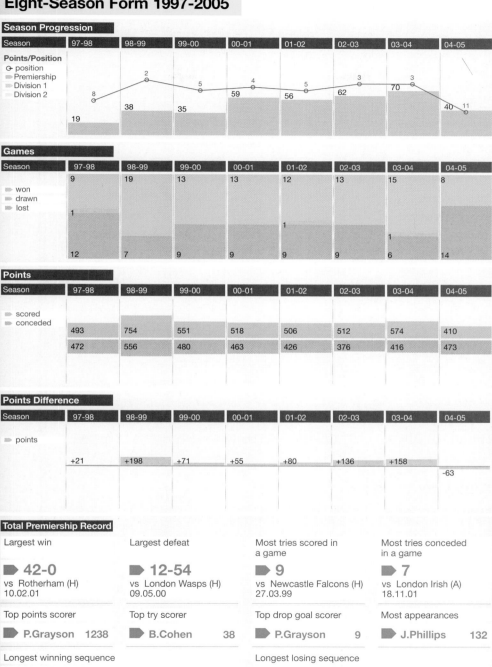

Position line: 8, 2, 5, 4, 5, 3, 3, 11
Points bars: 19, 38, 35, 59, 56, 62, 70, 40

## Games

| Season | 97-98 | 98-99 | 99-00 | 00-01 | 01-02 | 02-03 | 03-04 | 04-05 |
|--------|-------|-------|-------|-------|-------|-------|-------|-------|
| ➡ won | 9 | 19 | 13 | 13 | 12 | 13 | 15 | 8 |
| ➡ drawn | 1 | | | | 1 | | 1 | |
| ➡ lost | 12 | 7 | 9 | 9 | 9 | 9 | 6 | 14 |

## Points

| Season | 97-98 | 98-99 | 99-00 | 00-01 | 01-02 | 02-03 | 03-04 | 04-05 |
|--------|-------|-------|-------|-------|-------|-------|-------|-------|
| ➡ scored | 493 | 754 | 551 | 518 | 506 | 512 | 574 | 410 |
| ➡ conceded | 472 | 556 | 480 | 463 | 426 | 376 | 416 | 473 |

## Points Difference

| Season | 97-98 | 98-99 | 99-00 | 00-01 | 01-02 | 02-03 | 03-04 | 04-05 |
|--------|-------|-------|-------|-------|-------|-------|-------|-------|
| ➡ points | +21 | +198 | +71 | +55 | +80 | +136 | +158 | -63 |

## Total Premiership Record

| Largest win | Largest defeat | Most tries scored in a game | Most tries conceded in a game |
|-------------|----------------|-----------------------------|-------------------------------|
| ➡ **42-0** | ➡ **12-54** | ➡ **9** | ➡ **7** |
| vs Rotherham (H) 10.02.01 | vs London Wasps (H) 09.05.00 | vs Newcastle Falcons (H) 27.03.99 | vs London Irish (A) 18.11.01 |

| Top points scorer | Top try scorer | Top drop goal scorer | Most appearances |
|-------------------|----------------|----------------------|------------------|
| ➡ P.Grayson  1238 | ➡ B.Cohen  38 | ➡ P.Grayson  9 | ➡ J.Phillips  132 |

| Longest winning sequence | Longest losing sequence |
|--------------------------|-------------------------|
| ➡ **7 wins**  from 05.11.99 to 26.01.00 | ➡ **9 defeats**  from 18.09.04 to 28.11.04 |

# ENHANCED FIXTURE LIST
[does not include play-off data]

## GUINNESS PREMIERSHIP 2005-06 | Premiership History

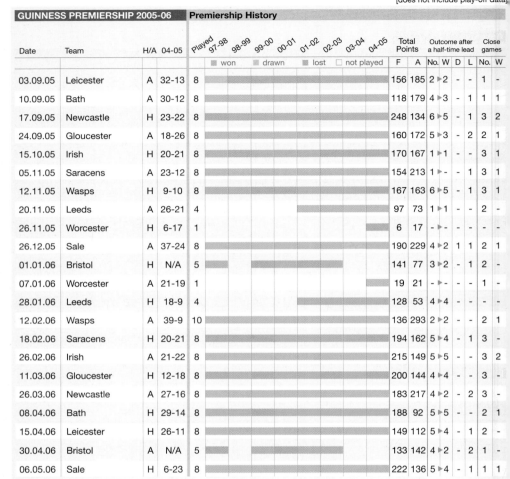

| Date | Team | H/A | 04-05 | Played | 97-98 | 98-99 | 99-00 | 00-01 | 01-02 | 02-03 | 03-04 | 04-05 | Total Points F | A | No. | W | D | L | Close games No. | W |
|---|---|---|---|---|---|---|---|---|---|---|---|---|---|---|---|---|---|---|---|---|
| | | | | | ■ won | | ■ drawn | | ■ lost | | □ not played | | | | | | | | | |
| 03.09.05 | Leicester | A | 32-13 | 8 | | | | | | | | | 156 | 185 | 2 ▶2 | | - | - | 1 | - |
| 10.09.05 | Bath | A | 30-12 | 8 | | | | | | | | | 118 | 179 | 4 ▶3 | | - | 1 | 1 | 1 |
| 17.09.05 | Newcastle | H | 23-22 | 8 | | | | | | | | | 248 | 134 | 6 ▶5 | | - | 1 | 3 | 2 |
| 24.09.05 | Gloucester | A | 18-26 | 8 | | | | | | | | | 160 | 172 | 5 ▶3 | | - | 2 | 2 | 1 |
| 15.10.05 | Irish | H | 20-21 | 8 | | | | | | | | | 170 | 167 | 1 ▶1 | | - | - | 3 | 1 |
| 05.11.05 | Saracens | A | 23-12 | 8 | | | | | | | | | 154 | 213 | 1 ▶- | | - | 1 | 3 | 1 |
| 12.11.05 | Wasps | H | 9-10 | 8 | | | | | | | | | 167 | 163 | 6 ▶5 | | - | 1 | 3 | 1 |
| 20.11.05 | Leeds | A | 26-21 | 4 | | | | | | | | | 97 | 73 | 1 ▶1 | | - | - | 2 | - |
| 26.11.05 | Worcester | H | 6-17 | 1 | | | | | | | | | 6 | 17 | - ▶- | | - | - | - | - |
| 26.12.05 | Sale | A | 37-24 | 8 | | | | | | | | | 190 | 229 | 4 ▶2 | | 1 | 1 | 2 | 1 |
| 01.01.06 | Bristol | H | N/A | 5 | | | | | | | | | 141 | 77 | 3 ▶2 | | - | 1 | 2 | - |
| 07.01.06 | Worcester | A | 21-19 | 1 | | | | | | | | | 19 | 21 | - ▶- | | - | - | 1 | - |
| 28.01.06 | Leeds | H | 18-9 | 4 | | | | | | | | | 128 | 53 | 4 ▶4 | | - | - | - | - |
| 12.02.06 | Wasps | A | 39-9 | 10 | | | | | | | | | 136 | 293 | 2 ▶2 | | - | - | 2 | 1 |
| 18.02.06 | Saracens | H | 20-21 | 8 | | | | | | | | | 194 | 162 | 5 ▶4 | | - | 1 | 3 | - |
| 26.02.06 | Irish | A | 21-22 | 8 | | | | | | | | | 215 | 149 | 5 ▶5 | | - | - | 3 | 2 |
| 11.03.06 | Gloucester | H | 12-18 | 8 | | | | | | | | | 200 | 144 | 4 ▶4 | | - | - | 3 | - |
| 26.03.06 | Newcastle | A | 27-16 | 8 | | | | | | | | | 183 | 217 | 4 ▶2 | | - | 2 | 3 | - |
| 08.04.06 | Bath | H | 29-14 | 8 | | | | | | | | | 188 | 92 | 5 ▶5 | | - | - | 2 | 1 |
| 15.04.06 | Leicester | H | 26-11 | 8 | | | | | | | | | 149 | 112 | 5 ▶4 | | - | 1 | 2 | - |
| 30.04.06 | Bristol | A | N/A | 5 | | | | | | | | | 133 | 142 | 4 ▶2 | | - | 2 | 1 | - |
| 06.05.06 | Sale | H | 6-23 | 8 | | | | | | | | | 222 | 136 | 5 ▶4 | | - | 1 | 1 | 1 |

# Club Information

## Useful Information

**Founded**
1880
**Address**
Franklin's Gardens
Weedon Road
Northampton
NN5 5BG
**Capacity**
13,500 (11,500 seated)
**Main switchboard**
01604 751543
**Website**
www.northamptonsaints.
co.uk

## Travel Information

**Car**
From North:
Approaching on the M1, exit at junction 16 and take the A45 onto Weedon Road, which is signposted 'Town Centre'. Turn left into Ross Road and follow signs for the car park.
From South:
Approaching on the M1, exit at junction 15a and follow signs for Sixfields. Turn left to join the A45 onto Weedon Road. Then as route for North.

**Train**
Silverlink trains run from Milton Keynes Central or Coventry to Northampton station.
Silverlink Trains also run directly from London Euston to Northampton station.
From Northampton station, turn right and continue walking until you pass the bus station and enter a shopping area. Turn left, then left again down Abbey Street into the Northampton Saints Car Park.

## Maps

### Area Map

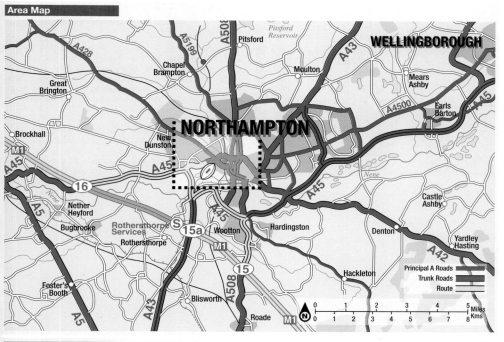

### Local Map

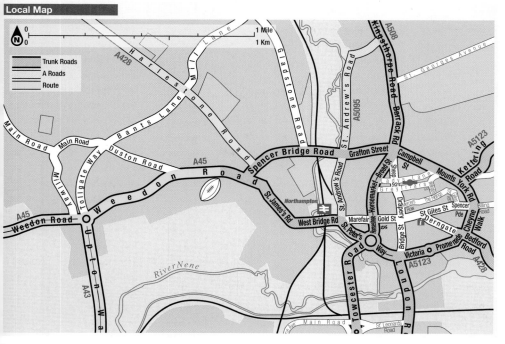

# Sale Sharks

## Season Summary

| Position | Won | Drawn | Lost | For | Against | Bonus Points | Total Points |
|---|---|---|---|---|---|---|---|
| **3** | **13** | **0** | **9** | **513** | **442** | **8** | **60** |

Although injured for some of the season, Bryan Redpath enjoyed another hugely influential year at Sale, his last before retirement. Charlie Hodgson continued to make a convincing case to be first-choice England fly half in a season when Sale lost the most players of any Premiership club during the international periods.

Mark Cueto, Steve Hanley and Jason Robinson scored more tries than the whole of any other club's back line, and Sébastien Chabal, unmistakeable with his wild mane and rampaging runs, was an instant hit with the fans. Expectations for the new season should be high.

**Director of Rugby:** Philippe Saint-Andre

**Club Honours**
Parker Pen Shield: 2002, 2005

# Season Squad

## Stats 2004-05

| Position | Player | Height | Weight | Apps | Rep | Tries | Points | Position | Player | Height | Weight | Apps | Rep | Tries | Points |
|---|---|---|---|---|---|---|---|---|---|---|---|---|---|---|---|
| BR | P.Anglesea | 6'3" | 16st 4lb | 3 | 7 | - | - | FL | M.Lund | 6'3" | 16st 9lb | 17 | 5 | 3 | 15 |
| FH/C | J.Baxendell | 6'0" | 14st 2lb | 14 | 1 | - | - | SH | S.Martens | 5'11" | 14st 7lb | 8 | 9 | - | - |
| FH | D.Blair | 5'9" | 11st 7lb | - | 1 | - | - | C/W | C.Mayor | 6'2" | 15st 0lb | 6 | 2 | 1 | 5 |
| P | S.Bozzi | 6'2" | 19st 9lb | - | 4 | - | - | FB | J.Moore | 5'10" | 11st 12lb | 2 | 2 | - | - |
| H | S.Bruno | 5'9" | 16st 9lb | 8 | 9 | 2 | 10 | C | J.Payne | 6'1" | 15st 7lb | 2 | 3 | - | - |
| BR | P.Caillet | 6'3" | 17st 0lb | 4 | 6 | - | - | FL | H.Perrett | 6'2" | 15st 0lb | - | 1 | - | - |
| FL | J.Carter | 6'3" | 17st 0lb | 7 | 6 | 2 | 10 | SH | B.Redpath | 5'7" | 12st 9lb | 14 | 6 | 2 | 10 |
| 8 | S.Chabal | 6'3" | 17st 0lb | 21 | - | 2 | 10 | W | O.Ripol Fortuny | 5'9" | 12st 6lb | 2 | 1 | - | - |
| P | B.Coutts | 6'3" | 18st 0lb | 1 | 2 | - | - | FB | J.Robinson | 5'8" | 13st 4lb | 16 | - | 4 | 23 |
| W | M.Cueto | 6'0" | 14st 9lb | 17 | - | 11 | 55 | H | J.Roddam | 5'9" | 15st 2lb | 6 | - | 1 | 5 |
| L | C.Day | 6'6" | 16st 10lb | 9 | 7 | - | - | L | D.Schofield | 6'6" | 18st 0lb | 21 | 1 | 2 | 10 |
| C | J.Duffy | 5'9" | 14st 8lb | - | 1 | - | - | P | A.Sheridan | 6'5" | 18st 10lb | 15 | 2 | 3 | 15 |
| L | I.Fernandez Lobbe | 6'5" | 17st 4lb | 2 | 2 | - | - | P | B.Stewart | 6'2" | 18st 0lb | 17 | 5 | - | - |
| P | M.Halsall | 5'11" | 17st 10lb | - | 1 | - | - | FB/C | J.Taumalolo | 5'10" | 15st 5lb | 2 | 2 | - | - |
| W | S.Hanley | 6'4" | 15st 12lb | 20 | - | 9 | 45 | H/FL | A.Titterrell | 5'8" | 14st 9lb | 9 | 9 | 1 | 5 |
| FB | B.Hayward | 5'8" | 12st 12lb | 2 | - | - | 17 | C | R.Todd | 5'11" | 16st 0lb | 21 | - | 3 | 15 |
| FH | M.Hercus | 5'9" | 12st 10lb | 7 | 5 | - | 53 | P | S.Turner | 6'0" | 17st 9lb | 11 | 11 | 2 | 10 |
| FH | C.Hodgson | 5'10" | 12st 13lb | 15 | 1 | 2 | 200 | FL/L | J.White | 6'5" | 18st 6lb | 16 | 1 | 1 | 5 |
| L/BR | C.Jones | 6'7" | 16st 1lb | 15 | 4 | 3 | 15 | SH | R.Wigglesworth | 5'9" | 13st 3lb | 3 | 7 | - | 2 |
| C | C.Jones | 6'2" | 15st 0lb | 10 | 6 | - | - | P | T.Woodman | 6'0" | 17st 7lb | 2 | 1 | - | - |

# Last Season Form

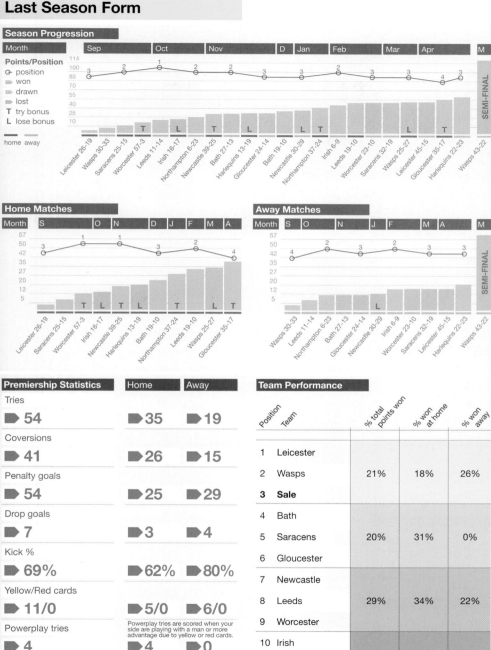

## Season Progression

| Month | Sep | Oct | Nov | D | Jan | Feb | Mar | Apr | M |

Points/Position
- G position
- won
- drawn
- lost
- T try bonus
- L lose bonus

home away

## Home Matches

| Month | S | O | N | D | J | F | M | A | M |

## Away Matches

| Month | S | O | N | D | J | F | M | A | M |

## Premiership Statistics

| | Home | Away |
|---|---|---|
| Tries | | |
| 54 | 35 | 19 |
| Conversions | | |
| 41 | 26 | 15 |
| Penalty goals | | |
| 54 | 25 | 29 |
| Drop goals | | |
| 7 | 3 | 4 |
| Kick % | | |
| 69% | 62% | 80% |
| Yellow/Red cards | | |
| 11/0 | 5/0 | 6/0 |
| Powerplay tries | | |
| 4 | 4 | 0 |
| Shorthand tries | | |
| 0 | 0 | 0 |

Powerplay tries are scored when your side is playing with a man or more advantage due to yellow or red cards.

Shorthand tries are scored when your side is playing with a man or more fewer due to yellow or red cards.

## Team Performance

| Position | Team | % total points won | % won at home | % won away |
|---|---|---|---|---|
| 1 | Leicester | | | |
| 2 | Wasps | 21% | 18% | 26% |
| 3 | **Sale** | | | |
| 4 | Bath | | | |
| 5 | Saracens | 20% | 31% | 0% |
| 6 | Gloucester | | | |
| 7 | Newcastle | | | |
| 8 | Leeds | 29% | 34% | 22% |
| 9 | Worcester | | | |
| 10 | Irish | | | |
| 11 | Northampton | 30% | 17% | 52% |
| 12 | Harlequins | | | |

# Sale Sharks

## Top Scorer

### Charlie Hodgson

| Total points | % team points | Home | Away |
|---|---|---|---|
| ▶ 200 | ▶ 37 | ▶ 126 | ▶ 74 |

### Points by Time Period

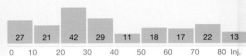

| 27 | 21 | 42 | 29 | 11 | 18 | 17 | 22 | 13 |
|---|---|---|---|---|---|---|---|---|
| 0 | 10 | 20 | 30 | 40 | 50 | 60 | 70 | 80 Inj. |

## Team Tries and Points

### Tries by Time Period

| 8 | 5 | 8 | 10 | 5 | 6 | 3 | 7 | 2 |
|---|---|---|---|---|---|---|---|---|
| 0 | 10min | 20min | 30min | 40min | 50min | 60min | 70min | 80 Injury time |
| 6 | 5 | 7 | 14 | 3 | 5 | 2 | 2 | 3 |

League Best

- ▬ scored
- ▬ conceded

### Tries by Halves

- ▬ scored
- ▬ conceded

| ▶ 54 | ▶ 31 | ▶ 23 | ▶ 57% | ▶ 43% |
|---|---|---|---|---|
| Total | 1st half | 2nd half | 1st half % | 2nd half % |
| ▶ 47 | ▶ 32 | ▶ 15 | ▶ 68% | ▶ 32% |

### How Points were Scored

- ▬ tries: 51
- ▬ conversions: 39
- ▬ penalty goals: 53
- drop goals: 7

### How Points were Conceded

- ▬ tries: 43
- ▬ conversions: 31
- ▬ penalty goals: 49
- drop goals: 6

### Tries Scored by Player

- ▬ backs: 32
- ▬ forwards: **22**

League Best

### Tries Conceded by Player

- ▬ backs: 33
- ▬ forwards: 12

### Tries Scored/Conceded Across the Pitch

| 4 | 4 | 2 | 2 | 3 | 3 | 2 | 1 | - | 1 | 3 | - | 4 | 4 | 1 | - | 2 | 3 | 2 | - | 1 | 1 | - | 6 | 2 |
|---|---|---|---|---|---|---|---|---|---|---|---|---|---|---|---|---|---|---|---|---|---|---|---|---|

- ▬ scored
- ▬ conceded

| 5 | 3 | 2 | 1 | 1 | 2 | - | 3 | - | 1 | - | 2 | 7 | 1 | - | 2 | - | - | 1 | 2 | 3 | - | 2 | 4 | 1 |
|---|---|---|---|---|---|---|---|---|---|---|---|---|---|---|---|---|---|---|---|---|---|---|---|---|

# Eight-Season Form 1997-2005

## Season Progression

| Season | 97-98 | 98-99 | 99-00 | 00-01 | 01-02 | 02-03 | 03-04 | 04-05 |
|--------|-------|-------|-------|-------|-------|-------|-------|-------|

**Points/Position**
- ○ position
- ■ Premiership
- ■ Division 1
- ■ Division 2

Position: 6, 11, 11, 10, 2, 4, 7, 3

Points: 22, 19, 18, 43, 69, 62, 53, 60

## Games

| Season | 97-98 | 98-99 | 99-00 | 00-01 | 01-02 | 02-03 | 03-04 | 04-05 |
|--------|-------|-------|-------|-------|-------|-------|-------|-------|
| ■ won | 10 | 9 | 7 | 8 | 14 | 12 | 9 | 13 |
| ■ drawn | | 1 | | 1 | | 2 | 3 | |
| | | | | | 1 | | | |
| ■ lost | 10 | 16 | 15 | 13 | 7 | 8 | 10 | 9 |

## Points

| Season | 97-98 | 98-99 | 99-00 | 00-01 | 01-02 | 02-03 | 03-04 | 04-05 |
|--------|-------|-------|-------|-------|-------|-------|-------|-------|
| ■ scored | 605 | 604 | 381 | 561 | 589 | 556 | 510 | 513 |
| ■ conceded | 558 | 731 | 633 | 622 | 517 | 470 | 472 | 442 |

## Points Difference

| Season | 97-98 | 98-99 | 99-00 | 00-01 | 01-02 | 02-03 | 03-04 | 04-05 |
|--------|-------|-------|-------|-------|-------|-------|-------|-------|
| ■ points | +47 | -127 | -252 | -61 | +72 | +86 | +38 | +71 |

## Total Premiership Record

**Largest win**

➤ **57-3**
vs Worcester Warriors (H)
24.09.04

**Largest defeat**

➤ **5-58**
vs London Wasps (A)
30.04.00

**Most tries scored in a game**

➤ **12**
vs Bristol Shoguns (H)
09.11.97

**Most tries conceded in a game**

➤ **9**
vs London Wasps (A)
30.04.00

**Top points scorer**

➤ C.Hodgson 840

**Top try scorer**

➤ S.Hanley 71

**Top drop goal scorer**

➤ C.Hodgson 12

**Most appearances**

➤ J.Baxendell 131

**Longest winning sequence**

➤ **6 wins** from 08.05.04 to 03.10.04

**Longest losing sequence**

➤ **7 defeats** from 20.12.98 to 14.02.99

# Sale Sharks EFL

## GUINNESS PREMIERSHIP 2005-06 | Premiership History

| Date | Team | H/A | 04-05 | Played | Total Points F | A | Outcome after a half-time lead No. | W | D | L | Close games No. | W |
|------|------|-----|-------|--------|----|----|----|----|----|----|----|----|
| 02.09.05 | Newcastle | H | 39-25 | 8 | 259 | 160 | 5 ▶4 | - | - | 1 | 1 | - |
| 10.09.05 | Gloucester | A | 24-14 | 8 | 134 | 256 | 1 ▶1 | - | - | 1 | 1 | 1 |
| 16.09.05 | Irish | H | 16-17 | 8 | 235 | 170 | 2 ▶2 | - | - | 4 | 4 | 1 |
| 25.09.05 | Saracens | A | 32-19 | 8 | 190 | 316 | 1 ▶- | - | 1 | 1 | 1 | - |
| 14.10.05 | Wasps | H | 25-27 | 8 | 180 | 224 | - ▶- | - | - | 4 | 4 | 1 |
| 05.11.05 | Leeds | A | 11-14 | 4 | 121 | 80 | 3 ▶3 | - | - | 1 | 1 | 1 |
| 11.11.05 | Worcester | H | 57-3 | 1 | 57 | 3 | 1 ▶1 | - | - | - | - | - |
| 18.11.05 | Leicester | H | 26-19 | 8 | 143 | 202 | 3 ▶2 | 1 | - | 1 | 1 | - |
| 27.11.05 | Bristol | A | N/A | 5 | 118 | 106 | 3 ▶3 | - | - | - | - | - |
| 26.12.05 | Northampton | H | 37-24 | 8 | 229 | 190 | 4 ▶4 | - | - | 2 | 2 | 1 |
| 02.01.06 | Bath | A | 27-13 | 8 | 130 | 203 | 2 ▶1 | - | 1 | 4 | 4 | - |
| 08.01.06 | Bristol | H | N/A | 5 | 197 | 127 | 4 ▶3 | - | 1 | 2 | 2 | 1 |
| 28.01.06 | Leicester | A | 45-15 | 8 | 112 | 255 | 2 ▶1 | - | 1 | 1 | 1 | 1 |
| 11.02.06 | Worcester | A | 23-10 | 1 | 10 | 23 | - ▶- | - | - | - | - | - |
| 17.02.06 | Leeds | H | 19-10 | 4 | 123 | 71 | 2 ▶2 | - | - | - | - | - |
| 26.02.06 | Wasps | A | 30-33 | 9 | 223 | 290 | 3 ▶2 | - | 1 | 2 | 2 | 2 |
| 10.03.06 | Saracens | H | 25-15 | 8 | 178 | 199 | 6 ▶5 | - | 1 | - | - | - |
| 25.03.06 | Irish | A | 6-9 | 8 | 144 | 157 | 3 ▶3 | - | - | 5 | 5 | 4 |
| 07.04.06 | Gloucester | H | 35-17 | 8 | 203 | 200 | 5 ▶3 | 2 | - | - | - | - |
| 16.04.06 | Newcastle | A | 30-29 | 8 | 130 | 213 | - ▶- | - | - | 4 | 4 | - |
| 28.04.06 | Bath | H | 19-10 | 8 | 186 | 155 | 4 ▶3 | - | 1 | 6 | 6 | 3 |
| 06.05.06 | Northampton | A | 6-23 | 8 | 136 | 222 | 3 ▶1 | - | 2 | 1 | 1 | - |

Legend: ■ won  ■ drawn  ■ lost  □ not played

# Club Information

## Useful Information

**Founded**
1861
**Address**
Edgeley Park
Hardcastle Road
Edgeley
Stockport
SK3 9DD
**Capacity**
5,678 (3,132 seated)
**Main switchboard**
0161 283 8888
**Website**
www.salesharks.com

## Travel Information

**Car**
From South:
Leave the M6 at junction 19 (towards Manchester Airport, Stockport A55), then turn right at the roundabout onto the A556. After approx four miles you reach a roundabout, turn right onto the M56 (towards Manchester). After approx a further seven miles, exit the M56 and join the M60 (signposted Stockport, Sheffield). Leave the M60 at junction 1 and follow the signs to Cheadle and Stockport County FC at the roundabout. Continue straight ahead at the first set of traffic lights, then right at the next set (keep following signs for Stockport County FC). After a mile, turn left onto the B5465 Edgeley Road, then after another mile turn right into Dale Street. Take the second turning on the left into Hardcastle Road to reach the stadium.

From North:
From the M62 join the M60 and continue south. Leave the M60 at junction 1, then as route for South.

**Train**
Stockport station is approx half a mile from the stadium. Arriva Trains Northern run services from Sheffield to Stockport. From London, Virgin Trains run from London Euston to directly to Stockport.

# Maps

## Area Map

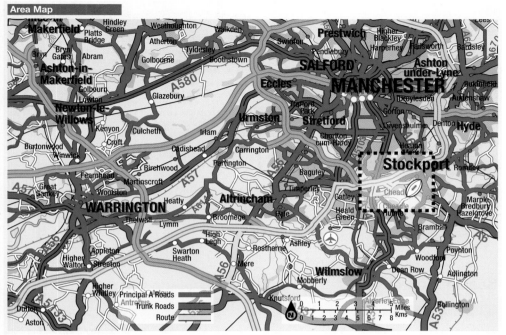

## Local Map

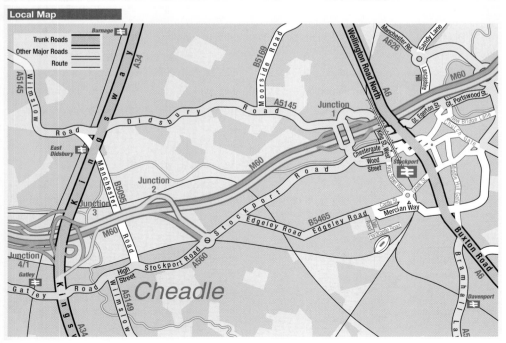

# Saracens

## Season Summary

| Position | Won | Drawn | Lost | For | Against | Bonus Points | Total Points |
|---|---|---|---|---|---|---|---|
| 5 | 12 | 2 | 8 | 384 | 428 | 5 | 57 |

Saracens looked strong by the end of the 2004-05 campaign. However, the talk of the town is the arrival of Andy Farrell from rugby league club Wigan, who will start at inside centre. Rod Kafer's sudden departure as Head Coach handed the reins to Steve Diamond, who turned round a poor start as his side went on to win seven of their last nine matches. After making the Wildcard play-offs, they secured a place in Europe for the first time since 2001.

Richard Hill is laid up for the long-term, but Alex Sanderson should make a good impression after recovering from injury.

**Head Coach:** Steve Diamond
**Director of Rugby:** Mike Ford

**Club Honours**
Pilkington Cup: 1998

## Season Squad

### Stats 2004-05

| Position | Player | Height | Weight | Apps | Rep | Tries | Points | Position | Player | Height | Weight | Apps | Rep | Tries | Points |
|---|---|---|---|---|---|---|---|---|---|---|---|---|---|---|---|
| FL | S.Armitage | 5'9" | 16st 8lb | - | 1 | - | - | P | N.Lloyd | 6'0" | 16st 9lb | 1 | 18 | - | - |
| C | P.Bailey | 6'0" | 12st 8lb | 4 | 5 | 3 | 15 | L | S.Raiwalui | 6'6" | 18st 13lb | 16 | 3 | - | - |
| C | M.Bartholomeusz | 5'9" | 13st 8lb | 17 | 2 | - | 6 | BR | T.Randell | 6'2" | 17st 4lb | 20 | - | 2 | 10 |
| SH | K.Bracken | 5'11" | 13st 0lb | 14 | - | - | - | SH | M.Rauluni | 5'10" | 13st 7lb | 3 | 15 | 1 | 5 |
| P | B.Broster | 5'11" | 16st 9lb | 10 | 1 | 1 | 5 | FH | B.Russell | 6'2" | 13st 3lb | 1 | - | - | - |
| H | M.Cairns | 5'11" | 16st 0lb | 14 | 8 | 2 | 10 | BR | B.Russell | 6'3" | 15st 10lb | 4 | 4 | 2 | 10 |
| FH | T.Castaignede | 5'9" | 13st 3lb | 16 | 1 | 3 | 47 | BR | A.Sanderson | 6'2" | 16st 1lb | 2 | 1 | - | - |
| L | K.Chesney | 6'6" | 18st 4lb | 13 | 9 | 1 | 5 | FB | D.Scarbrough | 6'1" | 13st 3lb | 6 | 1 | 1 | 5 |
| L | I.Fullarton | 6'7" | 16st 12lb | 14 | 3 | - | - | BR | D.Seymour | 5'11" | 14st 2lb | 13 | 4 | - | - |
| C | D.Harris | 5'10" | 15st 12lb | 13 | - | 1 | 5 | BR | B.Skirving | 6'4" | 16st 12lb | 2 | 8 | - | - |
| W | R.Haughton | 6'2" | 13st 7lb | 12 | 1 | 4 | 20 | C | K.Sorrell | 5'11" | 13st 8lb | 12 | 7 | 1 | 5 |
| BR | R.Hill | 6'2" | 16st 0lb | 7 | 1 | 1 | 5 | 8 | S.Taylor | 6'4" | 16st 7lb | - | 1 | - | - |
| H | R.Ibanez | 5'11" | 15st 2lb | 8 | 10 | 1 | 5 | W | T.Vaikona | 6'2" | 16st 2lb | 14 | 1 | 1 | 5 |
| FH | G.Jackson | 5'11" | 13st 6lb | 8 | 3 | 1 | 77 | P | C.Visagie | 6'1" | 18st 0lb | 12 | 1 | - | - |
| C | B.Johnston | 6'3" | 16st 7lb | 17 | 1 | 4 | 23 | BR | H.Vyvyan | 6'6" | 16st 0lb | 19 | - | 2 | 10 |
| C/FH | R.Kydd | 5'11" | 14st 3lb | 8 | 1 | 2 | 38 | SH | M.Williams | 6'0" | 13st 0lb | 5 | 4 | - | - |
| FH | N.Little | 6'0" | 15st 0lb | 4 | 10 | 1 | 53 | P | K.Yates | 5'11" | 17st 12lb | 21 | - | 1 | 5 |

## Last Season Form

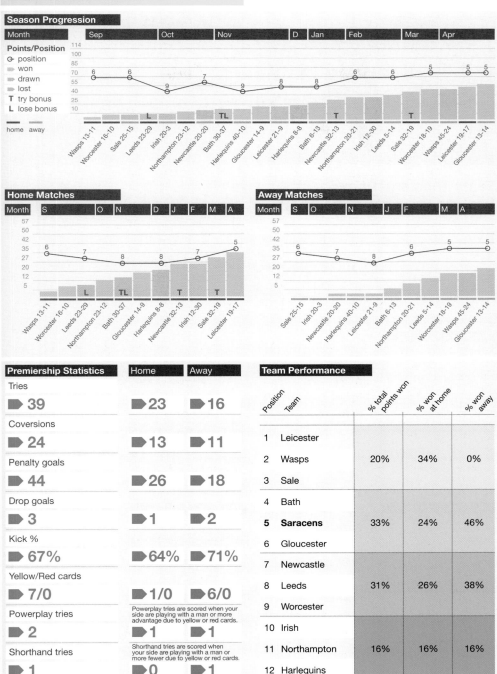

### Season Progression

| Month | Sep | Oct | Nov | D | Jan | Feb | Mar | Apr |

Points/Position
- G- position
- won
- drawn
- lost
- T try bonus
- L lose bonus

home away

### Home Matches

| Month | S | O | N | D | J | F | M | A |

### Away Matches

| Month | S | O | N | J | F | M | A |

### Premiership Statistics

| | Home | Away |
|---|---|---|
| Tries | | |
| 39 | 23 | 16 |
| Coversions | | |
| 24 | 13 | 11 |
| Penalty goals | | |
| 44 | 26 | 18 |
| Drop goals | | |
| 3 | 1 | 2 |
| Kick % | | |
| 67% | 64% | 71% |
| Yellow/Red cards | | |
| 7/0 | 1/0 | 6/0 |
| Powerplay tries | | |
| 2 | 1 | 1 |
| Shorthand tries | | |
| 1 | 0 | 1 |

Powerplay tries are scored when your side is playing with a man or more advantage due to yellow or red cards.

Shorthand tries are scored when your side are playing with a man or more fewer due to yellow or red cards.

### Team Performance

| Position | Team | % total points won | % won at home | % won away |
|---|---|---|---|---|
| 1 | Leicester | | | |
| 2 | Wasps | 20% | 34% | 0% |
| 3 | Sale | | | |
| 4 | Bath | | | |
| 5 | **Saracens** | 33% | 24% | 46% |
| 6 | Gloucester | | | |
| 7 | Newcastle | | | |
| 8 | Leeds | 31% | 26% | 38% |
| 9 | Worcester | | | |
| 10 | Irish | | | |
| 11 | Northampton | 16% | 16% | 16% |
| 12 | Harlequins | | | |

---

# Saracens

## Top Scorer

### Glen Jackson

### Points Facts

| Total points | % team points | Home | Away |
| --- | --- | --- | --- |
| 77 | 20 | 44 | 33 |

### Points by Time Period

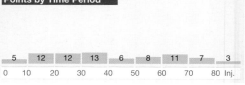

| 5 | 12 | 12 | 13 | 6 | 8 | 11 | 7 | 3 |
| --- | --- | --- | --- | --- | --- | --- | --- | --- |
| 0 | 10 | 20 | 30 | 40 | 50 | 60 | 70 | 80 Inj. |

## Team Tries and Points

### Tries by Time Period

| 2 | 7 | 3 | 8 | 4 | 4 | 3 | 7 | 1 |
| --- | --- | --- | --- | --- | --- | --- | --- | --- |
| 0 | 10min | 20min | 30min | 40min | 50min | 60min | 70min | 80 Injury time |
| 10 | 5 | 3 | 5 | 4 | 4 | 3 | 5 | 4 |

- scored
- conceded

### Tries by Halves

- scored
- conceded

| | Total | 1st half | 2nd half | 1st half % | 2nd half % |
| --- | --- | --- | --- | --- | --- |
| scored | 39 | 20 | 19 | 51% | 49% |
| conceded | 43 | 23 | 20 | 53% | 47% |

### How Points were Scored

- tries: 39
- conversions: 24
- penalty goals: 44
- drop goals: 3

### How Points were Conceded

- tries: 43
- conversions: 30
- penalty goals: 47
- drop goals: 4

### Tries Scored by Player

- backs: 23
- forwards: 13

### Tries Conceded by Player

- backs: 31
- forwards: 12

### Tries Scored/Conceded Across the Pitch

| 4 | 5 | - | 2 | - | 1 | - | 2 | 1 | 1 | - | 1 | 7 | 3 | - | - | - | - | 1 | 2 | 1 | 1 | 2 | 1 | 3 | 1 |
| --- | --- | --- | --- | --- | --- | --- | --- | --- | --- | --- | --- | --- | --- | --- | --- | --- | --- | --- | --- | --- | --- | --- | --- | --- | --- |

- scored
- conceded

| 4 | 6 | 2 | - | - | 2 | - | - | 1 | - | 6 | 2 | - | 2 | - | 3 | 2 | 3 | 1 | - | - | 4 | 2 | 3 |
| --- | --- | --- | --- | --- | --- | --- | --- | --- | --- | --- | --- | --- | --- | --- | --- | --- | --- | --- | --- | --- | --- | --- | --- |

# Eight-Season Form 1997-2005

## Season Progression

| Season | 97-98 | 98-99 | 99-00 | 00-01 | 01-02 | 02-03 | 03-04 | 04-05 |
|---|---|---|---|---|---|---|---|---|
| **Points/Position** O position — Premiership — Division 1 — Division 2 | 37 | 33 | 37 | 58 | 34 | 42 | 39 | 57 |

Positions: 2, 3, 4, 5, 10, 8, 10, 5

## Games

| Season | 97-98 | 98-99 | 99-00 | 00-01 | 01-02 | 02-03 | 03-04 | 04-05 |
|---|---|---|---|---|---|---|---|---|
| won | 18 | 16 | 14 | 12 | 7 | 8 | 8 | 12 |
| drawn | | 1 | | | | | 1 | 2 |
| lost | 1 / 3 | 9 | 8 | 10 | 15 | 14 | 13 | 8 |

## Points

| Season | 97-98 | 98-99 | 99-00 | 00-01 | 01-02 | 02-03 | 03-04 | 04-05 |
|---|---|---|---|---|---|---|---|---|
| scored | 584 | 748 | 729 | 589 | 425 | 499 | 397 | 384 |
| conceded | 396 | 583 | 514 | 501 | 671 | 587 | 543 | 428 |

## Points Difference

| Season | 97-98 | 98-99 | 99-00 | 00-01 | 01-02 | 02-03 | 03-04 | 04-05 |
|---|---|---|---|---|---|---|---|---|
| points | | +188 | +165 | +215 | +88 | -246 | -88 | -146 | -44 |

## Total Premiership Record

| | |
|---|---|
| **Largest win** | **Largest defeat** |
| ▶ **59-5** vs Rotherham (H) 24.09.00 | ▶ **13-55** vs London Irish (H) 22.11.01 |
| **Most tries scored in a game** | **Most tries conceded in a game** |
| ▶ **9** vs Bedford Blues (A) 16.04.00 | ▶ **7** vs Newcastle Falcons (A) 15.05.02 |

| | |
|---|---|
| Top points scorer | Top try scorer |
| ▶ G.Johnson 363 | ▶ T.Diprose 23 |
| Top drop goal scorer | Most appearances |
| ▶ A.Goode 9 | ▶ K.Chesney 131 |

Longest winning sequence

▶ **7 wins** from 29.04.98 to 11.10.98

Longest losing sequence

▶ **6 defeats** from 04.01.03 to 06.04.03

# Saracens `EFL`

## ENHANCED FIXTURE LIST
[does not include play-off data]

### GUINNESS PREMIERSHIP 2005-06 — Premiership History

Legend: ■ won ■ drawn ■ lost □ not played

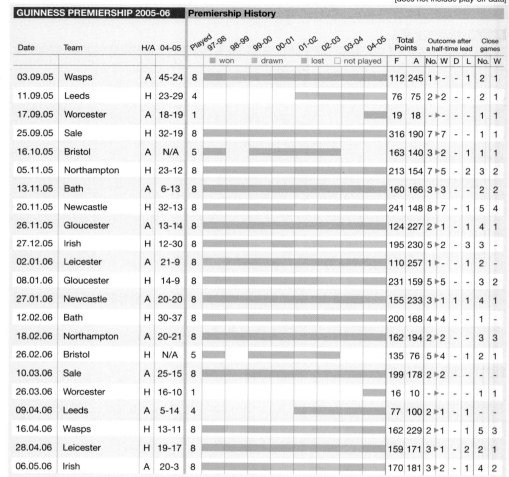

| Date | Team | H/A | 04-05 | Played | 97-98 | 98-99 | 99-00 | 00-01 | 01-02 | 02-03 | 03-04 | 04-05 | Total Points F | A | Outcome after a half-time lead No. | W | D | L | Close games No. | W |
|---|---|---|---|---|---|---|---|---|---|---|---|---|---|---|---|---|---|---|---|---|
| 03.09.05 | Wasps | A | 45-24 | 8 | | | | | | | | | 112 | 245 | 1 | - | - | 1 | 2 | 1 |
| 11.09.05 | Leeds | H | 23-29 | 4 | | | | | | | | | 76 | 75 | 2 | 2 | - | - | 2 | 1 |
| 17.09.05 | Worcester | A | 18-19 | 1 | | | | | | | | | 19 | 18 | - | - | - | - | 1 | 1 |
| 25.09.05 | Sale | H | 32-19 | 8 | | | | | | | | | 316 | 190 | 7 | 7 | - | - | 1 | 1 |
| 16.10.05 | Bristol | A | N/A | 5 | | | | | | | | | 163 | 140 | 3 | 2 | - | 1 | 1 | 1 |
| 05.11.05 | Northampton | H | 23-12 | 8 | | | | | | | | | 213 | 154 | 7 | 5 | - | 2 | 3 | 2 |
| 13.11.05 | Bath | A | 6-13 | 8 | | | | | | | | | 160 | 166 | 3 | 3 | - | - | 2 | 2 |
| 20.11.05 | Newcastle | H | 32-13 | 8 | | | | | | | | | 241 | 148 | 8 | 7 | - | 1 | 5 | 4 |
| 26.11.05 | Gloucester | A | 13-14 | 8 | | | | | | | | | 124 | 227 | 2 | 1 | - | 1 | 4 | 1 |
| 27.12.05 | Irish | H | 12-30 | 8 | | | | | | | | | 195 | 230 | 5 | 2 | - | 3 | 3 | - |
| 02.01.06 | Leicester | A | 21-9 | 8 | | | | | | | | | 110 | 257 | 1 | - | - | 1 | 2 | - |
| 08.01.06 | Gloucester | H | 14-9 | 8 | | | | | | | | | 231 | 159 | 5 | 5 | - | - | 3 | 2 |
| 27.01.06 | Newcastle | A | 20-20 | 8 | | | | | | | | | 155 | 233 | 3 | 1 | 1 | 1 | 4 | 1 |
| 12.02.06 | Bath | H | 30-37 | 8 | | | | | | | | | 200 | 168 | 4 | 4 | - | - | 1 | - |
| 18.02.06 | Northampton | A | 20-21 | 8 | | | | | | | | | 162 | 194 | 2 | 2 | - | - | 3 | 3 |
| 26.02.06 | Bristol | H | N/A | 5 | | | | | | | | | 135 | 76 | 5 | 4 | - | 1 | 2 | 1 |
| 10.03.06 | Sale | A | 25-15 | 8 | | | | | | | | | 199 | 178 | 2 | 2 | - | - | - | - |
| 26.03.06 | Worcester | H | 16-10 | 1 | | | | | | | | | 16 | 10 | - | - | - | - | 1 | 1 |
| 09.04.06 | Leeds | A | 5-14 | 4 | | | | | | | | | 77 | 100 | 2 | 1 | - | 1 | - | - |
| 16.04.06 | Wasps | H | 13-11 | 8 | | | | | | | | | 162 | 229 | 2 | 1 | - | 1 | 5 | 3 |
| 28.04.06 | Leicester | H | 19-17 | 8 | | | | | | | | | 159 | 171 | 3 | 1 | - | 2 | 2 | 1 |
| 06.05.06 | Irish | A | 20-3 | 8 | | | | | | | | | 170 | 181 | 3 | 2 | - | 1 | 4 | 2 |

## Club Information

### Useful Information

**Founded**
1876
**Address**
Vicarage Road Stadium
Vicarage Road
Watford
Herts
WD1 8ER
**Capacity**
22,000 (all seated)
**Main switchboard**
01923 475222
**Website**
www.saracens.com

### Travel Information

**Car**

From North:
Leave the M1 at junction 5, taking the third exit from the roundabout and follow signs to Watford Town Centre. When joining the ring road get into the middle lane, before moving into the left lane after the second set of traffic lights. Follow signs for Watford General Hospital, which is next to Vicarage Road.

From West:
Leave the M25 at junction 19, and follow the A411 Hempstead Road, signposted Watford. Go straight over the first roundabout, then left at the second. Follow the signs towards Watford General Hospital, which is next to Vicarage Road.

**Train**

Watford High Street station is approx 10 minutes walk from the stadium. North London Railway trains run from London Euston station.

**Tube**

Watford tube station is approx 20 minutes walk from the stadium, on the Metropolitan Line.

# Maps

## Area Map

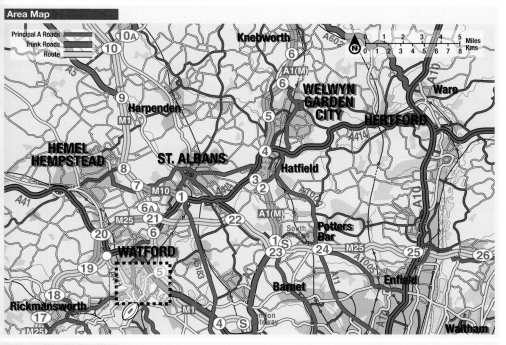

## Local Map

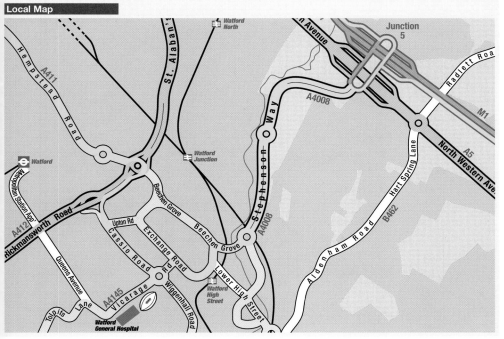

# Worcester Warriors

## Season Summary

| Position | Won | Drawn | Lost | For | Against | | Bonus Points | Total Points |
|---|---|---|---|---|---|---|---|---|
| 9 | 9 | 0 | 13 | 365 | 493 | | 6 | 42 |

There are few who would have wanted to see Worcester, one of the big success stories of the professional era, get relegated. As skipper, Pat Sanderson had a tremendous season, and Matt Powell and James Brown made a great halfback combination.

The incoming Andy Gomersall and Shane Drahm should not take a starting place for granted. Andy Keast has gone, but he and John Brain should share the credit for last season's work. While Brain builds the club at a sensible but slow pace, they won't set the Premiership alight, but should maintain their place in the top flight.

**Head Coach:** Anthony Eddy
**Director of Rugby:** John Brain

**Club Honours**
N/A

## Season Squad

### Stats 2004-05

| Position | Player | Height | Weight | Apps | Rep | Tries | Points |
|---|---|---|---|---|---|---|---|
| L | R.Blaze | 6'7" | 18st 0lb | - | 1 | - | - |
| FH | J.Brown | 5'10" | 11st 2lb | 16 | - | 1 | 113 |
| SH | N.Cole | 5'11" | 12st 6lb | 5 | 3 | - | - |
| L | T.Collier | 6'6" | 21st 3lb | 18 | 1 | 1 | 5 |
| FL/H | B.Daly | 6'2" | 17st 0lb | 8 | 7 | - | - |
| FB | T.Delport | 6'2" | 14st 6lb | 20 | 1 | 1 | 5 |
| P | L.Fortey | 5'10" | 16st 3lb | 2 | 9 | 1 | 5 |
| L | M.Gabey | 6'5" | 18st 9lb | 3 | 4 | - | - |
| L | C.Gillies | 6'7" | 17st 8lb | 21 | - | - | - |
| W | B.Gollings | 5'8" | 12st 9lb | 6 | 2 | - | 2 |
| BR | L.Greeff | 6'4" | 15st 11lb | 6 | - | - | - |
| H | C.Hall | 5'10" | 13st 9lb | - | 5 | - | - |
| FH | T.Hayes | 6'0" | 14st 4lb | 8 | 7 | - | 75 |
| BR | D.Hickey | 6'3" | 15st 12lb | 20 | 2 | 1 | 5 |
| C | B.Hinshelwood | 6'2" | 15st 10lb | 13 | 1 | 5 | 25 |
| P | C.Horsman | 6'2" | 17st 6lb | 12 | - | - | - |
| W | S.Kepu | 6'2" | 18st 0lb | - | 2 | 1 | 5 |
| C | T.Lombard | 6'2" | 13st 5lb | 19 | - | 4 | 20 |

| Position | Player | Height | Weight | Apps | Rep | Tries | Points |
|---|---|---|---|---|---|---|---|
| P | N.Lyman | 6'1" | 18st 10lb | 6 | - | - | - |
| BR | B.MacLeod-Henderson | 6'4" | 15st 9lb | 10 | 5 | - | - |
| BR | N.Mason | 6'2" | 14st 8lb | - | 1 | - | - |
| L | P.Murphy | 6'7" | 17st 6lb | 5 | 8 | - | - |
| P | C.Noon | 5'11" | 18st 3lb | 2 | 1 | - | - |
| W | D.O'Leary | 6'0" | 15st 0lb | 13 | 2 | - | - |
| W/C | G.Pieters | 6'1" | 15st 4lb | 12 | - | 4 | 20 |
| SH | M.Powell | 5'10" | 13st 9lb | 16 | 1 | 3 | 15 |
| C | D.Rasmussen | 6'2" | 14st 12lb | 18 | - | 2 | 10 |
| C | D.Roke | 6'2" | 14st 2lb | - | 3 | - | - |
| W/FB | P.Sampson | 5'9" | 14st 12lb | 1 | 4 | 1 | 5 |
| BR | P.Sanderson | 6'2" | 14st 8lb | 22 | - | 3 | 15 |
| P | S.Sparks | 5'10" | 16st 9lb | 1 | 9 | 1 | 5 |
| SH | C.Stuart-Smith | 5'9" | 13st 7lb | 1 | 5 | - | - |
| C | G.Trueman | 6'0" | 14st 2lb | 6 | 4 | 1 | 5 |
| BR | S.Vaili | 6'4" | 17st 6lb | 5 | 6 | 2 | 10 |
| H | A.Van Niekerk | 5'10" | 16st 12lb | 14 | 6 | - | - |
| P | T.Windo | 6'0" | 16st 12lb | 21 | 1 | 2 | 10 |

# Last Season Form

## Season Progression

| Month | Sep | Oct | Nov | D | Jan | Feb | Mar | Apr |
|---|---|---|---|---|---|---|---|---|

**Points/Position**
- position
- won
- drawn
- lost
- T try bonus
- L lose bonus

home  away

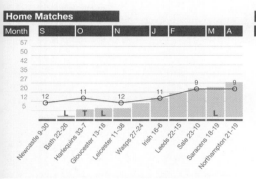

## Home Matches

| Month | S | O | N | J F | M | A |
|---|---|---|---|---|---|---|

## Away Matches

| Month | S | O | N | D J | F | M | A |
|---|---|---|---|---|---|---|---|

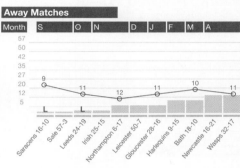

## Premiership Statistics

| | Home | Away |
|---|---|---|
| **Tries** | | |
| 36 | 22 | 14 |
| **Coversions** | | |
| 25 | 15 | 10 |
| **Penalty goals** | | |
| 39 | 23 | 16 |
| **Drop goals** | | |
| 6 | 2 | 4 |
| **Kick %** | | |
| 66% | 63% | 70% |
| **Yellow/Red cards** | | |
| 10/0 | 3/0 | 7/0 |
| **Powerplay tries** | | |
| 4 | 3 | 1 |
| **Shorthand tries** | | |
| 1 | 1 | 0 |

Powerplay tries are scored when your side are playing with a man or more advantage due to yellow or red cards.

Shorthand tries are scored when your side are playing with a man or more fewer due to yellow or red cards.

## Team Performance

| Position | Team | % total points won | % won at home | % won away |
|---|---|---|---|---|
| 1 | Leicester | | | |
| 2 | Wasps | 17% | 27% | 0% |
| 3 | Sale | | | |
| 4 | Bath | | | |
| 5 | Saracens | 9% | 10% | 6% |
| 6 | Gloucester | | | |
| 7 | Newcastle | | | |
| 8 | Leeds | 29% | 20% | 45% |
| 9 | **Worcester** | | | |
| 10 | Irish | | | |
| 11 | Northampton | 45% | 43% | 49% |
| 12 | Harlequins | | | |

**Worcester Warriors**

## Top Scorer

**James Brown**

### Points Facts

| Total points | % team points | Home | Away |
|---|---|---|---|
| 113 | 31 | 64 | 49 |

### Points by Time Period

| 10 | 16 | 8 | 20 | 8 | 17 | 9 | 16 | 9 |
|---|---|---|---|---|---|---|---|---|
| 0 | 10 | 20 | 30 | 40 | 50 | 60 | 70 | 80 Inj. |

## Team Tries and Points

### Tries by Time Period

| 5 | 7 | 5 | 3 | 3 | 3 | 1 | 5 | 4 |
|---|---|---|---|---|---|---|---|---|
| 0 | 10min | 20min | 30min | 40min | 50min | 60min | 70min | 80 Injury time |
| 5 | 5 | 9 | 7 | 9 | 5 | 6 | 6 | 1 |

*League Best*

- scored
- conceded

### Tries by Halves

- scored
- conceded

| | Total | 1st half | 2nd half | 1st half % | 2nd half % |
|---|---|---|---|---|---|
| scored | 36 | 20 | 16 | 56% | 44% |
| conceded | 53 | 26 | 27 | 49% | 51% |

### How Points were Scored

- tries: 36
- conversions: 25
- penalty goals: 39
- drop goals: 6

### How Points were Conceded

- tries: 53
- conversions: 39
- penalty goals: 46
- drop goals: 4

### Tries Scored by Player

- backs: 23
- forwards: 11

### Tries Conceded by Player

- backs: 35
- forwards: 17

### Tries Scored/Conceded Across the Pitch

| 2 | 3 | 2 | - | - | 1 | - | 3 | - | - | 1 | 1 | 5 | 2 | - | - | 1 | 1 | 2 | 1 | - | 2 | 1 | 1 | 6 | 1 |
|---|---|---|---|---|---|---|---|---|---|---|---|---|---|---|---|---|---|---|---|---|---|---|---|---|---|

- scored
- conceded

| 10 | 3 | 1 | 2 | - | 3 | 2 | 3 | - | 1 | 1 | 2 | 4 | 2 | 2 | 1 | - | - | 2 | 3 | 1 | 1 | 2 | 1 | 4 | 2 |
|---|---|---|---|---|---|---|---|---|---|---|---|---|---|---|---|---|---|---|---|---|---|---|---|---|---|

# Eight-Season Form 1997-2005

## Season Progression

| Season | 97-98 | 98-99 | 99-00 | 00-01 | 01-02 | 02-03 | 03-04 | 04-05 |
|---|---|---|---|---|---|---|---|---|
| **Points/Position** | | | | | | | | |
| ⊙ position | 1 | 3 | 3 | 2 | 2 | 2 | 1 | 9 |
| ▬ Premiership | | | | 112 | 108 | 114 | 125 | |
| ▬ Division 1 | 48 | 34 | 38 | | | | | 42 |
| ▬ Division 2 | | | | | | | | |

## Games

| Season | 97-98 | 98-99 | 99-00 | 00-01 | 01-02 | 02-03 | 03-04 | 04-05 |
|---|---|---|---|---|---|---|---|---|
| ▬ won | 24 | 18 | 19 | 23 | 23 | 23 | 26 | 9 |
| ▬ drawn | | | | | | | | |
| ▬ lost | 2 | 8 | 7 | 2 | 3 | 3 | | 13 |

## Points

| Season | 97-98 | 98-99 | 99-00 | 00-01 | 01-02 | 02-03 | 03-04 | 04-05 |
|---|---|---|---|---|---|---|---|---|
| ▬ scored | 1001 | 716 | 865 | 844 | 941 | 1185 | 1119 | 365 |
| ▬ conceded | 331 | 409 | 450 | 387 | 364 | 431 | 340 | 493 |

## Points Difference

| Season | 97-98 | 98-99 | 99-00 | 00-01 | 01-02 | 02-03 | 03-04 | 04-05 |
|---|---|---|---|---|---|---|---|---|
| ▬ points | +670 | +307 | +415 | +457 | +577 | +754 | +779 | -128 |

## Total Premiership Record

| | |
|---|---|
| **Largest win** | **Largest defeat** |
| ▶ **33-7** | ▶ **3-57** |
| vs Harlequins (H) 02.10.04 | vs Sale Sharks (A) 24.09.04 |
| **Most tries scored in a game** | **Most tries conceded in a game** |
| ▶ **5** | ▶ **8** |
| vs Harlequins (H) 02.10.04 | vs Sale Sharks (A) 24.09.04 |
| **Top points scorer** | **Top try scorer** |
| ▶ J.Brown 113 | ▶ B.Hinshelwood 5 |
| **Top drop goal scorer** | **Most appearances** |
| ▶ J.Brown 5 | ▶ T.Windo 22 |

**Longest winning sequence**
▶ **3 wins** from 04.02.05 to 25.02.05

**Longest losing sequence**
▶ **4 defeats** from 10.10.04 to 13.11.04

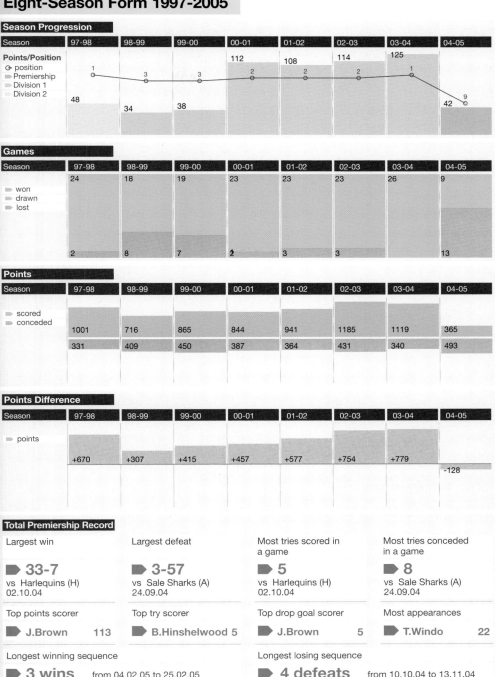

# Worcester Warriors EFL

## ENHANCED FIXTURE LIST
[does not include play-off data

| GUINNESS PREMIERSHIP 2005-06 | | | | Premiership History | | | | | | | | | Total Points | | Outcome after a half-time lead | | | | Close games | |
|---|---|---|---|---|---|---|---|---|---|---|---|---|---|---|---|---|---|---|---|---|
| Date | Team | H/A | 04-05 | Played | 97-98 | 98-99 | 99-00 | 00-01 | 01-02 | 02-03 | 03-04 | 04-05 | F | A | No. | W | D | L | No. | W |
| | | | | ■ won | | ■ drawn | | | ■ lost | | □ not played | | | | | | | | | |
| 04.09.05 | Gloucester | H | 13-18 | 1 | | | | | | | | | 13 | 18 | 1 | - | - | 1 | 1 | - |
| 11.09.05 | Irish | A | 25-15 | 1 | | | | | | | | | 15 | 25 | - | - | - | - | - | - |
| 17.09.05 | Saracens | H | 18-19 | 1 | | | | | | | | | 18 | 19 | 1 | - | - | 1 | 1 | - |
| 25.09.05 | Wasps | A | 32-17 | 1 | | | | | | | | | 17 | 32 | - | - | - | - | - | - |
| 14.10.05 | Leeds | H | 22-15 | 1 | | | | | | | | | 22 | 15 | 1 | 1 | - | - | 1 | 1 |
| 04.11.05 | Leicester | H | 11-38 | 1 | | | | | | | | | 11 | 38 | - | - | - | - | - | - |
| 11.11.05 | Sale | A | 57-3 | 1 | | | | | | | | | 3 | 57 | - | - | - | - | - | - |
| 18.11.05 | Bristol | H | N/A | - | | | | | | | | | - | - | - | - | - | - | - | - |
| 26.11.05 | Northampton | A | 6-17 | 1 | | | | | | | | | 17 | 6 | 1 | 1 | - | - | - | - |
| 26.12.05 | Bath | H | 22-26 | 1 | | | | | | | | | 22 | 26 | - | - | - | - | 1 | - |
| 01.01.06 | Newcastle | A | 16-21 | 1 | | | | | | | | | 21 | 16 | 1 | 1 | - | - | 1 | 1 |
| 07.01.06 | Northampton | H | 21-19 | 1 | | | | | | | | | 21 | 19 | 1 | 1 | - | - | 1 | 1 |
| 28.01.06 | Bristol | A | N/A | - | | | | | | | | | - | - | - | - | - | - | - | - |
| 11.02.06 | Sale | H | 23-10 | 1 | | | | | | | | | 23 | 10 | 1 | 1 | - | - | - | - |
| 18.02.06 | Leicester | A | 50-7 | 1 | | | | | | | | | 7 | 50 | - | - | - | - | - | - |
| 24.02.06 | Leeds | A | 24-19 | 1 | | | | | | | | | 19 | 24 | - | - | - | - | 1 | - |
| 10.03.06 | Wasps | H | 27-24 | 1 | | | | | | | | | 27 | 24 | 1 | 1 | - | - | 1 | 1 |
| 26.03.06 | Saracens | A | 16-10 | 1 | | | | | | | | | 10 | 16 | 1 | - | - | 1 | 1 | - |
| 08.04.06 | Irish | H | 16-6 | 1 | | | | | | | | | 16 | 6 | 1 | 1 | - | - | - | - |
| 15.04.06 | Gloucester | A | 28-16 | 1 | | | | | | | | | 16 | 28 | - | - | - | - | - | - |
| 29.04.06 | Newcastle | H | 9-30 | 1 | | | | | | | | | 9 | 30 | - | - | - | - | - | - |
| 06.05.06 | Bath | A | 18-10 | 1 | | | | | | | | | 10 | 18 | - | - | - | - | - | - |

# Club Information

## Useful Information

**Founded**
1871
**Address**
Sixways
Pershore Lane
Hindlip
Worcester
WR3 8ZE
**Capacity**
5,000 (3,700 seated)
**Main switchboard**
01905 454183
**Website**
www.wrfc.co.uk

## Travel Information

**Car**
Take Junction Six off the M5 motorway. Take the A4538 to Droitwich and Sixways is 300 yards on the left.

**Train**
Depart at Worcester Shrub Hill Station. There is a taxi rank outside the station. A taxi to Sixways will cost approximately £6.
Match Days Only - Park and Walk: Take Junction Six off the M5 motorway and follow the turning to 'Warndon Villages' and 'Shires Industrial Estate'. Follow the yellow signs marked 'Worcester Rugby – Park and Walk'. The club is approximately 15 minutes walk from the car parks and is signposted.
Match Days Only – Park and Ride: Take Junction Seven off the M5 motorway and follow the yellow AA 'Worcester Rugby – Park and Ride' signs to County Hall.

# Maps

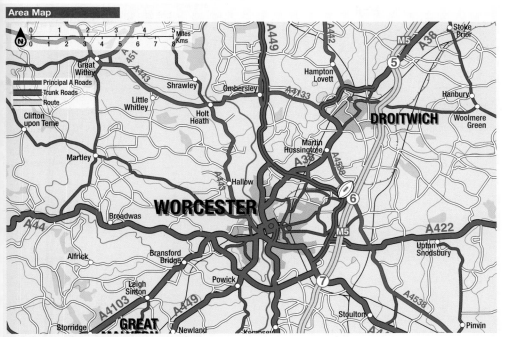

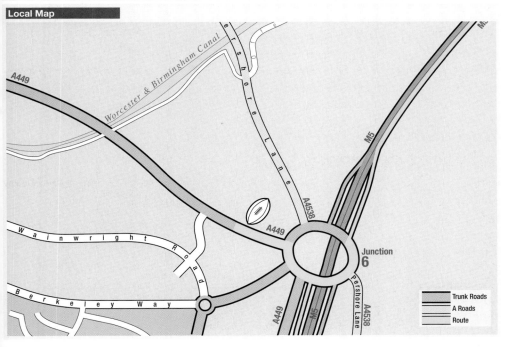

# Premiership Fixture Grid 2005-06

| Worcester | Saracens | Sale Sharks | Northampton | Newcastle | London Wasps | London Irish | Leicester Tigers | Leeds Tykes | Gloucester | Bristol Rugby | Bath Rugby | HOME / AWAY |
|---|---|---|---|---|---|---|---|---|---|---|---|---|
| 26/12 | 12/02 | 28/04 | 08/04 | 25/09 | 20/11 | 05/11 | 17/09 | 08/01 | 25/02 | 04/09 | | Bath Rugby |
| 18/11 | 26/02 | 08/01 | 01/01 | 11/09 | 04/11 | 24/09 | 06/05 | 10/02 | 25/03 | | 15/04 | Bristol Rugby |
| 04/09 | 08/01 | 07/04 | 11/03 | 19/02 | 26/12 | 20/11 | 12/11 | 30/04 | | 18/09 | 15/10 | Gloucester |
| 14/10 | 11/09 | 17/02 | 28/01 | 06/05 | 26/03 | 15/04 | 11/03 | | 31/12 | 13/11 | 25/11 | Leeds Tykes |
| 04/11 | 28/04 | 18/11 | 15/04 | 26/02 | 10/09 | 08/01 | | 25/09 | 11/02 | 27/12 | 25/03 | Leicester Tigers |
| 08/04 | 27/12 | 16/09 | 15/10 | 11/11 | 30/04 | | 26/11 | 03/09 | 28/01 | 12/03 | 18/02 | London Irish |
| 10/03 | 16/04 | 14/10 | 12/11 | 27/11 | | 31/12 | 08/04 | 18/09 | 06/05 | 19/02 | 28/01 | London Wasps |
| 29/04 | 20/11 | 02/09 | 17/09 | | 08/01 | 12/02 | 14/10 | 27/12 | 05/11 | 09/04 | 11/03 | Newcastle |
| 07/01 | 05/11 | 26/12 | | 26/03 | 12/02 | 26/02 | 03/09 | 20/11 | 24/09 | 30/04 | 10/09 | Northampton |
| 11/02 | 25/09 | | 06/05 | 16/04 | 26/02 | 25/03 | 28/01 | 05/11 | 10/09 | 27/11 | 02/01 | Sale Sharks |
| 17/09 | | 10/03 | 18/02 | 27/01 | 03/09 | 06/05 | 02/01 | 09/04 | 26/11 | 16/10 | 13/11 | Saracens |
| | 26/03 | 11/11 | 26/11 | 01/01 | 25/09 | 11/09 | 18/02 | 24/09 | 15/04 | 28/01 | 06/05 | Worcester |